GW00731710

HOW MANY MORE WOMEN?

Certain sections of this book have been redacted on legal advice, due to the possibility that the timing of its publication may coincide with the date of the criminal trial concerning allegations of rape made by Brittany Higgins where the accused has pleaded not guilty.

JENNIFER ROBINSON
KEINA YOSHIDA

HOW MANY MORE WOMEN?

ENDEAVOUR

Originally published by Allen & Unwin in 2022
Cammeraygal Country
83 Alexander Street
Crows Nest NSW 2065
Australia

First published in Great Britain in 2023 by Endeavour, an imprint of
Octopus Publishing Group Ltd,
Carmelite House,
50 Victoria Embankment,
London EC4Y 0DZ
www.octopusbooks.co.uk

An Hachette UK Company
www.hachette.co.uk

ISBN 978 1 80419 020 3
A CIP catalogue record for this book is available from the British Library.

Set in 13/17.5 pt Granjon by Midland Typesetters
Printed and bound in UK.

10 9 8 7 6 5 4 3 2

This FSC® label means that materials used for the product have been
responsibly sourced.

FSC
www.fsc.org

MIX
Paper from
responsible sources
FSC® C104740

CONTENTS

To the many women who are silent, who have been silenced and who have broken their silence. This book is written in the hope that we can better protect women to transform silence into action—and change.

A NOTE ON LANGUAGE

Many of those speaking out are women and girls who seek to shine a spotlight on sexual and gender-based violence. In this book, we will often refer to women and girls in an inclusive sense but are acutely aware that misconduct, harassment, abuse and rape affect people of all genders, including those who are trans, non-binary and gender non-conforming. This is important. In Japan, for example, rape laws excluded men and boys until very recently. Men and boys are also victims and survivors of sexual abuse, rape and harassment. That beacon of feminist thinking bell hooks reminds us that 'patriarchy has no gender'. She has explained that 'The enemy of feminism isn't men. It's patriarchy. And patriarchy is not men. It is a system. And women can support the system of patriarchy just as men can support the fight for gender equality.' Her work seeks to emphasise the tyranny of patriarchy and toxic masculinity. Thus, while we focus here on women and girls' experiences, we do not exclude men and boys and much of what we say will be relevant to everyone. But focusing on women and girls is important, as it allows us to shine a spotlight on sexism, gender stereotyping and patriarchal laws that tend to oppress and discriminate against women and girls.

HOW MANY DISCLAIMERS?

It is necessary for us to make a disclaimer. In fact, a few of them.

This book should not be taken as asserting the truth or as claiming to know the truth about the allegations of gender-based violence contained within its pages.

Every man named in this book vehemently denies all allegations—allegations that often relate to matters that typically happen in private, behind closed doors.

This book isn't really about the truth of any of these allegations: it is not an assessment of the evidence or a statement of facts. We raise the allegations to prompt discussion of a series of questions: what happens when women speak out about their alleged experience of gender-based violence? Have we created a legal system that is just, fair and equitable? Do we think the right balance is being struck between protecting a man's privacy and reputation and allowing women to speak about their experiences?

We are not saying that any man or lawyer or judge named in this book is intentionally silencing women—not even the men bringing or threatening legal action. They are seeking to protect their reputation, their privacy and the confidentiality promised to them under contract. We are merely pointing to the effect and impact of the law.

This legal disclaimer is one of the results of these laws. The team of lawyers who combed over our draft for defamatory imputations are a result of these laws. The ever-present threat of legal action for any material published about these allegations is a result of these laws. It would of course be a great irony if we were to be sued and silenced for this book, which is itself about how women are sued and silenced. But irony is no protection in the law.

And one final disclaimer:

This book is not, and should not be taken as, legal advice. There are civil and criminal laws on privacy, contract, defamation, contempt of court and anonymity that are jurisdiction-specific and apply depending on where you are and the individual circumstances of each woman and each case. If you have experienced gender-based violence and want to speak out, you should always seek independent, specialist legal advice. These areas of law are notoriously difficult to navigate, and decisions taken on the spur of the moment can have long-lasting consequences.

We want to say one more thing: we believe you. Not in the sense that we believe anything and everything any woman says, but in the sense that every woman's truth deserves to be taken seriously. And we believe that your right to speak about it should be better protected. We have written this book as a way of passing on what we know in the hope it might be useful to you in some way.

In care and solidarity,
Jen and Keina

Prologue

HIS INTENTION WAS TO SILENCE, NOT TO KILL

In December 2012, Nicola Stocker posted a comment on the Facebook status update of her ex-husband's new partner, Deborah Bligh. This prompted an exchange of comments between the women about Mr Stocker's history of violence:

NICOLA STOCKER: 'Wouldn't bring it up last time I accused him of cheating he spent a night in the cells, tried to strangle me. Police don't take too kindly to finding your wife with your handprints round her neck.'

. . .

DEBORAH BLIGH: 'why did terry get arrested?'

NICOLA STOCKER: '. . . Which time?'

DEBORAH BLIGH: 'why has he been arrested???'

NICOLA STOCKER: 'well u know about him trying to strangle me, then he was removed from the house following a number of threats he made and some gun issues I believe and then the police felt he had broken the terms of the non molestation order.'

NICOLA STOCKER: 'All quite traumatic really'

The Facebook comments were read by Bligh and a few of her family and friends. Mr Stocker sued Nicola for defamation—and, at trial, he won. The problem was Nicola's statement that Mr Stocker had 'tried to strangle me'. Nicola's account that Mr Stocker had violently grabbed her around the throat was supported by police evidence that red marks were visible around her neck when they attended two hours after the incident. But Mr Stocker still won the case.

Nicola would spend another five years in legal battles, with crippling financial costs, to defend her account of domestic violence—and her freedom of speech. In 2019, she was vindicated in the highest court in England and Wales, the Supreme Court, which ultimately ruled in her favour.

The most shocking aspect of this case isn't that Nicola was sued by her ex-husband for comments she made on a Facebook wall, or how long the legal process took, or how much it cost—it was the finding of the High Court trial judge in Mr Stocker's favour. After hearing the evidence about how Mr Stocker had placed his hands around his ex-wife's throat, the judge concluded:

> The most likely explanation about what happened is that he did in temper attempt to silence her forcibly by placing one hand on her mouth and the other on her upper neck under her chin to hold her head still. His intention was to silence, not to kill.

The judge concluded that Nicola had libelled her ex-husband for saying 'he tried to strangle me' because the technical legal definition of strangulation, according to the judge and the dictionary he consulted, requires an intent to kill. It didn't matter what Nicola intended with her words—that he had constricted her neck forcefully and painfully, threatening her— it mattered what the judge said her words meant ('an attempt to kill by strangulation'). She could prove he had assaulted her by placing his hands around her neck, that the police had observed red marks on her neck hours after that assault, that he breached a non-molestation order prohibiting him from threatening or intimidating her, and that he had been arrested three times. But she couldn't prove that he had intended to kill her, or indeed that he had attempted to kill her. On this basis, the judge concluded that Nicola did not meet the 'sting of the posting [Facebook post] that the claimant was a dangerous man'. Despite the evidence Nicola had of his threats, intimidation and assault, the judge found that her statement and its suggestion that Mr Stocker was dangerous—at least to any woman he lived with—was not true, and was therefore defamatory.

For obvious reasons, the High Court decision received fierce criticism. 'A greenlight for men who abuse women', read one headline. The judge's reasoning was criticised by women's rights non-government organisations (NGOs) and frontline domestic violence organisations, which raised their concerns about the implications of the judgment. As the Centre for Women's Justice stated:

The majority of women who have been raped or subjected to domestic abuse do not even report their allegations through shame, victim blaming and the fear of reprisals and of disbelief. For those that do report, ultimately few get justice as they face numerous hurdles negotiating their way through the criminal justice system. The impression created by MeToo that now women are free to speak out about sexual violence is sadly far from the truth and the willingness of lawyers and the courts to collude with the silencing of women must stop.

Despite these criticisms, the judge's decision was later upheld by the Court of Appeal. Commenting before the Supreme Court judgment, Harriet Wistrich, a leading women's rights campaigner and lawyer in the United Kingdom, noted:

> This case has chilling implications for women who speak out about male violence. The judgment reveals a shocking ignorance amongst members of the judiciary of the realities of domestic violence. The fact that Mr Stocker was arrested and red marks were observed by the police on the victim's neck is a serious warning of escalation of violence regardless of whether he had any intent to kill. In fact, strangulation is a warning marker in standardised police risk assessments. We are appalled that a woman speaking out about an accepted incident of domestic violence has been silenced and severely financially penalised.

How was it that the courts could find that Nicola Stocker had defamed her ex-husband for saying he tried to strangle her when, as the Supreme Court would later note, it 'was beyond dispute that Mr Stocker grasped his wife by the throat so tightly as to leave red marks on her neck visible to police officers two hours after the attack took place'? The judge had found that Mr Stocker had intended to silence Nicola. By finding that she had defamed the man who had assaulted her, the judge was prohibiting her from repeating the allegation—effectively silencing her. Couldn't the judge see the irony and perverse logic of his judgment? For years Nicola could not speak about her abuse. For speaking out and attempting to warn her ex-husband's new partner about his history of violence, she faced hundreds of thousands of pounds in costs and damages.

For us, Nicola's case was the last straw. We kept thinking about those words: 'his intention was to silence, not to kill'. How could this outcome be *possible* in any legal system, let alone be considered justice? What had happened to Nicola's right to speak about her experience of violence?

We believed there were important arguments on the right of free speech about gender-based violence, equality and the need to prevent the silencing of women about their abuse that weren't being heard or considered by the courts. For this reason, we applied to intervene in Nicola's case on behalf of Liberty, Britain's leading human rights organisation. We argued that the courts had so far failed to recognise Nicola's rights: her right to speak, and her right to live a life free of gender-based violence.

The Supreme Court declined to hear us. Ultimately, Nicola would win—but for very different reasons.

On 3 April 2019, the Supreme Court found that the trial judge was wrong to conclude that Nicola's words meant that her ex-husband had intended to kill her, and that her language, expressed as it was on social media, should not be given such a technical meaning. The late Lord Justice Kerr, a liberal and compassionate voice on the court, pointed out that the fact Mr Stocker had assaulted her and violated a non-molestation order would be considered by many (though not the trial judge) to be sufficient to show he was a dangerous man. Lord Kerr also questioned how the trial judge had reached a conclusion 'more benevolent to Mr Stocker than any version of the facts which could reasonably have been advanced', having sought as he did 'to explain the red marks on a basis which Mr Stocker never argued for'. Despite Nicola's evidence, and the police evidence supporting her account, the trial judge had come up with his own hypothesis about what had happened in order to exonerate Mr Stocker. This is what is known as 'himpathy'— and gender bias—in action.

But the Supreme Court did not call it that, nor was the judge's gender bias stated as a reason to overturn his findings. Nor did the Supreme Court, anywhere in its decision, mention the importance of freedom of speech about gender-based violence, or the need for women to be able to talk about their experience of abuse. Instead, the judgment was all about the need for courts to consider the context of social media posts, whatever their content or subject matter. While the Supreme Court decision is important for all future social media defamation cases, it was in our view a missed opportunity to underline the importance of protecting the rights of survivors to speak about their abuse— online or anywhere else.

Nicola Stocker's legal case is an important illustration of the difficulties people face when trying to speak out about or make allegations of domestic violence, sexual violence or sexual harassment. But her case is also just one example of a much broader trend in Australia, the United Kingdom and around the world of survivors, journalists and advocacy groups being silenced by asphyxiating, expensive civil litigation.

We wrote this book to put forward the arguments the Supreme Court declined to hear. We want to show how these laws are failing, and silencing, women. And we want to inform more women than we could ever meet in person in our chambers about the kinds of risks they face.

What happens when the law that is meant to protect us is instead used to silence? And what can we do about it?

INTRODUCTION

HOW MANY WOMEN?

I remember him saying, 'Don't tell anybody.' I remember him saying, 'Don't make a sound.'

Well, hear me now. Using my voice, amongst a growing chorus of voices that will not be silenced.

Grace Tame spoke these words after being named Australian of the Year in January 2021.

In a lot of ways, this was a peak of the MeToo movement—a survivor being recognised, and speaking on a national platform about her experience of challenging a law that prevented her from talking about the abuse she suffered. This was a shift, and an acknowledgement of the change that was happening.

MeToo, at its core, is a movement about survivors speaking out and finding solidarity in one another. In a culture of shame and silence, where survivors are kept siloed and isolated from each other, speaking is a powerful act. It has shown how powerful silence was in protecting perpetrators. That cultural silence—and the status quo—was finally breaking, along with the impunity perpetrators had enjoyed for too long. MeToo was started by Tarana Burke all the way back in 2006 as a means of letting victims and survivors know that they were not alone, but in 2017 the movement went viral.

In a sense, the MeToo movement is a response to legal systems that do not serve women and girls, either because the laws are inadequate or because the response of the legal system to victims and survivors is flawed. Many women and girls have lost faith in the police and the legal system to provide justice to survivors of sexual harassment, misconduct, abuse and rape—and understandably so.

In Australia, Canada, the United Kingdom and the United States, only 14 per cent of sexual violence victims report the assault to police. And even if sexual assault and rape are reported to police, prosecutions and convictions remain depressingly low. For example, in the United Kingdom only 1.6 per cent of rapes reported to the police result in a charge—a rate so low that the UK Victims Commissioner, Dame Vera Baird, has said that 'we are witnessing the de-criminalisation of rape'.

Even if a matter does get to trial, most of the time it doesn't feel much like 'justice'. Many survivors talk about being re-traumatised by police and by cross-examination, and many more experience victim-blaming attitudes and gender bias in the courtroom. Even smaller again is the number of men who are actually convicted. In the United Kingdom, less than 1 per cent of rape cases result in conviction. And even where men are convicted, judges' biased sentencing remarks regularly minimise or excuse their offending.

The system fails survivors at so many points—from not educating children about consent to failing to tackle the misogynistic ideas about sex and violence that pervade our culture, our police and our courts. In this context, speaking out about it is the only way many survivors feel they can agitate for change. They want to tell their story to protect others, to stop the violence from happening again, and to start a serious conversation about violence against women. In speaking out, survivors also find solidarity and support, and are no longer alone in a shame that should never have been theirs to carry.

The crux of the problem is that women and girls are speaking out about abuse and violence because not enough is being done to stop it—and we need to be able to talk about it so that governments can do better. We can't act if we don't know.

The success of MeToo has been in how it is breaking down cultural silence about gender-based violence, encouraging women to speak out and enabling us—the public and policymakers—to understand the extent of the problem. Around the world, thanks to MeToo, police and rape crisis services saw a massive spike in women reporting their abuse, and we have seen increased public discussion about violence against women and policy discussions about how we might better address it. The resistance and bravery of those speaking out has brought to light 'a collective experience of powerlessness against systemic injustice'.

For human rights experts at the United Nations, MeToo marked 'a tipping point' for women's rights and foreshadowed the end of indifference and impunity as 'the shame and fear begin to shift from the victims to the side of abusers and perpetrators of sexual violence'. This change is urgently needed to address what is an urgent and widespread human rights crisis. As UN Women reports, violence against women and girls is the most prevalent human rights violation in the world, suffered by one in three women, and a problem that disproportionately affects women of colour, First Nations women and those with disability—who are each far more likely to face abuse. The UN Committee on the Elimination of Discrimination Against Women (CEDAW) has described gender-based violence as pervasive, reminding all governments that it is prohibited under international law and that they have an obligation to protect women from violence, to punish those responsible and to put an end to violence. As CEDAW makes clear, freedom of speech—and the ability for survivors to talk about their abuse and the media to report on it—is an essential aspect of violence prevention.

But something has been happening as a reaction to this movement. As women have been empowered to break their silence, they have also been facing a different kind of silencing: the silencing of women who speak out by and through the law.

The spike in survivors speaking out has been followed by a spike in legal actions against them and the journalists who want to report their stories—in defamation, in contract, in privacy and in breach of confidence. We have seen this in our practice and have watched it happen all around the world. The law is being wielded to reinforce the culture of silence and protect the status quo. The courts have become the battlefield, where judges grapple with competing rights: her right to speak about gender-based abuse and his right to reputation.

The UN-appointed expert on freedom of expression, Irene Khan, calls this 'the perverse twist of MeToo' and 'gendered censorship'. It is a problem so big that she dedicated her entire report to the UN General Assembly in 2021 to it and explained why free speech is also an equality issue.

We agree—and in this book we show why.

As we saw in Nicola Stocker's case—and in the many cases we highlight in this book—the same gender bias, victim-blaming and harmful stereotypes about sexual and domestic violence that impede the ability of the criminal justice system to deliver justice are also found in this flood of civil cases which silence. The difference, however, is that these cases are initiated not by the state but by (mostly) powerful and wealthy individuals. The costs of these cases are borne not by the state but by those facing the legal action: the women who speak out, the journalists who report on it or the advocacy groups that seek to campaign about it. And the costs are crippling. In many cases it is an alleged perpetrator suing his victim, and the law enables him to turn his victim into the defendant. Using the law in this way is a legally sanctioned way to victim-blame. As psychologist Jennifer Freyd explains, it offers abusive men a legal mechanism for the age-old strategy of 'deny, attack and reverse victim and offender' (known as DARVO). Many women who are sued by their perpetrator experience litigation as another form of abuse, a legally sanctioned means by which he continues to torment, humiliate and control her long after she has left him.

Using the law in this way is also a legally sanctioned way to say 'Don't tell anybody'. It enables men with wealth and power to repeat that refrain: 'Don't make a sound.'

The cost of speaking out

As human rights barristers, we are often approached by women for advice on the risks they face if they choose to speak out. Many survivors speak out without considering the legal implications, and only come to us after receiving legal threats or when facing legal action. There is a worrying pattern of actions emerging that we want women to be aware of.

In general terms, a typical scenario is as follows:

A young woman suffers abuse or harassment at the hands of a rich and powerful man. The rich and powerful man negotiates a settlement to buy her silence. The young woman subsequently decides to speak out about her experiences. The rich and powerful man seeks to protect his reputation, strenuously denies the allegation and calls the woman a liar. He (or his lawyers) threatens to sue the woman, and/or the newspaper or news outlet if they print the allegation. He might seek an injunction to prevent publication of the allegation, or (if the information is already out) claim she is lying and use defamation or libel laws to cast doubt on her allegation, obtain an apology from the news outlet and seek monetary compensation for damage to his reputation—as well as an injunction to prevent her or the publication from repeating the allegation and to deter other journalists from doing their own reporting about it.

The problem we continue to see is that the women making the accusations and the journalists printing them are being sued in costly, technical and stressful legal proceedings. Rich, privileged and powerful men have teams of lawyers at their disposal to suppress allegations and stop newspaper stories. Individual women, frontline services and advocacy groups, and journalists find themselves fighting against censorship and silencing, being sued for defamation and vilified in court, in public and online. The costs are crippling—financially and emotionally. As Jia Tolentino has argued, women, rather than being able to speak out in their own terms, 'have had to be painfully careful about how we speak'.

How many women?

In 2017, when allegation after allegation began to surface about film producer Harvey Weinstein, we were working with journalists and newspapers in the United Kingdom who were breaking what has come to be known as the MeToo story. After decades of Weinstein's behaviour being an open secret, suddenly there was a push to publish. It was as if the walls of a dam had burst. Newspapers finally felt able to print serious allegations against one of Hollywood's most powerful producers.

But why now? How was he able to silence the allegations for so long? How many women had to accuse this man before they would be believed? How many women had to accuse him before the newspaper would run a story about it? How many women needed to come forward before he would be prosecuted? At the time the first Weinstein story ran, he had not been arrested or put on trial. But thanks to the collective power of women speaking out, and the power of the pen, he is now in prison. But how many women had suffered because of the silence that had protected him for so long?

This question—how many women?—haunted us as we worked with news organisations to publish this and many other MeToo stories. As we wrote this book, it kept coming up. How many women will be raped or killed before we fix the system? How many women are scared to walk home alone? How many women actually receive justice in our courts? How many women need to speak out before things change? How many women will be sued for defamation for speaking out? How many women have been silenced by non-disclosure agreements (NDAs)? How many women do we need in parliament before laws are changed? How many women need to protest before society changes the way women are treated? The question came up so often, and in so many contexts, that it became an exasperated refrain.

This book reflects our own journey in thinking through these issues separately and together since 2012, and long before MeToo.

In this book, we sometimes refer to our own cases, but only in relation to material that is in the public domain or with our clients' permission. Jen has advised journalists, media organisations, survivors and frontline services organisations, and has advised and worked with high-profile women who have spoken out.

Keina has been working on women's human rights and intersectional discrimination since 2008. Keina's international work has led her to meet many of the silence-breakers we interviewed for the book, who are using the law in Colombia, Japan and Kenya to fight back.

We have also acted together in cases, including some that never made it to court, and we write this book informed by those stories and our experience of how the law works in practice.

As barristers in England and Wales, we have also advised organisations on publication risks, with stints in-house and advising major national newspapers and broadcasters in London, working with journalists to break stories. We have seen, from the inside, the challenges journalists face investigating these stories, as well as the legal threats and other harassment and pressure they face for their reporting.

We have talked with survivors, journalists and human rights activists from around the world who have been spied on, sued or prosecuted, and who have faced jail time, bankruptcy, online abuse and threats, and even exile for speaking out or reporting on abuse. In this book we show how it is not just powerful and privileged men who have been bringing these cases: governments and state officials have also been active or complicit in the silencing. We show, too, how discriminatory criminal laws serve to silence and punish women for speaking their truth, and slap down and silence activism on women's rights issues. But we also show how brave survivors and silence-breakers are fighting back and using the law in creative and interesting ways to counter the backlash and advocate for necessary law reform.

This book is not about the criminal justice system and how it is failing women. There are many great books about this, including those written by our Doughty Street Chambers colleagues about what is happening in the United Kingdom. From Baroness Helena Kennedy KC's books, *Eve Was Framed* (1992) and *Eve Was Shamed* (2018), to Harriet Johnson's recent manifesto, *Enough: The violence against women and how to end it* (2022), it is clear that too many women are failed by the criminal justice system—through systemic racial and gender bias, gender stereotypes or sexist reasoning from police, lawyers and judges. We need a criminal justice system that works better for everyone. And we need to build a society in which women and girls can live free from violence.

We firmly believe that this begins with being able to talk about it. That is why we are concerned about how the law is being used as a weapon to silence women, and why we argue there is a clear public interest in speaking about these issues. If we want to end violence against women, we must be able to speak about it.

How many women will be silenced before we make the structural changes we need to empower them to speak?

Chapter 1

SILENCING JUSTITIA

If you have been into a courtroom—in Australia, the United Kingdom, Europe or Latin America—you have likely seen a statue of a blindfolded woman, a sword in one hand and a set of scales in the other. This is Justitia, or Lady Justice, the personification of justice in ancient Rome and the symbol of moral force in our judicial systems today. The scales represent the weighing of interests in the pursuit of justice; the blindfold represents objectivity and equality before the law. She is there to remind all those working in our courts of their obligations.

Justitia represents the ideal and the objective of our legal systems: it matters not who you are, your wealth or your status—or your gender—justice will be delivered. It is deeply ironic, then, that justice is depicted as a woman, given that women have historically been excluded from systems of justice and denied both rights and justice.

The reality is that nations' laws have largely been written by and for men. It is overwhelmingly men who have written them in parliaments, and male judges who have interpreted and applied them in the courts, relying on the arguments of courtroom advocates who are also predominately men.

Understanding this legal history is essential to understanding the operation of the law today. Laws and rights were created for men, not for women. Patriarchal interests have been protected and privileged over all else, with little regard for or consideration of women's rights and lived experiences. The lingering legacy of this are myths about sexual and domestic violence: pervasive attitudes and beliefs that are generally false and serve to deny and even justify male violence against women. These myths permeate society, the media and the legal system.

The fact is that parliaments and the upper echelons of both the media and the legal profession have been, and still are, dominated by men. This matters and it has lasting consequences today. It can be seen in laws about gender-based violence and the laws regulating women's ability to speak about it. It can also be seen in media coverage of gender-based violence, and in the laws regulating the way the media can report it. And it affects the way these laws operate in practice to silence women.

Silencing Olympe de Gouges

This book traces the ways in which the law silences women. So let's begin with the history of human rights and women's right to free speech—and the fact that we were not originally entitled to it at all.

Human rights law is said to reflect and protect the essence of what it means to be human, and it defines our rights in society, including our right to freedom of speech. These rights are now found in most democratic constitutions (except in Britain, where there is no codified constitution, and in Australia, where the written constitution doesn't really protect human rights at all, and the courts had to imply limited free speech protections). But the right to free speech has not always protected women. Indeed, until about the last century, women didn't have many rights at all—in international or national law.

The history of human rights is intertwined with the histories of class and gender. While they are said to be human rights, not all humans had their rights protected equally. For the United Kingdom, Australia and the rest of the common law world, the foundation for human rights began with the *Magna Carta Libertatum* (or 'Great Charter of Freedoms'), signed in England in 1215. The Magna Carta limited the power of the King of England and introduced some limited but important rights, such as the right to due legal process. But these rights only applied to noblemen—that is, to certain wealthy white men. Rights were only for the rich and powerful, not for all people—and certainly not for women and people of colour.

The first comprehensive legal declaration of human rights is said to have come in 1789, after the Enlightenment and the French Revolution, when the French National Constituent Assembly drafted the 'Declaration of the Rights of Man and of the Citizen'. This was a declaration of rights for the people— not just for the ruling class. It embodied what we now see as modern natural and civil rights.

As Susie Alegre points out in *Freedom to Think* (2022), the declaration was radical in its time, but not so radical as to extend equality to anyone other than white men. The seventeen principles were designed to protect and respect the rights of men and ensure the happiness of men—and exclusively men. It established the rights of liberty, property, due process, security and resistance to oppression. It established the pillars of modern democracy and defined the relationship between man and government, by establishing the rule of law, the separation of powers and accountability of government to the all-male electorate.

It also protected—for the first time—the right to freedom of speech. Again, this was only for men. But, as Alegre writes, just a few years after this was drafted, a woman dared to point out the limitations of this male-led Enlightenment political thinking and their failure to include women in their so-called *égalité*. It did not end well for her.

This was Olympe de Gouges—a pen name she chose for herself when she sought her destiny as a revolutionary in Paris. As an activist, she fought for the right for women to be included in the social reforms sweeping France. In 1791, she wrote the 'Declaration of the Rights of Woman and of the Female Citizen', in which she stated: 'A woman has the right to be guillotined; she should also have the right to debate.'

This turned out to be disturbingly prophetic: after upsetting many powerful figures through her political activism and writings (including Robespierre, whom she called a tyrant), she was convicted of treason, and executed. Her execution was seen as a warning to all politically active women—and generally to women who dared to speak out—many of whom were executed in the years that followed.

But it would be a mistake to think that advocating for equality for women began in revolutionary France. In fact, hundreds of years earlier, in the 1630s, the Ethiopian philosopher and intellectual Zera Yacob was an advocate for equality for all, including women. Yacob believed that equality was for all humans: this meant that women should be treated equally and that slavery was unjustifiable.

And yet it wasn't until after World War II, when women were needed in the workforce, that women's rights were formally—and finally—recognised, when they were included in the Universal Declaration of Human Rights (UDHR). But even then, the first draft of the document opened with the words 'All men are brothers' and it looked like we might end up with another declaration of men's rights. It was in fact a formidable Australian woman, Jessie Street, who—together with the few other women invited to the founding conference of the United Nations, held in San Francisco in 1945—insisted that women be included and the wording 'All men are brothers' be dropped.

Street was the sole woman on the Australian delegation, and was instrumental in creating the Commission on the Status of Women (CSW), on which she served as the inaugural vice-president. Street also served on the UDHR drafting committee, which was led by Eleanor Roosevelt, a feminist, social justice activist and former US First Lady. Street insisted, after banding together with the small group of women delegates, that 'if you don't refer expressly to women, they will be excluded from rights'. Their efforts ensured that Article 1 of the UDHR states: 'All human beings are born free and equal in dignity and rights', and that human rights would be for all, women included. Street may have succeeded on this, but another of her important points was ignored: she had argued for the inclusion of the right of women to freedom from violence. As we explain in Chapter 8, it would take another half a century for this right to finally be recognised—and governments are still failing to give it effect.

The law is man-made

The law, as Justitia reminds us, is meant to be blind—and applied equally to all. But what happens when the law, as it is made, is blind to women? What happens when the law itself is only written from the perspective of men?

Until the early 20th century, parliaments were made up of all men, voted in by men because women did not have the vote. Cases before the courts were argued by men, and decided by men because women were not allowed to study and practise law or become judges. Although a woman could feel the full force of the law, and be punished by the law, she had no ability to shape or influence the law. She was excluded from the so-called democracy which legislated her life, her body and her relationships. This historical reality did not end when women were given the right to vote. While there have been huge efforts towards correcting unjust and discriminatory laws, the very foundation and architecture of the system, with its gender bias and male perspective, still impacts upon law and practice today.

In their seminal book *Women and the Law* (1984), co-authors Susan Atkins and Brenda Hoggett (who later become a UK Supreme Court judge, Baroness Hale) showed how the law in the United Kingdom has reflected men's interests and a patriarchal world view, which has led to discrimination and injustice towards women. Study after study in jurisdictions around the world have highlighted this same problem elsewhere and how it results in legal systems that fail women. And even though societal views are changing, the law lags along behind it, and many biases and myths continue to persist in society, and in the law and its practice. This is particularly true when we look at gender-based violence, which is overwhelmingly perpetrated by men against women.

Let's start with sexual offences.

Your body or mine? Sexual violence and women as property

Historically, sexual violence was not criminalised for the effect it had on women. It was a crime that centred on the trespass of property—that is, based on women being the property of their father or husband—and was concerned with how a sexual assault of a woman would affect those men. The law was a means by which men secured legitimate heirs and bargainable daughters: therefore, as Atkins and Hoggett explain, when it came to rape, the law was primarily concerned with penile penetration because it might lead to pregnancy. There was far less concern for other forms of sexual assault, which also violated women's bodily autonomy but did not risk impregnation.

As Atkins and Hoggett write, men went to even greater lengths to protect themselves from other men: the harshest penalties in law were preserved for non-consensual vaginal intercourse and for buggery of men, whether consensual or non-consensual. There was far less concern for punishing female homosexuality—after all, that didn't concern men. (In modern times, some countries—such as Sri Lanka—amended their criminal laws to make sex between women an offence. Keina successfully challenged this law before the Committee on the Elimination of Discrimination Against Women (CEDAW) as a violation of women's rights to equality and privacy.)

For centuries, the law condoned rape within marriage: women were, upon marriage, the property of their husband and had no right to refuse sex. Husbands had complete immunity from criminal prosecution for rape. The origin of this rule of common law is an oft-quoted statement from Sir Matthew Hale published in 1736: '[T]he husband cannot be guilty of rape upon his lawful wife, for by their mutual matrimonial consent and contract the wife hath given up herself in this kind unto her husband, which she cannot retract.' Marriage was therefore an irrevocable contract for sex. If a man was violent with his wife in order to have sex with her, he could be prosecuted for assault, but not for rape.

In the United Kingdom, it wasn't until 1991 that the courts removed this immunity. Finally, the British courts recognised that Sir Matthew's statement that a woman gave up her right not to consent to sex upon marriage was 'a common law fiction which has become anachronistic and offensive'. The same can be said of Sir Matthew's views on abortion, but that has not stopped the US Supreme Court from citing him in 2022 to deny women rights over their own body. Justice Samuel Alito's majority opinion overturning *Roe v. Wade*—which put an end to women's constitutional right to an abortion in the United States—cited the same treatise, *The History of the Pleas of the Crown*, in which he described abortion as 'a great crime'. Sir Matthew's 17th-century views of the law and women—which included putting women to death for witchcraft—clearly have not yet been consigned to the history books.

In Australia, it was not until 1976 that 'marital rape' was partially criminalised, and only in South Australia. It took until 1994 for all the other states and territories to catch up. Despite this, recent surveys in both Australia and the United Kingdom show that an alarming number of people still do not consider forced marital sex to be rape; clearly many still believe that women in relationships have an obligation to have sex with their partner, even if they don't want to.

According to the United Nations in 2021, some 43 countries still don't have legislation criminalising marital rape. Even worse, in some countries the law can grant this immunity retrospectively: twenty countries still permit a man to escape criminal prosecution for rape if he marries his victim. Morocco recently repealed the law after a young woman committed suicide after being forced to marry her rapist. How many women will speak out about their rape if it might mean being forced to marry the man who raped her? The effect of these laws is to silence victims.

Even in countries where these laws have been repealed, the attitude persists that marriage atones for rape. In India in 2021, Chief Justice Sharad Arvind Bobde told an accused rapist: 'If you want to marry her, we can help you. If not, you lose your job and go to jail.' The defendant had been accused of stalking, gagging and repeatedly raping the girl, and of threatening to douse her in petrol, set her alight and kill her brother. This was despite a 2013 Supreme Court decision that said 'rape is not a matter for the parties to compromise and settle'. In India, defence lawyers reportedly still often propose that the defendant will marry the victim in the hope of receiving a more lenient sentence for rape.

Rape was historically seen and defined as an offence of honour, committed against the property of husband or father, rather than an act which violated women's bodily autonomy. As Professor Jessica Clarke explains, in the United States— and elsewhere—rape historically could not be committed against a female victim of previously unchaste character. This is why rape only used to be prosecuted when the victim was a 'respectable woman'. Sex workers were deemed to have given up their right to refuse consent—and the right to deny their services—to the world at large.

This underlying architecture is still present in modern-day cases of sexual assault and rape around the world. In India, until recently, differential sentences were given to men for rape depending on the woman's previous sexual activity. We interviewed a leading Indian barrister, Karuna Nundy, who redrafted India's sexual offences law after the now-infamous Delhi gang rape in 2012. She explained: 'If the woman was a virgin and deemed "pure", the sentence was higher; if she was married or otherwise sexually active, the sentence was less. In fact, pursuant to the hierarchy of "purity", rapists of women who are sexually active but not married receive the lowest sentences.' The test to assess whether women were 'habituated' to sex was the two-finger test, where a doctor inserts their fingers into the vagina of a woman to test her hymen and vaginal laxity.

The two-finger test is a virginity test used in many parts of the world despite the fact that the World Health Organization (WHO) has long condemned its use for medical and ethical reasons, including because it can't prove whether sexual intercourse took place or not. But it wasn't until 2013 that the Supreme Court of India declared the practice unlawful on the grounds that it violated women's privacy and dignity.

Karuna also explained that Indian law was—as in the United Kingdom—male-centric and therefore only penalised penile penetration of the vagina as rape. Karuna has worked with others to change this by redefining the law from a feminist perspective: any non-consensual form of penetration or sexual touching is now a crime. But even today, Karuna told us, judges in India still talk about 'honour' in rape cases, despite it bearing no relevance to the law as it now stands.

This is a familiar pattern around the world: long after the requirement that a woman must be chaste to be considered a rape victim has been removed, a woman's sexual history continues to be brought up by defence lawyers to undermine a victim's credibility. As Harvard law professor Catharine MacKinnon has written, this is a perpetuation of 'the rape myth that women who have had sex are inherently not credible . . . having apparently lost our credibility along with our virginity'. Baroness Helena Kennedy KC has written extensively about her experience in sexual crimes trials in *Eve Was Framed* (1992) and *Eve was Shamed* (2018). She writes how complainants in rape trials are 'required to be the ideal victim, preferably sexually inexperienced and at least respectable'. Throughout her career, women complainants were 'still asked questions which are never put to men', including about her sexual history, her clothing, whether she had anything to drink, why she was out alone, why she was at the pub or nightclub. Women who had uncommitted consensual sex were treated as having consented to sex in any context, which Helena writes 'seems to be the price paid for woman choosing to be as independent as a man'. In one case, she describes a male defence counsel saying 'You are not a true victim. You are the victim of your own behaviour that evening.' As Helena wrote, '[t]rue victimhood has very demanding standards'. And it worked with juries: she referred to research in Canada that showed that the more a jury heard about a woman's previous sexual history, the less likely they were to convict.

In many jurisdictions today, including Australia, the United Kingdom and the United States, evidence about a victim's sexual history is now barred in sexual offence trials—though this has been a relatively recent development. But the history and architecture of bias in the law is hard to break. Despite all the new guidance and jury directions in the United Kingdom that aim to educate police, prosecutors, juries and judges about these myths in sexual offence trials, they persist.

In 2020, a whistleblower came forward to show how UK police and prosecutors were declining to prosecute sexual offence cases based on these very myths. In one case, prosecutors declined to prosecute a rape case because the complainant 'enjoyed an adventurous sex life'. Even more shockingly, as we explain in chapters 6 and 7, there are no protections in civil defamation trials—before judges or juries—about this. In the high-profile *Depp v. Heard* defamation case in the United States, where an issue before the jury was whether or not Johnny Depp had subjected his then wife Amber Heard to domestic and sexual violence, Amber told us that she faced questions in depositions about her sexual history and whether she had worked as a stripper and sex worker—all of which was irrelevant to whether or not Depp had hit her or raped her.

Real rapes, real victims

The laws on the books are one part of the problem. But there is the less visible problem of how myths and stereotypes are still pervasive—and how they are used to discredit and silence victims.

As Professor Jessica Clarke points out in *The Global #MeToo Movement*, the law has treated rape cases with 'extraordinary scepticism both because women were thought to fabricate accusations and because the crime was penalised by the harshest of sanctions, including the death penalty'. Because the consequences were so serious for the accused (who were overwhelmingly men), the law imposed special requirements on victims (who were overwhelmingly women), which were not seen in any other area of assault law. They included that a man could not be convicted of rape without corroboration: juries were warned that the woman's evidence alone was not enough; it had to be backed up by other evidence before a jury could convict. In the words of one Judge Sutcliffe to a jury in 1971, 'it is well known that women in particular and small boys are liable to be untruthful and invent stories'. Thanks to feminist campaigning, this requirement was removed in the United Kingdom in 1994. A credible account from a victim now can and should form the basis of a prosecution and a conviction. That is, unless you are in countries like Iran where the Islamic Penal Code requires that, for a rape conviction, a woman must also have four male eyewitnesses, an obviously near-impossible evidential standard. The word of the victim, even where corroborated by several female witnesses, is not enough.

This old requirement of corroboration was based upon, and perpetuated, the myth that women making allegations of abuse could not be trusted—and survey after survey in Australia, the United Kingdom and elsewhere show that alarming numbers of people continue to hold this belief.

Another special requirement imposed on victims of sexual assault was, as Professor Clarke explains, that the victim had to show that she had physically resisted during her assault, as well as actually saying 'no'. Presumably the requirement of physical resistance was put in place so that the man could be shown to clearly understand that she did not want to have sex; saying or even screaming 'no' was not enough. This denies the reality of most women's experience: freezing is the most common reaction to rape, with the victim unable to resist. Physically resisting a man is likely to provoke further violence during rape, even risking death, and many women don't resist for this reason.

These requirements were never designed to prioritise the experience of rape victims or to protect them. Instead, they were developed to ensure that men were not wrongfully convicted. The result is a law that bears little relation to the reality of the crime or women's experience of it, and that means many rapes have gone unpunished.

The requirement that a woman physically resist has—like the requirements of prompt reporting and corroboration—been removed in the United States, the United Kingdom and other democratic countries. But, as Professor Clarke explains, these myths and 'outdated ideas continue to influence' cases today—determining whether the police investigate, whether the prosecutor's office decides to press charges and what is convincing to juries—and inform popular ideas about 'real victims' and 'real rapes'.

The old requirement that there be an element of force for rape to be prosecuted as a crime also contributes to outdated myths. For example, as Professor Clarke explains, early US courts had borrowed from the old English definition of rape: 'carnal knowledge of a woman forcibly and against her will'. The requirement of force has been removed from the laws of many countries, including in the United Kingdom and Australia, where the law is based on consent. But it has perpetuated the myth that 'real rapes' are stranger rapes, perpetrated by force—even though the statistics show that the overwhelming majority of rapes are committed by intimate partners or acquaintances.

Force remains a requirement of rape in many jurisdictions, including in Japan and in countries across Europe, although women are fighting to make rape a consent-based offence. Even in jurisdictions where force is no longer a legal requirement, the UN Special Rapporteur on Violence Against Women notes that this myth has resulted in judges, juries and prosecutors being more likely to believe women's accusations of rape when it is accompanied with physical injury, and more likely to give lighter sentences for rape by acquaintances. So who, then, does this law really protect? And what use is the law if it doesn't reflect the real conditions in which that crime is committed?

We see a similar pattern with the old 'prompt reporting' requirement. Victims who don't report a rape right away are seen as unreliable or seeking revenge—or so it was said. Of course, contemporaneous reporting enables evidence to be taken when memories are fresh. Trauma responses, fear of retaliation (particularly when perpetrators are powerful) and being afraid of not being believed are all common reasons that it can take some victims time—sometimes years or even decades—to report their abuse. Experts agree that there are many legitimate psychological and cultural reasons why survivors take time to report, and that a delay is not, in and of itself, any bar to the successful prosecution of crimes.

For this reason, many countries have removed the 'prompt reporting' requirement to better reflect the reality of victims' lived experiences. But some countries have kept it: in Italy, it remains a requirement that victims report within six months of the alleged crime. This is considered 'protection against false complaints or blackmail'. Again, this justification is rooted in the myth that 'real victims' report immediately.

In some countries where the 'prompt reporting' requirement has been removed, there still exist statutes of limitations, ranging between five and fifteen years, for criminal and civil claims for rape and sexual assault. This was how the US comedian Bill Cosby avoided prosecution in all but one of 50 cases: the women had remained silent, or had not been believed by police, for too long. Only Andrea Constand's case against Cosby alleging sexual assault could be prosecuted, because all other cases were statute-barred and out of time.

Limitation rules are designed to protect the due process rights of the accused: memories fade and evidence deteriorates over time, which can potentially make convictions less reliable. But in many jurisdictions, limitation periods apply in respect of prosecution for rape (committed overwhelmingly by men against women), but not for murder (overwhelmingly committed against men, except—of course—in relation to intimate partner murder). Campaigners say this unfairly denies rape survivors justice, and they have campaigned for extensions to the time limits in order to recognise the reality of victims' lived experiences.

They have had some success: in the United Kingdom, for example, there is now no time limit on prosecuting sexual assault or murder. The extension of time limitations for civil claims relating to historical sexual abuse in California has enabled a number of women to make civil claims against Cosby for sexual assault.

Domestic violence justified

The history of family law, on divorce and domestic violence, shows how it disadvantaged women in order to protect the interests of men. Despite changes to the law since, we still see the same myths play out in the family courts and in defamation cases involving domestic violence.

The starting point in family law and divorce was the indivisible matrimonial union and the protection of patriarchal propriety interests. Like the laws on rape, the laws around divorce and adultery were designed to protect men's lineage and succession from women who might lie. Divorce was permitted for a man if his wife committed adultery, but not for a woman if her husband did. As the Lord Chancellor explained in 1857, '[T]he adultery of the wife might be a means of palming spurious offspring upon the husband, while the adultery of the husband could have no such effect with regard to the wife.' As Atkins and Hoggett explained, this inequality persisted in the United Kingdom until 1923.

For women, it was hard to get a divorce even if your husband was violent. As far back as the 1700s, a woman could get a divorce for cruelty if she suffered domestic violence, but only if 'she was a woman of good temper' and had 'always behaved dutifully to her husband'. The law of provocation set out all the ways in which her behaviour would justify male violence in marriage and would deny her the right to divorce him for cruelty. Atkins and Hoggett described provocation as 'the most insidious concept' in cruelty and domestic violence cases. As they explained, 'the alleged provocative act is usually an affront to the husband's exclusive rights of possession': adultery, withdrawal of sex, neglect of household duties. Women behaving in this way 'provoked' their husbands and therefore had no remedy. In this way, victim-blaming was legally sanctioned.

Until the late 1960s, you can find cases where a man's violence was excused because his wife 'provoked' him. Atkins and Hoggett outline different cases where his violence was deemed to be justified. In one case, a woman went to visit her relatives after her husband told her not to, so his beating her did not constitute cruelty because she had disobeyed his orders. In another case, a judge stated that a woman's withdrawal of sex and neglect of household duties justified 'very considerable violence'. Provocation could even extend to nagging. If a man beat his wife after she had been nagging him, it would not constitute cruelty in law, and if he murdered her, the crime would attract a lesser prison sentence. These attitudes persist in domestic violence myths, which continue to be rolled out in cases today to discredit victims: if she wasn't passive, if she wasn't faithful or if she nagged him, then she deserved it and is not a 'real victim'. This stands in stark contrast to the behaviour expected of rape victims: if she did not resist she is not a 'real victim'. But when it comes to domestic violence, if she does resist she is not a 'real victim'. Women's credibility is questioned for not resisting or resisting too much.

The law also imposed a difficult standard of proof on women seeking a divorce due to domestic violence. Until the 1970s in the United Kingdom, women were not able to divorce violent husbands with a history of abuse unless they could prove there was a risk that the men would be violent again. As Atkins and Hoggett explain, a past history of abuse, even with evidence, was not enough to meet this evidentiary bar. They also highlight a 1975 textbook on matrimonial offences which explained that, in the law, some 'rough and tumble' was deemed to be the 'wear and tear' of married life. The textbook author explained it was a 'natural part' of marriage, and opined that 'an occasional thrashing' was considered by some as 'a sign of their husband's affection'.

In a famous case in 1983, *Bergin v. Bergin*, a judge found that a beaten woman who did not go to the police or seek medical attention, despite having black eyes, had accepted the violence and so had no remedy. As we explain in Chapter 6, similar attitudes continue to be expressed in cases argued today. Of course, there are many reasons women don't report violence at home or otherwise attempt to hide their injuries from others, including to protect their partner because they still love him and to keep their children's father out of jail.

Even when women did make reports to the police, it didn't necessarily result in action. For many years, as Atkins and Hoggett and others have written, police rationalised their failure to act against domestic violence as a desire not to disrupt a marriage or a family home, as that was seen as 'private' and beyond the realm of the law. What happened in the home stayed in the home, and the police wouldn't intervene even if there was evidence of violence. Domestic violence was also seen and treated as somehow less serious than other forms of violence, with violent offences by strangers in the street attracting longer sentences than domestic violence. In her books, Helena Kennedy has also written of her extensive experience in criminal trials involving battered women, who 'still face the prospect of being condemned by popular mythology about domestic violence'. Over her decades in practice, Helena saw how these harmful myths and stereotypes were deployed in court to let men get away with it: 'Within the male stronghold of the court it is all too easy to create the feeling that a woman had it coming to her. Pictures of nagging, reproachful, bitter termagants who turn domestic life into hell on earth are painted before the jury,' she writes. Women are judged by impossible standards of a 'real victim', despite the reality that '[t]o onlookers the response of a battered woman seems abnormal, but to her it is a rational response to her abnormal circumstances'. According to Helena, understanding domestic violence is a challenge for the police, lawyers and judges, and 'misconceptions litter the court and are reflecting in the verdicts of juries'.

These problems continue today. A super-complaint filed by the Centre for Women's Justice against the British police in 2020 exposed ongoing failings in how women are treated when reporting domestic abuse in the United Kingdom. These include the failure to properly investigate abuse allegations, the arresting of abused women instead of perpetrators, and police themselves displaying victim-blaming attitudes.

Male violence myths, silencing and injustice

The legacy of these laws, and of the ongoing gendered myths and stereotypes that they embodied, has a silencing effect on victims. Many survivors report that they don't recognise themselves in what society—and the law—have told them a 'real victim' looks like. Others report that the men who assaulted them don't look like 'real abusers'.

Law professor Julie Macfarlane has written about this from her perspective as both an academic and a survivor. In her book, *Going Public: A survivor's journey from grief to action*, Professor Macfarlane explains the difficulty she faced in speaking out about her abuse by an Anglican priest. She had been groomed and sexually assaulted by an Anglican priest when she was sixteen, but only felt able to speak out about it and take action 30 years later, after the MeToo movement began. Even as a respected academic and white woman, she experienced victim-blaming from the church over her delayed report. The church also claimed she had consented to her abuse. After she spoke out to the media, the church claimed that if she was, in fact, abused (i.e. was a 'real victim'), her post-traumatic stress would have prevented her from being able to speak out about it. From her experience and her research, Professor Macfarlane writes about how these myths reinforce survivors' concerns that they will not be believed if they speak out or report their abuse—and how they therefore silence many women. The myth that a 'nice guy' cannot also be a perpetrator is one of the most insidious. Each time a person or group of people (his friends, family or colleagues) says a man has been nice to them so he couldn't possibly be a perpetrator, they perpetuate this myth to undermine her credibility.

Studies that also show that women who are confronted by these harmful myths and victim-blaming attitudes from police and prosecutors—which is known as 'secondary victim-isation' and even 'judicial rape'—often withdraw their report and their support for prosecution. Psychiatrist Judith Lewis Herman has written about how these myths are deployed by men as tools to silence victims after they speak out: 'If secrecy fails, the perpetrator attacks the credibility of his victim. If he cannot silence her absolutely, then he tries to make sure no one listens.' These attacks happen in public, in the media, on social media and in the courtroom. Sadly, they work—in the court of public opinion and in the courts of law.

Professor Macfarlane explains that the research shows that juries are overwhelmingly influenced by myths about rape and abuse when evaluating evidence and determining guilt or innocence. Studies have shown that men are more likely to believe these myths and tend to have more negative reactions to women victims. However, both men and women—of all ages and backgrounds—are affected by rape myths and demonstrate victim-blaming views. These include beliefs that victims who are voluntarily intoxicated are responsible for their rape; that it's a woman's fault for not properly communicating her lack of consent; that it is not rape if she hasn't been injured; that a delay in reporting an alleged rape is suspicious; and that women often lie or report men in order to take revenge. Studies also show that less blame was attributed to the man when there was a prior relationship with the victim, or where she was seen to have somehow 'participated', whether by what she was wearing or by her behaviour, including flirting.

However, the studies also show that this bias and prejudice can be addressed by judge and juror education, and by judges giving appropriate directions to juries. In the United Kingdom, for example, judges are now required to warn juries about the dangers of myths and stereotypes about both perpetrators and victims when deciding sexual offence cases. This shows there is a need to actively counteract these damaging mythologies, which jurors are now told are 'misleading and capable of leading to injustice'.

But as our colleague Harriet Johnson states in her 2022 manifesto *Enough*, no such jury directions are given in cases of domestic violence—and directions are needed, because myths and victim-blaming remain pervasive in all cases involving gender-based violence in the criminal justice system. As we explain in Chapter 6, there is no requirement for giving jury directions about such harmful myths in civil defamation cases decided by juries—even though juries in defamation cases are increasingly dealing with cases involving sexual and domestic violence.

Male violence mythbusting

Myths and male-centric attitudes about sexual and domestic violence are so problematic and pervasive that guides have been created for judges, for police and for the public to prevent their perpetuation and remove obstacles to more effective prosecution of gender-based violence. For example, the Australian government in 2017 prepared a guide for police to help them challenge misconceptions about sexual offending, setting out different myths and providing the empirical evidence that debunks them. The UK Crown Prosecution Service (CPS) issued similar guidance in 2020. These myths include:

- *Easy to report, hard to defend.* It is in fact difficult for most women to report sexual offences (in Australia, the United Kingdom, the United States and Canada, as few as 14 per cent of sexual violence victims ever report). And it is manifestly not a difficult charge to defend (in Australia, the average conviction rate is just 12.5 per cent).
- *Real victims report immediately.* In fact, the majority of victims don't report at all (83 per cent of Australian women), child abuse victims typically don't report until adulthood, and delay is common for a range of psychological reasons and fear, particularly when the perpetrator is an intimate partner, family member or acquaintance.
- *Real rapes are perpetrated by strangers.* In fact, the majority of rapes are committed by someone known to the victim (a 2016 UK study found the figure to be 70 per cent).
- *Rapes are not perpetrated by boyfriends or husbands.* Consent to sex on one occasion does not imply consent on a later occasion. There is no immunity for rape in marriage anymore.
- *Rape involves violence and force; real victims physically resist.* Most rapes don't involve physical violence, given the prior relationship between victim and offender, and victims are more likely to freeze and cooperate (one US study showed that 81 per cent of rape victims do not resist at all).

- *False accusations of rape are common*. They just aren't. Studies estimate that 5 per cent of rape allegations are false (and this figure is based only on rapes that are reported, so the true figure is, in fact, likely to be even lower). The police guidance makes clear that the incorrect assumption about false allegations contributes to under-reporting.

In Australia, there is also guidance for judges on domestic violence. The *National Domestic and Family Violence Bench Book* reminds judges that the behaviour of a victim does not excuse domestic violence, that victims do not need to be weak, passive or powerless to be a 'real victim', and that women may physically resist violence or defend themselves (i.e. provocation is not a thing anymore, nor does it amount to 'mutual abuse'). It also makes clear that domestic violence includes sexual violence, not just physical violence (i.e. there is no immunity for raping your wife anymore), and that attempts to control a partner can be as serious as physical violence. Other debunked myths include that men and women are equally victims of domestic violence (when in fact women are predominantly the victim of domestic violence), that victims of domestic violence can always 'just leave' an abusive relationship (when it is never that simple), and that women make false or exaggerated claims in order to obtain tactical advantage in family claims or divorce proceedings (they rarely do).

There is clearly still a need for judges to be given these warnings. One UK example is the 2017 Family Court case concerning Afsana Lachaux, an award-winning campaigner for women living in the United Arab Emirates. Afsana had accused her ex-husband of abuse, including coercive control, and sought to challenge a UAE court decision to deny her custody of her son in the UK courts. She returned to the United Kingdom to campaign for custody of her son and received support from Southall Black Sisters, a feminist organisation working against all forms of domestic violence. The case became high-profile: the media reported her story about her allegations of her ex-husband's abuse and he sued the media for defamation.

In the family court, Mr Justice Mostyn reviewed the evidence and concluded that Afsana had—using a well-known trope—'given as good as she got' in the relationship, and that she could not have been the victim of coercive control because she had been able to have a sexual relationship after separating from her husband. Pragna Patel, a former head of Southall Black Sisters, told us the judge's conclusions revealed a fundamental misunderstanding of domestic violence and coercive control. Afsana could not get her son back, but she was also silenced from speaking about her experience. She told us her ex-husband threatened her and her family with defamation action. As we explain in Chapter 6, the media later lost the defamation case.

Laws made by women, for women

The reason the law has historically reflected male interests is because women had no role or voice in political life and law-making. In most places around the world, women were not permitted to vote until the 20th century. At a national level, women were first enfranchised in New Zealand, in 1893, with Saudi Arabia being the last country to allow it, in 2015. History shows that once lawmakers are accountable to women voters, laws change in material ways that are meaningful for women.

It is no coincidence that the year after women got the vote in the United Kingdom and Australia, sweeping laws were passed giving women more rights. In 1919, the UK Parliament passed a law to enable women to join professions and professional bodies, and be awarded degrees. Before that, for example, women had been barred from practising law because they were not considered 'persons' under the *Solicitors Act 1843*. In Australia, the year after women got the vote, Victoria's parliament passed the *Women's Disabilities Removal Act 1903* (since being a woman was considered a disability in relation to work), which allowed women to join professions, become lawyers and sit on juries. Studies have since shown that the inclusion of women on juries increases conviction rates for sexual offences against women. Women are more likely to believe women—and listen to them.

The vote has not meant the end of inequality or discrimination caused by laws that were made and applied by men. But we know that when we have more women MPs, more laws are passed that better protect the interests of women (though, of course, it should never be taken for granted that all women act in the best interests of other women, or that all self-proclaimed feminists enact feminist laws and policies).

Women are still very under-represented in parliaments around the world. Australia was the first country in the world to allow women to sit in parliament, but this came about after a miscalculation by Ebenezer Ward, a vocal opponent of women's rights in the South Australian Legislative Council. Ward devised a ploy to kill a bill which proposed to give women the right to vote. His plan was to add an amendment to the bill saying that women would not only be allowed to vote, but could also run for parliament. He believed this would ensure that the bill was voted down. But it passed, 31–14. Queen Victoria called it a 'mad, wicked folly'—but gave it her royal assent in 1895. But it would take decades before Australia had its first woman parliamentarian, when Edith Cowan was elected to the Western Australian Legislative Assembly in 1921. And it would take until 1975 before the Australian Senate even bothered to install toilet facilities for women.

Life still isn't easy for women in parliament, as evidenced by Julia Gillard's famous speech on misogyny and the 'Ditch the Witch' placards she faced as Australia's first female prime minister. The experience for women of colour in politics is even worse: studies show that Diane Abbott, who in 1987 became the first Black woman MP in the British Parliament, continues to receive—by far—the highest number of online attacks and threats.

Things are not yet equal. In the United Kingdom in 2021, only 34 per cent of parliamentarians in the House of Commons were women—and this was an all-time high. Australia had 38 per cent representation in the federal House of Representatives.

It wasn't until 1983 that Susan Ryan—a senator and later the first woman to serve in a Labor cabinet—introduced the first draft legislation outlawing sex discrimination. The opposition to it was as fierce as it was hysterical: opponents said it would result in a totalitarian regime, the creation of a unisex society, and the demise of the nuclear family. However, according to the National Museum of Australia, the law has since had 'a profound impact on women's position in Australian society', 'encouraged more women to seek an education and employment, which raised families' incomes', and has meant more opportunities for single mothers and more women being appointed to more senior and visible roles. The vehement and even hysterical opposition to progressive change for women is worth reflecting upon as we engage in debates today about women's rights—and their right to speak.

Women MPs and peers played a similarly important role in ensuring the passing of the equivalent legislation in the United Kingdom: the *Sex Discrimination Act 1975*, which created similarly positive outcomes for women. Without it, Jen would not have received her scholarship to Oxford: it was only after this legislation that the Rhodes Scholarship had to be open to women applicants—and even then only after Education Secretary Shirley Williams (at the time the only woman in cabinet) signed a statutory order to remove the words 'manly' and 'qualities of manhood' from Cecil Rhodes' will. Feminist MPs like Stella Creasy, Jess Phillips and Maria Miller, with their work on domestic and sexual abuse and discrimination against women, demonstrate the importance of having women in parliament. The continuing need for more focused attention on issues affecting women and necessary law reform within parliament was underscored by the creation of the Women and Equalities Committee in 2015—the work of which we consider in Chapter 5.

Laws judged and applied by men

It is not enough to improve the law to better protect women. We need also to look at how the law is applied by the courts. The just application of the law might be represented by Justitia, a woman balancing the scales of justice, but in practice those responsible for this task have been men. In the United Kingdom and Australia, the judiciary has always been dominated by privileged white men—and this remains so today. As a former Chief Justice of Western Australia, Wayne Martin, has said, Australia's judiciary is 'pale, stale and male'. And this lack of judicial diversity—and perspective—matters.

Reflecting on progressive legal reforms for women over the past 40 years, Susan Atkins notes how judges' application of the law—and their male-centric perspectives—have often undermined intended reforms or limited their effectiveness. For example, the British courts ruled that discrimination on the grounds of pregnancy was not sex discrimination under the *Sex Discrimination Act 1975*, because discrimination required a comparison between a man and a woman in the same circumstances and men could not be pregnant. This ruling was, thankfully, overturned by the European Court of Justice (a correction that today would not be possible, in this post-Brexit world). As Atkins explains, judges tended only 'to understand the law from a female point of view when they realised that if men were treated in the same way, it would be unfair'. Her best example of this was a case in which women were excluded from ordering drinks at a bar—an injustice any man can empathise with. Attempts to provide better protection against domestic violence were also undermined. When the parliament legislated to increase the courts' powers to grant injunctions to remove violent men from their homes in order to protect women from domestic violence, Atkins notes, judges showed reluctance to deny husbands their right to occupy the family home, calling the injunctions 'draconian', even where they were required to protect the wife from further violence.

This is not ancient history. We could write an entire book on the unjust decisions caused by gender bias. The organisation Women's Link Worldwide has an annual awards ceremony for the best and worst legal decisions that demonstrate this, and that emphasise the need for a gender balance on the bench.

In 2017, there were so many examples of sexist judicial comments that the journalist Sarah Friedman compiled her top picks for the year, which included Canadian judge Robin Camp asking a sexual assault survivor why she couldn't 'just keep her knees together' to 'prevent' the assault. In 2019, in Indonesia, a judge acquitted a defendant of rape because the alleged victim was not a virgin and had 'a drinking habit'. In a case about the capacity of a woman with learning difficulties to consent to sex with her husband in 2019, a British judge said, 'I cannot think of any more obviously fundamental right than the right of a man to have sex with his wife,' sparking outrage and reminders from women's groups that rape in marriage was criminalised back in 1991. In 2016, Judge Aaron Persky's comments in the United States, when sentencing Brock Turner for sexually penetrating an unconscious woman, caused national and international outrage: he justified a lenient sentence by referring to the 'huge collateral consequences' for Turner, ignoring the damage his assault had caused to the survivor, Chanel Miller. Turner served just three months in prison.

In Australia in 2021, Judge Robert Sutherland quashed the conviction of Nicholas Drummond, making comments which caused controversy. There was no dispute on the facts: the former student of the private boys' school Knox Grammar had drunkenly punched two people outside a pub. This included punching one woman in the back of the head after yelling at her 'Put your tits away' and calling her a 'slut'. Using his discretion at sentencing, Justice Sutherland granted Drummond a good behaviour bond. He commented that Drummond's comments were 'lewd' and 'completely inappropriate', but that they were made to someone 'whose dress . . . might have been perceived by a 20-year-old former student from Knox to be provocative'. The judge's comments sparked outrage, including from the victim, who said 'it made me feel as if his actions were almost justified'. Activist Chanel Contos, who founded Teach Us Consent to highlight the pervasiveness of sexual assault perpetrated by private schoolboys in Australia, said this decision showed the injustice in the courts in relation to gender-based violence and the lack of accountability for men with privilege.

How many women will speak out about their abuse—and seek justice—if this is how they are treated by the courts? The effect of decisions like these is to silence women.

Having women in positions of power can influence the law and create meaningful change. Feminist legal critics Susan Atkins and Brenda Hoggett are two women who put their understanding into practice. After publishing *Women and the Law*, their seminal 1984 text highlighting the injustices arising from a male-dominated interpretation of the law, both women made career changes in order to have a more direct impact on policymaking and legal interpretation. Atkins joined the civil service and worked at the Equal Opportunities Commission, while Hoggett became a judge—and eventually, as Baroness Brenda Hale (having reverted to her pre-marriage surname), the first woman on the UK Supreme Court, and the first woman to be its president.

In her time on the bench, Hale drafted and handed down decisions that have markedly improved the lives of women in the United Kingdom: from abortion rights to the protection of asylum-seeking mothers and their children. When asked about her all-time favourite judgments, Hale mentions *Yemshaw v. London Borough of Hounslow* (2011), which established that domestic violence need not be physical and included coercive control. This was a law reform that she and Atkins had argued for almost 40 years earlier in the first edition of *Women and the Law*.

Hale's impact shows just how important it is to have women on the bench, but also just how slow law reform can be. Hale has been criticised for her work, with one *Daily Mail* piece describing her as 'subverting family values'. But it's the same work for which she has deservedly gained cult status in the United Kingdom, akin to that of Ruth Bader Ginsburg (also known as RBG) in the United States, who was a Supreme Court justice and became a feminist icon. While RBG was known for her elaborate lace collars, Lady Hale became known for the coat of arms she chose upon her appointment to the House of Lords, which bears the motto *Omnia Feminae Aequissimae*, meaning 'women are equal to everything'.

There is growing recognition that an all-male judiciary—and perspective on the law—is no longer acceptable. In 2001, Sonia Sotomayor, now a US Supreme Court justice, stated: 'I would hope that a wise Latina woman with the richness of her experiences would more often than not reach a better conclusion than a white male who hasn't lived that life.' In the United Kingdom, judges have been making statements calling for a more diverse judiciary, more women judges and more transgender judges in recognition of the 'rainbow lives of the law'. As a former Australian High Court justice, Michael McHugh, said back in 2004, 'When a court is socially and culturally homogenous, it is less likely to command public confidence in the impartiality of the institution.'

Change is happening, even if it is happening slowly. In Australia, there are now three women judges on the High Court (an all-time high), and in 2021 India appointed three women judges to its Supreme Court. But there is still a long way to go. In both Australia and the United Kingdom, women still only represent just over one-third of judges, despite the fact there are more women than men graduating from law. Only two of the eleven Supreme Court judges in the United Kingdom are women. According to the Diversity Council Australia, international research shows that Indigenous people and minorities are under-represented in the judiciary. Justice Sotomayor's nomination to the US Supreme Court in 2009 made her only the third person of colour appointed to that court in its 222-year history. At the time of writing, we could not find any official statistics on the race and ethnicity of Australian judges, which is itself a problem: you can't understand what you don't measure. One study of the profession shows that while Asian Australians make up almost 10 per cent of the population, they make up only 0.8 per cent of the judiciary. In the United Kingdom in 2021, Black, Asian and minority ethnic men and women accounted for only 5 per cent of judges in post.

Why are there still so few women judges? And how many more women judges do we need on the bench to ensure the law is interpreted to better protect women?

Women in the law

If we are to have more women judges, then we need more women lawyers not just entering the profession but reaching the top of the profession. It might be more than 100 years since the prohibition on women practising law was lifted—and women like Helena Normanton in the United Kingdom and Flos Greig in Australia began practising as lawyers—but the figures show we still have a long way to go.

History shows that having women lawyers in practice has been game-changing for women's rights.

RBG could not get a job at a law firm when she graduated in 1959 because law firms asserted a right to discriminate against women. As a law professor, she wrote about sex discrimination and later argued *Moritz v. Commissioner of Internal Revenue*, a case about discrimination against a man in order to lay the foundations for discrimination against women under the Fourteenth Amendment to the US Constitution. RBG went on to set up and lead the American Civil Liberties Union's women's rights project in 1972, with the support of Pauli Murray, a Black lawyer and academic who had pushed for a women's rights agenda at the ACLU. Murray's scholarship had compared the legal status of women and African Americans, using the term 'Jane Crow'. Their names appear together on the brief for *Reed v. Reed*, the first case in which the US Supreme Court applied the Equal Protection Clause of the Fourteenth Amendment to strike down a law that discriminated against women.

When Sarah Weddington graduated from law school in Texas in the 1960s, she couldn't get a job in a law firm because they didn't hire women. Instead, like RBG and other women of her generation, she became a law professor—one of the few ways she was allowed to use her degree. In 1973, at age 27, she filed what would become one of the most important and hotly contested women's rights cases in US history: *Roe v. Wade*. Weddington argued the case all the way to the US Supreme Court and won, ensuring that women across the United States had the constitutionally protected right to choose to have an abortion (at least until 2022, when it was taken away).

One of Jen's law heroes is Elizabeth Evatt, whose career in the law was one of many 'firsts': she was the first woman to win the University Medal for Law at the University of Sydney, the first woman to be appointed to an Australian federal court,

the first Chief Justice of the Family Court and the first Australian
to serve on the United Nations Human Rights Committee
(UNHRC) and the Committee on the Elimination of Discrimination Against Women (CEDAW). During her career, she
became a prominent reformist lawyer and later jurist. One of
her early cases as a young barrister saw her defending a woman
charged with causing the death of a young woman during an
abortion. This case made it clear to her that there was a need
for Australian women to have access to legal and safe abortion.
From then on, she became an advocate for law reform on
abortion and its decriminalisation in New South Wales. She
chaired the Royal Commission on Human Relationships
(1974–77), which made recommendations on contraception,
rape, child abuse and abortion, and recommended reforms to
better protect women from violence and to ensure equality in
divorce. In her work with the United Nations, Evatt developed
international human rights jurisprudence, including to protect
women against discrimination.

Progress has been made since these women started out in the
law, but the numbers don't lie: more women than men start out
in law, but this has not translated into senior roles or judicial
appointments. And this is a problem when talking about who
has the power to shape our laws and how they are applied.

In the United Kingdom, less than 40 per cent of practising
barristers are women. Judges are typically selected from among
silks, but only 18 per cent of Queen's Counsels are women. The
UK Bar Council has starkly warned that at this rate, women
will never take silk in equal numbers to men, which does not
bode well for achieving gender parity at the bar or on the bench.
In Australia, the figures are worse: in New South Wales, Jen's
home state—women are only 24 per cent of barristers and

less than 9 per cent of silks. When women are appointed silk in Australia, they are almost immediately tapped for judicial appointment because supply simply does not meet demand.

Why aren't more women progressing to the top of the profession? Structural discrimination, the studies all say. As Margaret Thornton wrote in 1996, despite the increase in numbers of women in law, women were still 'fringe-dwellers in the jurisprudential community' and would remain so until structural discrimination in legal practice was addressed. In 2021, Thornton said that while things have slowly improved, the implicit bias and 'boys' club' mentality have continued. The law remains, as it was before, a good case study of discrimination against women.

Jen's perspective

As a law student in Australia, I didn't see women doing the work I wanted to be doing. Until I started working as a barrister in the United Kingdom, all of my mentors were men. The human rights lawyers I had read about in books at university and had seen in the media were mostly men. I've since been fortunate to be able to work with many of those men, including Australian barrister and co-founder of Doughty Street Chambers, Geoffrey Robertson KC, Spanish jurist Baltasar Garzón, and the late Michael Ratner, a prominent US civil rights attorney and co-founder of the Center for Constitutional Rights. My work with them led me to women like Nancy Hollander in the United States and Baroness Helena Kennedy KC in the United Kingdom, who both forged the path for women at the bar and have both become dear friends and mentors. Their stories of the early days at the bar for women are a reminder of how far we have come, and they continue to inspire me.

'Gentleman, approach the bench.' This was how judges would address Nancy and her male opposing counsel when she started out in the early 1970s. One day she had had enough of it. When the judge asked them to approach, she remained in her seat. The judge looked up and asked her if there was a problem. 'I am clearly not a man,' she replied. From then on, the judge would ask 'counsel' to approach. As a single mother, Nancy overcame discrimination, prejudice and structural obstacles to build a successful practice and become the first woman president of the National Association of Criminal Lawyers in the United States. Her work defending Guantanamo detainees was portrayed in the 2021 Hollywood film *The Mauritanian*, in which she was played by Jodie Foster.

We stand on the shoulders of women like Nancy and Helena. I often think of Ada Evans, the first woman to graduate from law school in Australia in 1902. At law school, Ada was told she 'had not the physique' to become a lawyer. But she persisted. She was not allowed to practise until 1921 because of laws discriminating against women, but her efforts made sure I now can.

My own experience—and that of women of my generation at the bar—is a reminder of how far we still have to go. As a law student in Australia, I suffered sexual harassment in two of the three law firms I worked at before I even graduated. For many women, this is enough to kill their passion for the law, if not their willingness to work in such an unsafe environment. In my early days of practice in the United Kingdom, I was often mistaken for the secretary. Alexandra Wilson, a criminal defence barrister and the founder of Black Women in Law, has spoken about how she has been mistaken for the defendant in criminal courts. Even today, when I'm asked in social situations what I do, a surprisingly common response is, 'You don't look like a lawyer'. 'What does a lawyer look like?' I ask in response. And I have the benefit of white privilege. It is so much more difficult for women of colour and those women whose English accent reveals their class as quickly as my Australian vowels and intonation, or Keina's Northern Irish lilt, reveal our roots. I also have educational privilege. I may be a colonial upstart in London, but my scholarship-funded Oxford education eased my path to the Bar.

There are more women at the bar in London where we practise than there are in my home state of New South Wales in Australia. But when I joined the bar in early 2017, I quickly became aware of how few women barristers there are. When I went into the storied Ede & Ravenscroft on Chancery Lane to buy my wig and gown, I added my name to the handwritten list of women barristers who have gone before me, proudly listing my little country hometown of Berry in the book—a small but surprisingly emotional reminder of my unlikely trajectory. Flicking through the book, I noticed that it wasn't very many pages before me that Cherie Blair KC had signed her name. Cherie is another brilliant, pioneering woman in the law who I have since had the privilege of working with, and who—like Helena and Nancy—has forged a path for us. Later in 2017, my pupil supervisor and leading light on women's rights, Caoilfhionn Gallagher KC, took silk. When you take silk, you are given your number: she was only the 398th woman to take silk since the first in 1949. To put this in perspective, there are around 1500 male silks in practice in the United Kingdom today, before we even consider the number across history.

As Caoilfhionn was preparing for her silk ceremony, we discovered that the shoes she was required to wear did not come in a size small enough for her. This is just one of the small, seemingly unimportant but significant ways we, as women, are told we don't belong in the law. Indeed, it was only in 2020, a century after women began practising as barristers, that our colleague Karlia Lykourgou established the first ever legal outfitter devoted to and designed specifically for women. Her company is called Ivy & Normanton, named for the first two women to practise at the bar in England and Wales. For 100 years women have been wearing ill-fitting legal attire designed for men. 'Finally, a collar that actually fits and won't pull my hair,' remarked one of our colleagues.

We are fortunate to be members of Doughty Street Chambers, which was founded to further human rights and civil liberties for all. Each year we have an event for International Women's Day to celebrate the work of Doughty Street women, and all women in the law, in pursuit of women's rights. Each year I marvel at the remarkable work done by our colleagues: challenging laws criminalising abortion in Northern Ireland, suing prisons for their failure to provide women prisoners adequate sanitary supplies, defending battered women prosecuted for killing their abusive husbands or sued for defamation for speaking about their abuse, defending women arrested for protesting for women's rights and suing the police for failing to protect women from their abuser. And each year I am horrified to hear the stories about how women barristers and solicitors are treated in our courts and in the media. Not so long ago, a woman KC explained how, when in a heated argument with a male silk, a judge cautioned her not to be 'hysterical'—a gendered comment that would never be levelled at a man. But things are changing: in 2022, a barrister was disciplined and fined for using this language.

How we are represented in the media matters too. When Amal Clooney walked into the European Court of Human

Rights to argue a case with Geoffrey Robertson KC for Armenia about genocide denial, a male journalist stopped her to ask her what she was wearing. With the quick wit and humour typical of my brilliant friend and colleague, Amal laughed, pointed to her barrister's robe and said, 'Ede & Ravenscroft'. No one asked Geoffrey what he was wearing. In the media, women lawyers are too often defined by our appearance and fashion choices.

After I won the Rhodes scholarship, I got a call from an Australian magazine wanting to profile me. It was my first national media profile. I thought they might be interested in the fact I was the first Rhodes scholar from my region, and a woman (at the time, men still dominated the scholarship: only three of eleven scholars that year were women). The photographer called me to discuss the concept: they wanted me pictured in nothing but an academic robe and 'sexy stilettos'. I was to be their real-life version of Elle Woods, Reese Witherspoon's character in *Legally Blonde*. I refused, telling them it was already hard enough to be taken seriously as a young woman in the law. After some negotiation, I was pictured in a ball gown with the robe. I can't imagine Tony Abbott or Malcolm Turnbull, or any other male Rhodes scholar since, having to have that conversation.

It has continued since I have become a lawyer: like Ada Evans more than a century before me, my physique is apparently still relevant. In 2011, a piece in *The Monthly* about the Julian Assange extradition trial described me as 'the curvy, blonde barrister'. There was no description of the 'rotund' or 'slim' male lawyers in the room—it was only my physique that got a mention.

If it's not about how we look, then it's about how we behave. We are judged for doing our jobs—on the one hand, for being not being 'womanly' enough, and, on the other, for not being enough like a lawyer. Conservative columnist Gerard Henderson once described me as 'the sassy Assange lawyer'. He was using 'sassy' in the pejorative manner it was used back when Ada Evans was at law school: I was too big for my boots, even though I was saying exactly what Geoffrey Robertson KC was saying about the same case. (It made me laugh to think that, whatever Henderson meant by it, 'sassy' means something entirely different and positive to younger generations of women.) Another profile headline described me as the 'hardnosed' lawyer, as if I needed another adjective to ensure readers understood I had the characteristics required of a lawyer. Notice next time you read a description in the media of a woman lawyer being 'aggressive' for doing her job. Would it be said of a man?

And all of this continues today. During the Johnny Depp defamation trial in the United Kingdom, the media coverage often perpetuated myths and sexism, including about us as women lawyers. I was counsel for Amber Heard and assisting News Group Newspapers defend against Depp's claim, which alleged Amber lied about him abusing her. As the trial opened, a *Daily Mail* story was devoted to profiling me and lead counsel for the newspaper, Sasha Wass KC, an eminent woman in the law with decades of experience. The headline proclaimed we were 'Amber's Avengers'. The article described my personal life and 'figure-hugging outfit' and Sasha's 'elfin face' and 'penchant for wearing leather boots'. But even more problematic than the focus on our appearance and fashion choices, was the headline: 'Ms Heard is banking on this formidable legal duo to slip a stiletto into Johnny Depp'. The newspaper had chosen a gendered, violent metaphor to describe women lawyers doing their job: our job was depicted as perpetrating violence on Depp, when our job was to prove that Depp had violently assaulted Amber (see Chapter 7). Would a male lawyer doing their job ever be described as beating or stabbing the opposing client with their shoe? And how could the trial be complete without an Elle Woods reference: a front-page *Daily Mail* image of me comforting Amber as we prepared to enter court was captioned 'Legally Blonde'.

When working on high-profile and controversial cases, women lawyers—like women journalists and politicians—face online attacks and threats. It is sadly not unusual for me or for my colleagues and clients to receive threats. The online attacks we face as women are typically gendered and sexualised: commenting on our appearance, our families, our personal relationships, or making threats of gender-based violence. Over the years, I have received rape and death threats, marriage proposals and indecent images. When I spoke with Rebekah Giles, a well-known media lawyer in Australia who has represented high-profile feminists, women making accusations of abuse and men accused of abuse, she told me she had faced the same. Rebekah pointed out that despite working on many of these cases on teams that included male lawyers, it was only the women lawyers who faced this kind of abuse. She told me, 'At times, it's very unsettling. Some days I wonder, am I going to get my throat slit on the way to the carpark?' And this is our experience in Australia and the United Kingdom. Women lawyers I've worked with in countries like Colombia, Mexico, India and South Africa face serious threats of physical violence. As we explain later, this is just another of the ways women are told to be quiet, play small, and stay out of public and professional life.

We also know that women barristers are paid less and briefed less—and, again, it's worse for women of colour. Studies show we are interrupted more in court—a fact that holds true all the way to the US Supreme Court. Workplace culture still makes it incredibly difficult for women with children to succeed in the law, which I think partly explains why so few women remain in the profession, and why we have so few women taking silk and becoming judges.

All of this matters. It matters because we need a diversity of perspectives in the way the law is argued, shaped and applied. We need more women lawyers and judges, and more lawyers trained and educated not to pander to outdated and false myths about male violence. As Harriet Johnson argues in *Enough*, a more representative legal system is vital not just to ensure public confidence but to ensure fair treatment of women. Johnson writes about the injustices resulting from sexist arguments in criminal cases about gender-based violence, but, as we will show in Chapter 8, these same problems also arise in civil cases that focus on women's rights to speak about it.

Malestream media

Was the MeToo movement a legitimate attempt to break the silence on sexual assault or a baseless witch-hunt?

Well, that depends on which newspapers you read—and on which journalists are writing about it.

Newspapers, journalists and commentators around the world, from Italy to Germany, from Australia to China, India and beyond, have described MeToo as 'a witch-hunt' and condemned the 'media trials' of the accused men. In India, one newspaper described MeToo as 'an epidemic that would destroy Indian culture and civilisation'. In Hong Kong, media reports claimed that 'real victims' should report to the police, not the media, and that MeToo was 'the dumbest movement so far of the century'. In other coverage, women have been depicted as liars and had their credibility questioned, with reference to all the same harmful myths we have been discussing in this chapter.

When we talk about violence against women, we also need to ask what role the media plays in perpetuating these harmful myths and stereotypes. How many women will speak out about their abuse if they see other women who speak out being vilified and attacked in the media? How many more women would speak out if they were treated with the respect they deserve?

The United Nations has asserted that the media can play a role in ending violence against women if it challenges harmful myths and social norms that condone discrimination and violence—and if it reports more stories about it to raise awareness. Media coverage that perpetuates those myths and trivialises male violence, UN Women warns, can even encourage the reproduction of violent acts.

A 2016 media content analysis report by Australia's National Research Organisation for Women's Safety (ANROWS) confirmed that stories often minimised or sensationalised violence against women. Australian journalist Jane Gilmore (see @JaneTribune on Twitter) started a project called 'Fixed It' to highlight this problem. Taking headlines from the Australian media, she 'fixes' them—crossing out the actual headline and substituting her own, which more accurately reports the case at hand:

> ~~Man claims violent sex attack was agreed rape fantasy~~ Woman alleges man raped her three times and threatened to kill her (*Courier Mail,* Australia)

Gilmore's aim is to demonstrate how the media regularly preferences male perpetrators' versions of events when reporting on abuse cases and minimises male violence.

To address this problem, the United Nations recommends the media achieves gender parity. This is because the media, like the law, has a problem with diversity. The media is so heavily dominated by men that UN discrimination expert Alda Facio has dubbed it the 'malestream media'. A 2016 study by the Reuters Institute showed that more than half of journalists in the United Kingdom are men, and 94 per cent are white. A study in 2020 by Women in Journalism, a networking, training and campaigning organisation for UK journalists, concluded that there was a 'shocking lack of media diversity' in the country, with only 30 per cent of experts shown on TV being women. The Australian media also preferences male voices and experts. For example, in 2021 women were quoted less frequently than men (just 31 per cent of the time) and were even less likely to be quoted by male journalists. Our research shows that these figures are replicated in countries around the world: from Nepal to Nigeria and from Bangladesh to Brazil.

Why does diversity matter? Because reporters, and the larger media ecosystems, decide what gets reported on—and how it gets reported.

While women remain in the minority of journalists, it is consistently women journalists who are at the forefront of reporting on issues about gender-based violence and the failure of accountability. In Australia, all the key high-profile stories about allegations of gender-based violence in recent years were the result of reporting by women: Samantha Maiden (News Corp), Lisa Wilkinson (Ten Network), Louise Milligan (the ABC), Nina Funnell (freelance journalist), and Jacqueline Maley and Kate McClymont (Nine Media), including reporting on the Brittany Higgins and Christian

Porter stories, as well as the sexual harassment allegations against former High Court judge Dyson Heydon (which we examine in Chapter 3). In the United States, Jodi Kantor and Megan Twohey broke the Weinstein story, as they explain in their book, *She Said*. In Colombia, Catalina Ruiz-Navarro and Matilde de los Milagros Londoño at *Volcánicas* magazine have done groundbreaking work reporting stories of abuse and harassment that the mainstream media wouldn't touch (see Chapter 2). Indeed, *Volcánicas* was set up specifically to report these stories because the malestream media refused to report it—or reported it badly.

Yet the women who choose to report on stories about gender-based violence face additional threats, attacks and online harassment—all of which are forms of attempted silencing. The Association for Progressive Communications (APC) has identified that women journalists are one of the most frequently targeted groups when it comes to online violence, attacks which are often sexualised, make references to personal and family relationships, and use insults involving physical appearance and intellectual capability. Intimidation rarely comes as a direct response to women's ideas or arguments, but focuses instead on their identity as women who think for themselves and speak out.

British newspaper *The Guardian* commissioned research into 70 million comments left on its site since 2006, which made some significant findings: eight of the ten most abused writers were women (the two men were black); articles written by women—regardless of subject—attracted more abusive and dismissive trolling than those written by men; and articles about feminism or rape attracted the highest levels of blocked comments.

When we spoke to Pragna Patel, an intersectional feminist, she raised growing concerns about the wider context of silencing and the lack of a wider discussion of women's rights to freedom of speech and expression. Although her experiences of silencing relate to speaking out about violence against women and girls in particular, 'it is in a climate where the spaces to speak out are not just shrinking, but are becoming intimidating spaces, threatening spaces, [because of] the rise of authoritarianism around the world'. Pragna told us that we are living in a moment in which people who are campaigning and attempting to change the law face violence and intimidation, and that this is silencing feminist speech. Attacks on women speaking out, on the journalists who report on them, and on the lawyers who are defending their right to do so are all forms of attempted silencing.

When considering the role of the media in reporting on gender-based violence, and the media's role as the vehicle for women to speak out, it is important to understand these structural issues. As we will see in chapters 4 and 6, the way a story is reported matters, and can have serious consequences for the women who speak out.

Removing the gag

Justitia is depicted in our courts as holding the scales while blindfolded. But for the many women silenced by the law and by our justice systems, it would be more realistic to depict her as gagged—as she is on the cover of this book. This needs to change, and this is why we argue, just as RBG did, that women belong in all places where decisions are made—in parliament, in the courts and in the media. Many more women.

Laws made by men and judged by men have historically protected men, and those same laws have failed—and silenced—women. This structural issue affects how the law regulates gender-based violence. Harmful stereotypes and gender bias pervade how violence against women is reported in the media. and how it is treated in the justice system. This is the reality women are coming up against. As we will explain, it also can affect the outcome of cases involving women speaking out about gender-based violence.

Chapter 2

HOW MANY WOMEN ARE SILENCED?

In 2021, Chinese tennis star Peng Shuai accused a former vice premier of the Chinese State Council, Zhang Gaoli, of coercing her into having sex. She posted the accusations on the Chinese social media site Weibo. The allegation was the first to be made against one of China's most senior political leaders.

After she posted the accusation in November 2021, Peng Shuai was not seen or heard from for several weeks. The original post disappeared and news reports began to circulate that her personal feed had been censored. The BBC reported that search terms such as Peng Shuai's name were also temporarily blocked from social media.

International concern mounted for her wellbeing, with the United Nations requesting proof that she was safe and well and able to speak in her own terms. Serena Williams, Naomi Osaka and Novak Djokovic, some of the biggest stars in world tennis, spoke out and raised their own concerns. The Women's Tennis Association (WTA) pulled out of all tournaments in China the following month.

Then, in December, Peng Shuai gave an interview with media, wearing a red national tracksuit. In the interview, she walked back her accusations, saying, 'I never said anyone had sexually assaulted me in any way.' She has since been seen on social media and in person, but many are still concerned for her welfare. Some even noted that, in the video of her interview, there was a mirror showing a man standing there—likely her minder. The WTA has maintained its concern, and no events are taking place in China in 2022.

Peng Shuai's case was a window into the censorship that has stifled the MeToo movement in China: the hashtag #MeToo is itself blocked, along with other key phrases, including 'rice bunny', a Chinese homonym for the MeToo campaign. Prominent MeToo figures like Xianxi, who was sued for defamation after raising sexual harassment allegations against CCTV presenter Zhu Jun, and their supporters, have been blocked from posting on Weibo too.

Others have been arrested and imprisoned. For example, Huang Xuequin, an investigative journalist who has been involved in several MeToo campaigns to provide support and assistance to survivors, is currently in prison on charges of 'subverting state power'. Human Rights Watch reports that many Chinese MeToo activists have been '[s]ilenced by their home country' and have fled overseas, where they have freedom to speak, post online and be heard.

Just as there is a continuum of violence against women, from wartime rape to all different forms of violence, abuse and harassment, there is also a continuum of silencing. In this chapter we set out how human rights activists, women advocating for sexual and reproductive rights, journalists reporting allegations of sexual abuse and harassment, and individuals speaking about their own experiences of abuse are being silenced through the use of the law. We explain how the law is being used around the world—in different places and in different ways—to silence. And with different levels of silencing. This is what the United Nations has called 'gendered censorship'. Women are being silenced and their right to free speech is not being protected, or respected. From the conviction of directors of domestic violence shelters for speaking out about violence, to the targeting of those advocating for the decriminalisation of abortion, to the detention of migrant women who report their abuse to the police, there has been a global failure to uphold and protect women's free speech when speaking out against violence and abuse and advocating for their rights.

Criminal laws that silence

Criminal laws are punitive. They can result in jail sentences. They can also silence women's accounts of sexual violence. As Indian superstar lawyer Karuna Nundy explained to us, different criminal laws can work to make women reticent to come forward about abuse and punish them when they do. For example, in some countries adultery (or sexual relations outside of marriage) is a criminal offence. The United Nations has noted how the criminalising of sexual relations between consenting adults is a violation of human rights, and how in some countries such laws penalise only women.

Such discriminatory laws and the criminalisation of adultery also mean that a woman faces legal penalties if she makes an accusation of rape or sexual violence and the man alleges it was consensual or the authorities decide that she should be punished. The UK public were shocked in 2016 when the BBC reported that a British woman was 'arrested in Dubai after reporting rape'. She reported that she was raped by two British men, but was then charged with having extramarital sex and detained. That media report followed the sentencing of a Norwegian woman to sixteen months' imprisonment for extramarital sex after she reported her rape to police in Dubai (though she was pardoned a few days after sentencing). Organisations such as Amnesty International have brought attention to extreme examples: girls as young as thirteen were stoned to death in 2008 after being accused of adultery following their rape in Somalia. None of the men accused of rape were arrested. The European Court of Human Rights heard how Polish authorities opened a criminal investigation into a fourteen-year-old girl for the crime of unlawful intercourse after she reported a rape and requested an abortion. The girl was deprived of her liberty, separated from her mother and treated 'in a deplorable manner', breaching her fundamental human rights.

Research carried out by experts at the United Nations has underlined that most of these laws are specific to women: it's fine for a man to have an affair, but a crime if a woman does. In Iran, if a woman was drinking alcohol when their rape occurs, they could face criminal prosecution for engaging in unlawful activity. How many women are going to come forward and report their rape, or even risk telling anyone about it, if they may be charged with adultery, sent to prison or stoned to death? How many women have been silenced from speaking about their abuse because of laws like these?

Discriminatory criminal laws also affect the LGBTQI+ community, who in many countries around the world remain at risk of criminalisation for reporting sexual abuse. It remains a crime in 78 countries, including 35 Commonwealth countries,

for LGBTQI+ people to engage in consensual intimate relationships. In some countries, including Iran and Pakistan,
the punishment is a death sentence. Such laws produce a
chilling effect: they prevent LGBTQI+ victims of sexual crimes
from going to the authorities to seek protection from violence
or justice for abuse for fear of their own criminalisation. If a
same-sex rape is reported by a victim, the moment the perpetrator claims it was consensual, the victim may face prosecution
themselves. Societal notions of heteronormativity continue
to discriminate against queer communities. This means that
sexual and gender minorities live in fear of persecution by the
state and fear of others who use criminal laws to blackmail and
exploit queer people. How many women—or men—would
report their sexual or domestic abuse if it meant their own
arrest? How many queer people have been silenced because of
laws like these? Who is going to come forward to speak when
the law fails to protect you?

This was the problem explained by Rosanna Flamer-Caldera,
a leading LGBTQI+ activist in Sri Lanka, in her legal challenge
against the laws criminalising consensual sex between women.
Keina acted for Rosanna in her case before the UN Committee
on the Elimination of Discrimination Against Women. Rosanna
explained that the criminalisation of same-sex conduct meant
that lesbian, bisexual and trans women were too scared to report
gender-based violence or abuse to the police, since it could lead
to their own arrest. CEDAW ruled that Sri Lanka had violated
Rosanna's rights by enacting a law to criminalise same-sex
conduct between women, finding that it prevents people from
coming forward to seek protection.

In England, there is a campaign to introduce a law that
would protect undocumented migrant women from violence

by safeguarding their ability to report it without risk of criminalisation and deportation. We have seen through our work
that when migrant women try to speak out about their abuse,
they often find themselves in an impossible dilemma: do they go
to the police for protection and risk being arrested and placed
in immigration detention, or do they remain silent and thus
vulnerable to the abuse? Migrant women, and the organisations representing them, have been advocating for a law to
make sure that when they come forward to report sexual or
domestic violence, they are not arrested and detained for immigration offences or deported. In response to this blind spot in
the Domestic Abuse Bill in the UK, Baroness Meacher said:

> Migrant women with insecure immigration status are, in my
> view very understandably, reluctant to report domestic abuse to
> the statutory services. Would you, one might ask, particularly
> to the police? This reluctance is due to the current data-sharing
> agreements between statutory services, including the police
> and the Home Office, for immigration control purposes. This
> means that women affected cannot seek support or a safe place
> to go, with the most appalling consequences, as one can very
> easily imagine. Perpetrators are not being brought to justice.

And vulnerable women are being silenced about their abuse.
It is reported that 60 per cent of UK police forces share information with the Home Office. In response to the problem,
Southall Black Sisters and the Centre for Women's Justice filed
a super-complaint against the police to challenge this practice.
Following the super-complaint, the UK policing authorities
issued a report in 2010, *Safe to Share?* The report found that in
25 out of 36 case examples, the police forces caused harm. This

included taking no action in response to the crime and leaving the perpetrator of the abuse against the victim unchallenged; treating victims as perpetrators and detaining them in custody because of their immigration status; and telling victims to sort out their immigration status before reporting abuse, exposing them to further abuse. The report identified a risk that perpetrators use their victims' immigration status as a 'weapon' of control, and that this deters victims from coming forward. Clearly the law needs to change.

The enactment of a hostile environment policy for migrants stops women—especially Black women—from reporting violence by their intimate partners in the United Kingdom, for fear that they will be removed from the country. Women do not report violence to police because they do not trust that police will protect them. Associate Professor Marie Segrave of Monash University has explained that fear of deportation and loss of custody of children is a key barrier to temporary migrants reporting their abuse, and that these fears are often exploited by abusive family members.

In Australia, a long history of colonial and police violence—including high rates of Indigenous deaths in custody—means there is widespread distrust and fear of police. According to a 2020 report by Australia's National Research Organisation for Women's Safety, led by Professor Marcia Langton AO and Dr Kristen Smith, factors such as the fear of child removal and isolation from their family and community prevent First Nations women from reporting and speaking out about their abuse. To put this fear in context: Indigenous children are 9.7 times more likely to be removed from their families than non-Indigenous children, and one in every 16.6 First Nations children lives in out-of-home care.

For those paying attention, story after story shows how the authorities fail First Nations women, subject them to further violence and even to arrest and prosecution for reporting domestic violence. For example, Ms Dhu died in custody after her grandmother called the police to save her from domestic violence at home. When the police arrived, they didn't just arrest her violent partner, they also then arrested Ms Dhu over unpaid fines. She later died in custody from injuries sustained from the domestic violence, after what an inquest described as 'inhumane' handling by police, who had ignored her reports of pain.

In another case, in 2013, Tamica Mullaley was stripped naked and brutally beaten in the street by her boyfriend, who then fled the scene. When the police arrived, she was uncooperative, so they arrested her instead and left her baby at home. The infant was subsequently murdered by her boyfriend, the domestic violence perpetrator. It wasn't until 2022, after almost a decade of campaigning, that Tamica received an apology from the Western Australian government.

#LetHerSpeak: When speaking out is contempt of court

In Australia, Grace Tame's case—and her #LetHerSpeak campaign with journalist Nina Funnell—has led to much greater awareness of laws which silence victims of sexual assault. The campaign has shown not only that women often face public contempt for speaking out about their abuse, but also that speaking out itself can amount to contempt of court.

Contempt of court laws in Australia, England and Wales, and elsewhere are designed to protect against conduct or reporting that might prejudice a fair trial, and to sanction those who disobey or ignore court orders. This includes enforcing reporting restrictions or non-publication orders, which protect the anonymity of victims of sexual offences by making it a criminal offence to publish their names or otherwise reveal their identities. These laws aim to encourage women who might otherwise be deterred from reporting their abuse if they are publicly identified as victims of sexual assault to come forward and make complaints.

This makes sense—but the way the law has been drafted in some states has had unintended consequences, especially where victims want to tell their story and yet are not permitted to waive their right to anonymity in order to do so. For those survivors, like Grace Tame, the law functioned as a gag order, preventing them from talking about their assault, from naming their assailant and from telling their own story.

In England and Wales, all victims of sexual offences are autonomically guaranteed anonymity for life from the moment they make an accusation. This right to anonymity continues even if the accusation is withdrawn or the police decide to take no action. Victims and survivors have the power to waive their right to anonymity, provided they are over sixteen years old and they provide their consent in writing. Victims under sixteen cannot waive their right to anonymity.

Breaching contempt of court laws and identifying a victim of sexual assault is a criminal offence, and can result in a fine or even prison time. These laws aim to ensure the administration of justice by—for example—prohibiting behaviour such as shouting in a courtroom, disrupting court hearings or taking photographs during court proceedings. They also regulate what you can say publicly about a court case, in order to protect the right of the accused to a fair trial. For example, it is an offence for a newspaper to proclaim someone's guilt before a verdict is reached, or to publish anything that could prejudice a trial. Usually, victims of crime, witnesses and offenders under eighteen years of age cannot be named, or their images published, in the news media or on social media.

The rule ensuring anonymity for victims of sexual assault was introduced in the United Kingdom 1976 out of concern about the community shame associated with being a victim of sexual assault and how victims had been treated in the media. It makes a lot of sense, too, particularly in cultures and communities where sexual matters are taboo, or where there continues to be shame and stigma around being known as a victim of sexual abuse, which can lead to exclusion or retaliation. Ensuring victims and survivors can come forward without being associated with the abuse or the crime is important.

In Colombia, by contrast, as the feminist journalist Catalina Ruiz-Navarro explained to us, there is no law preventing sexual assault victims from being named. This means that women complainants in rape and sexual assault cases are identified in the media, and they are often vilified, their reputations attacked, and their names forever associated with the abuse. On the other hand, privacy laws and threats of libel suits keep the names of alleged abusers out of print, meaning that the crimes are associated only with the victims. For this reason, in countries like Colombia, there are efforts to introduce similar anonymity provisions to ensure that survivors do not face media intrusion and attacks, and are not forever defined by what was done to them. How many victims of abuse have been silenced after watching other women be attacked and vilified in the media for reporting theirs?

Contempt laws provide significant protections for those who want anonymity. We spoke to one of Australia's leading media lawyers, who sadly became the victim of what is colloquially known as 'revenge porn'. She did not want to be named but wanted to share her story. Her ex-partner pleaded guilty to threatening to share intimate images of her—images which, she said, she later found out did not exist. She was shocked when her name, and the details of the case, were suddenly all over the tabloids, and she had to obtain a court order to protect her right to anonymity. She explained how she discovered, through her own horrific experience, that when parliament had introduced new sexual assault laws to incorporate the non-consensual sharing of private images as an offence, the legislators forgot to extend anonymity protections to victims and survivors. It was an oversight that enabled the media to report about the case, naming her as the victim.

She shared her story for this book because she wanted to explain that—like many victims and survivors—she simply would not have come forward if she had known her anonymity would not be protected and the details of the story would be published to the world, and be online for her children to read. She also made the point that she was in a unique position to move quickly to protect her anonymity. How many women have the legal knowledge, networks and resources to instruct counsel and, if the material has been shared or published online, to get it taken down?

But there is a flipside to these laws, which has been seen most clearly in Australia. The desire to protect women from being identified has, inadvertently, led to women being silenced. In Tasmania, as in some other Australian states, women can't simply give their consent to waive their anonymity and tell their own story: they must get a court order and convince a judge that it is in the public interest.

Grace Tame's case brought this issue into the national spotlight. Her #LetHerSpeak campaign aims to abolish sexual assault victim gag laws—and led to her being named Australian of the Year in 2021. Tame was a victim of child sex abuse. As a vulnerable fifteen-year-old, she was groomed and repeatedly sexually assaulted by her 58-year-old teacher Nicolaas Bester. Bester was convicted and sentenced to two and a half years, serving just eighteen months.

After being released from prison, Bester started making vile, victim-blaming comments online about the sexual assault he had committed against Tame, including the tired old excuse that 'she wanted it'. She could not respond—under section 19K of the *Evidence Act* in Tasmania, it was illegal to identify someone as the victim of a sexual assault, even if that person was you. It was a strict liability offence, and newspaper editors or anyone else who published Tame's name could face up to twelve months in prison. Unlike in the United Kingdom, Grace couldn't simply waive her right to anonymity. She had to convince the courts that it would be in the public interest to let her speak.

This was not just a dormant law still on the books—it had been enforced as recently as 2012, when the Supreme Court of Tasmania fined the *Sunday Tasmanian* newspaper and its acting editor for contempt of court for publishing an article with the name, photograph and age of someone who said she was a victim of rape without first obtaining a court order. The Supreme Court stated:

Such a provision may encourage representatives of the media to pester victims to consent to publicity. It is undesirable to expose victims to this pressure at a time when they are likely to be in considerable emotional turmoil and may be ill-equipped to weigh up and assess the consequences of publicity.

Grace Tame's only option was to get a court order that would permit her to identify herself as a sexual abuse victim and speak about her experiences. It took two and a half years and cost $9000 of in-house legal fees and application fees to obtain that court order. It was only in August 2019, after her court order was granted, that Grace was able to speak out for the first time. The front-page story by Nina Funnell carried a picture of Grace with the headline: 'My name is Grace Tame and I am Jane Doe'.

As a result of her experience of silencing, Tame and Funnell started a campaign to change sexual assault victim gag laws around Australia and prevent other survivors from being silenced. Thanks to their #LetHerSpeak campaign, sexual assault victim gag laws in the Northern Territory, Victoria and Tasmania have now been amended to allow survivors of abuse to self-identify in the media where they consent to be named and where they will not identify another survivor.

Grace Tame's campaigning also resulted in another important change to the law. The Tasmanian criminal offence of 'maintaining a sexual relationship with a person under the age of 17' has been renamed as 'the persistent sexual abuse of a child', in order to properly reflect the abuse to which she was subjected as a child. As Tame explained in her campaigning, the description of the offence in the law diminished its seriousness and contributed to victim-blaming in the media. At the time of Bester's criminal trial for abusing her, some media and TV programs covered the story as 'an affair with a student', suggesting that Grace was somehow an equal participant in her own abuse, or that it was an illicit affair rather than a crime. The renaming of the offence calls it what it is: sexual abuse. It makes clear the gravity of the offence and its non-consensual nature—it is not a 'sexual relationship' between equals, it is the 'sexual abuse' of a child.

Far too often, survivors who speak out about their abuse face media intrusion, online trolling and unacceptable attacks. For this reason, anonymity should be ensured for the survivors who want and need that protection. But laws that result in the gagging of victims are not fit for purpose, and only end up harming those who want to speak out and those who feel it is healing to go public. This is why it is important to listen to victims and survivors when they speak. Tame's activism and her #LetHerSpeak campaign has not only changed the law, it has also started to change the national narrative: it is not shameful to have been abused, or to talk about being abused. You can talk about it if that is right for you, and you can be recognised and celebrated for speaking out.

———————

As we reflected on Tame's campaign, we began to notice a pattern whereby anonymity rules have prevented victims and survivors from speaking about their abuse. In the United Kingdom, there is a growing debate around anonymity provisions in family law cases, and it came to a head in late 2021 with the publication of the judgment in *Griffiths v. Griffiths*.

In family court settings, the normal order of things is that the matter remains secret in order to protect the privacy of the family and the children involved. When judgments are published, they are commonly anonymised to protect the identity of children. It is a contempt of court to speak about or publish what happens in family court proceedings without the permission of the court. Some have argued that while the privacy rights in family court proceedings provide important protections for children and for families who want to maintain anonymity, the laws also can have the inadvertent effect of silencing victims. Women may be isolated from important support networks if they are barred from being able to tell their friends and families about the abuse.

In 2020, a former Conservative MP, Andrew Griffiths, was found by a family court to have raped his then wife, Kate Griffiths, who is now also an MP, having taken over her ex-husband's seat. While Andrew Griffiths denies the allegations of rape and domestic violence, the family court found that, on the balance of probabilities, Kate Griffiths was telling the truth. Kate Griffiths gave evidence of coercive control, sexual assault and domestic violence inflicted over almost a decade, including while Andrew Griffiths was an MP.

Initially, the judgment in *Griffiths v. Griffiths* was not published—meaning the findings in relation to the rape and domestic abuse remained secret. Louise Tickle, a journalist for Tortoise Media, one of the organisations that challenged this secrecy, explained that this also meant Kate Griffiths was silenced: 'Kate Griffiths would have been banned—forever—from telling even her family and friends about what the court had determined had happened to her, had I at Tortoise, and Brian Farmer at PA Media, not fought for over a year to publish.'

The media organisation argued in court that the judgment should be published: it was in the public interest to do so because the public had a right to know that an elected MP had been found in law to have repeatedly raped and abused his wife while in office. Andrew Griffiths initially opposed the application made by the media, saying the judgment should never be published. He then changed his position and said the court should publish the judgment, but only on the condition that all names were removed—that is, the judgment would be anonymised so that he couldn't be identified.

The organisation Rights of Women, represented by our colleague Caoilfhionn Gallagher KC, intervened to support the media organisations' applications. In their intervention, Rights of Women argued that women who are victims of domestic abuse are entitled to choose between anonymity and publicity, and that they have a right to freedom of expression and 'informational self-determination'. In other words, women have the 'right to tell their own stories'.

Kate Griffiths supported the application by the media, and argued that the judgment—including her and her ex-husband's names—should be published. Her right to free speech and to share her experience as a survivor of rape and domestic abuse was affected.

As the judge summarised, she argued that she 'should not be "silenced" by the court, at the instance of the father [of her child]', and noted that 'if family proceedings had never been commenced, she would have been free to share publicly the abuse she had suffered, and she should not be barred from speaking publicly after seeking legal protection for the child through the family courts'.

In the High Court, Lieven J decided that the judgment should be published, along with their names, but that the identity of their child was to be protected. In reaching her decision, Lady Justice Lieven noted that Kate Griffiths had 'a right to speak to whomsoever she pleases about her experiences', and that the courts should be careful in situations where there have been findings of coercive control to ensure that proceedings didn't become a means of seeking further control. 'For women who have been the subject of domestic abuse to be unable to speak about their experiences, including their experiences through litigation, must often be extremely distressing. And may in some cases be re-traumatising.' Considering the balance between Kate Griffiths' right to speak and his right to privacy, the judge found that it tipped in favour of allowing publication of the judgment and the parents' names.

Tortoise Media has now published details of the many legal steps that it took to enable it to report the findings against Andrew Griffiths and to allow Kate Griffiths to speak.

These campaigns and cases raise important questions about who gets to speak and when—and whether the law is adequately protecting the right to free speech. How many women have been silenced from speaking about their experience of abuse by anonymity or non-publication orders? As a UK judge explained in a case called *Re Roddy*, free speech 'is the right, as a human being, to share with others—and, if one so chooses, with the world at large—one's own story'. The right to tell one's story is a fundamental part of who we are. The freedom to report the truth has been described by the courts as a basic right. Yet many women we have spoken to have described feeling like the Little Mermaid—having had their voices stolen from them by the law. The family courts are important venues for the protection of victims of domestic violence and abuse, and of children, but non-publication orders and the laws of contempt can also lead to silencing. These are just some of the legal battles that women face in order to tell their stories.

Silencing the campaigners

Should women face criminal charges for walking down the street with a large plastic vagina, or for marching for the right to have legal and safe abortions? While most places in the world advocate for freedom of expression, there seems to be a double standard when it comes to campaigning for women's rights. Religious freedom is often used as a means of silencing women, just as defamation is used not as a shield but as a sword.

In Spain and Latin America, ancient criminal laws on injury to religious feelings are used to prosecute and criminalise women's rights marches. For example, in Spain, a woman was given a criminal record for marching with a plastic vagina down a street because 'it was evidently with the intention of ridiculing and laughing in a gratuitous way at Catholic tradition'. The criminal investigation was instigated by a complaint from the conservative lawyers' association that carrying a 'powerful vulva' down a street is a hate crime. The convictions and the censorship of vaginas and vulvas are a ridiculous violation of the freedom of expression of those who march for greater respect of the rights of women to choose and to have bodily autonomy. It would all be funny—and ludicrously so—if women weren't ending up with criminal records.

In the United Kingdom, women have found themselves having to challenge bans on protests about women's rights and gender-based violence. A recent example is the vigil organised in the wake of Sarah Everard's disappearance, kidnapping and murder. Women and girls took to the streets en masse, to 'reclaim the streets', to advocate for the right to live a life free from violence, and to say enough is enough. The organisation Reclaim the Streets, represented by lawyers including two of our colleagues, had to go to court to challenge the Met Police's handling of the proposed vigil—which effectively banned them from organising an event to express their collective grief and to campaign for changes in attitudes and responses to violence against women. The Met threatened the organisers with fines and prosecutions if the event went ahead. The High Court found that the four organisers' human rights to free speech and freedom of assembly had been breached.

There is a long history of silencing women who campaign for the right to access safe abortions.

When Keina was a law student at Trinity College Dublin, one of her professors was Ivana Bacik, who is currently leader of the Labour Party in Ireland. Ivana was then a criminal law professor and well-known feminist activist. In 1989, she was threatened with prison. For what crime? Providing the phone numbers and addresses of abortion clinics in England to Irish women. She was prosecuted not for being involved in an abortion, but for simply giving information to women about where they could safely access an abortion outside the country. At that time in Ireland, many women were forced to travel to England, and pay a lot of money, for access to legal abortions. This was because abortion was unlawful in Ireland—and this remained the case until 2018, with the groundbreaking movement and referendum to repeal the Eighth Amendment to the Constitution of Ireland, which finally changed the law.

Ivana avoided prison, largely thanks to her lawyer, Mary Robinson—who would go on to become the first female president of Ireland. But her case showed that the law could be weaponised against women to stop them from sharing information. Information is a form of power—it educates and empowers women to know their rights and to take action for change—and, eventually, the law was changed. This shows the power of advocacy, but also the power of silence. Silencing women slows progress, if not preventing it altogether. And when there is a vested interest in silencing women to protect the status quo, the law can be and has been used as a blunt tool to shut us up. This should be deeply worrying—and should prompt us to question who is really entitled to freedom of speech, and why.

The weaponisation of the law to silence abortion activists occurs in a broader context, and often comes together with non-legal silencing techniques, including intimidation and harassment. Women speaking out and informing other women are facing legal threats, as well as physical and online attacks, and the ultimate silencing tactic: assassination attempts and extrajudicial killings. This builds on the broader continuum of silencing which is produced by the criminalisation of abortion. Women who have been raped are too scared to come forward and seek medical abortions when they fear criminalisation for doing so.

We recently caught up with the Colombian feminist and human rights activist Mónica Roa. Mónica is well known across Latin America for bringing a case that legalised abortion in Colombia, which paved the way for similar court decisions elsewhere in the region. She was only in her twenties when she brought that case, but it would change her life forever. She was sued, received death and rape threats, had to have 24/7 body-guards for years and her office was shot at; eventually she was forced to leave the country. Throughout and despite all this, she continued her work with Women's Link Worldwide, where Keina also worked, to implement the legal decision to make abortions available for women whose life or health was at risk or who had been raped.

After Mónica took and won the case that overturned the abortion ban, she filed another lawsuit on behalf of 1201 Colombian women, claiming that the state had violated their right to information by failing to provide accurate sexual and reproductive health information—including about how women could get an abortion. The lawsuit challenged misinformation by the inspector-general—the equivalent of a minister responsible for ensuring compliance with the constitution—and the government officials charged with implementing the Constitutional Court's decision on abortion.

'I had faced harassment and threats since the beginning from litigating abortion rights,' Mónica said. 'But when it became about the inspector-general, I had people walking up to me on the street, screaming at me, calling me a baby killer.'

She told us about how, in 2011, she was shot at while working in her office in Bogota. This was despite having 24/7 security guards provided by the state. After that, she told us, she realised she would never feel safe in Colombia, even with state protection. She received a huge number of threats online, many of which were motivated by religious extremism. She was sent emails with quotes from the Bible, such as 'the one who spills blood will be the one whose blood is spilled', and 'pictures of babies in clouds, saying they would send me to heaven too'. She recalled how people even 'threw shit at the door of the office'.

In 2012, out of the blue, Mónica was informed that a criminal investigation had been opened against her for criminal defamation. She learned via the press that she was being prosecuted, but her lawyers were unable to find out who had made the original complaint. She believes a powerful government official made the criminal complaint against her because of the 'right to information' lawsuit she filed before the Constitutional Court and her public statements calling for the state to make access to abortion care a reality. Mónica explained to us: 'It's difficult to understand, but the reason the government official denounced me for criminal defamation and calumny is simply because I filed a lawsuit.'

Women's Link Worldwide released a press statement raising its concerns that a high-level government official could file a criminal defamation complaint against a women's rights activist, and emphasised that women's rights would be seriously undermined if the state criminalised the work of human rights defenders. The American Bar Association wrote to the president of Colombia to outline its concerns over the attacks against Mónica Roa and the fact that a criminal defamation complaint had been made against her apparently in response to her filing of a legal case on sexual and reproductive rights.

Mónica decided to protect herself from retaliatory legal suits—and the risk to her life—and went to stay with Keina in London. Ten years later, Mónica continues to live outside Colombia. She continues to work on human rights, but she still faces security issues.

In 2019, when she travelled to Mexico, Mónica became a victim of digital kidnap, inhuman and degrading treatment, and sexual abuse. Digital kidnap is an emerging form of online violence whereby criminal groups intimidate and threaten someone by cloning their phone, and then they convince the victim's loved ones and friends that they have been kidnapped. At the same time, they make the victim believe that they are in a hostage situation.

Mónica took to Twitter to raise the alarm that she had been a victim of this new form of violence: she had been made to believe that she was in a hostage situation in her hotel room in Mexico, and at the same time her friends and family were told that she had been physically abducted. It was a nightmare for Mónica and her loved ones, until the Mexican and Colombian authorities stepped up and helped them. Monica's legal work underlines the personal impact and security challenges that many lawyers and activists face for standing up for human rights, protecting the environment and trying to ensure the world is a more equal place. It also shows how the law can be used against us. It is judicial harassment, and the organisation Frontline Defenders calls it out as such.

The trend of criminalising and silencing activists and those working on women's rights issues is also affecting those working in frontline domestic violence services. This silencing, and the fear of legal repercussions for speaking publicly about violence against women, is a problem that organisations often raise with us.

It is a serious issue for many small, grassroots and frontline organisations working with migrant women, Black-led women's organisations and rape crisis centres in the United Kingdom and elsewhere. It is especially a problem in countries where the law enables police officers, state officials or abusive men to file criminal defamation claims against those who report on their abuse or criticise their failings.

In Latin America, celebrated journalists such as Lydia Cacho have been arrested, detained and subjected to cruel, inhumane and degrading treatment on charges of criminal defamation. The Mexican journalist had written a book about corruption and child sexual exploitation. The powerful figures she criticised wanted to silence her, so they had her arrested for criminal defamation. The UN Human Rights Committee held that her rights had been violated, and that Mexico should repeal its criminal defamation laws. In Chile, the feminist dance group Las Tesis is also facing criminal charges of defamation for creating a song titled 'A Rapist in Your Path', and for calling out the police for their inaction on violence against women. The police filed a criminal defamation suit against Las Tesis.

These cases demonstrate how the state shuts down women's activism—in fact, it SLAPPs them down. 'SLAPP' stands for 'Strategic Litigation Against Public Participation', and it's a term that is increasingly being used around the world to explain legal actions in which the law is used as a weapon to silence.

When we spoke to Mónica Roa about her situation, she told us that we needed to speak to two Colombian journalists who were facing criminal and civil suits for reporting on MeToo allegations. Catalina Ruiz-Navarro had been the communications officer at Women's Link Worldwide at the time Keina had worked there and when Mónica had faced her criminal defamation suit in Colombia. When we spoke with Catalina, we were shocked to learn that she was facing multiple suits, along with her co-founder and editor-in-chief of the online feminist magazine *Volcánicas*. It was time to talk to Catalina.

Silencing the journalists

We caught up with Catalina Ruiz-Navarro and Matilde de los Milagros Londoño in early 2022. Catalina and Matilde are currently facing multiple lawsuits for reporting allegations of sexual misconduct made by eight women against Ciro Guerra, one of Latin America's most famous film directors.

Their commitment to feminist perspectives means that, on their website, you can find articles on the rising Colombian singer Lido Pimienta, on friendships, love and sex, on political protest, and on sexual and reproductive rights. You can also find an interview with the Colombian journalist Jineth Bedoya, who talks about how she was kidnapped, raped and tortured by paramilitaries while doing her job, and how she has since fought for justice, setting a landmark human rights precedent on the protection and rights of women journalists. *Volcánicas*, their website, also carries out investigative journalism into allegations of sexual impropriety.

Volcánicas was born from the debris of sexual harassment allegations which blew up the media outlet where Catalina used to work. That journal, which was based in Guatemala, promoted itself as a feminist organisation but was far from it. The founder was accused of sexual harassment, which Catalina later reported on—risking her personal safety and her financial security. But, as she recognises, Catalina was privileged enough to be married to someone with a stable job, so she could take that risk. And she did not live in Guatemala at the time.

Catalina published her article about her former boss in 2020, and the fallout was immense: the journal was shut down, international funders pulled out and her former boss's wife left him. She was concerned he might sue her, but he didn't. After her publication of the article online, Catalina and Matilde decided to start their own feminist-led news site—*Volcánicas*—and to prioritise feminist reporting, including on public-interest stories on gender-based violence.

Reporting on gender-based violence and sexual assault is extremely difficult in Latin American countries. Most outlets will not publish allegations without a verdict against the alleged perpetrator, because to do otherwise could open them up to liability for defamation, including criminal defamation. But prosecution and conviction rates for these crimes are extremely low, and this means only a fraction of the stories about sexual abuse cases are ever reported. There are many women and girls who experience sexual violence but never see justice, and they can never speak publicly about what happened to them. And this matters: we know that media reporting about sexual abuse encourages more women to come forward and report to police and to family. It also raises awareness and sparks protests about gender-based violence, and forces policy change.

Volcánicas saw that they could change this culture of reporting, or lack thereof—even though they were at risk of being sued. But both Catalina and Matilde felt it was important to tell the stories of women who chose not to go to the police—because they felt it would be hopeless if they did—and who just wanted the abuse to stop. As Matilde told us, the 'main goal' for these women 'in making their stories public was that they didn't want him to abuse and harass women again. The only thing they want is for their abuser to stop abusing. They didn't want him to go to jail, they didn't want money, they just wanted it to stop.'

On 24 June 2020, *Volcánicas* published allegations about Ciro Guerra, an Oscar-winning director. They named him in an article reporting accusations from eight different women of alleged sexual assault and abuse—all of which he vehemently denies. Guerra responded by launching a series of lawsuits against *Volcánicas*. He also launched a PR campaign that represented him as a loving father and husband, with statements of support from powerful industry figures.

In May 2021, the journalists published another article about Guerra, this time about the various lawsuits he had taken against them, accusing the director of 'a strategy of judicial harassment against them'. He had sued them in a civil claim for the equivalent of US$1 million, and initiated criminal defamation proceedings and a number of other legal actions against both journalists. In total, they have faced at least five different lawsuits so far for publishing the allegations.

As a small, new and independent media organisation, *Volcánicas* didn't have the money to defend the legal actions, so Catalina and Matilde had to find pro bono support from lawyers. The cases, which are ongoing, take up their time and expose them to massive risks: if they lose, Guerra could bankrupt them both. But they aren't backing down. The articles remain online, and the journalists stand by the women making the accusations and affirm their belief that there is clear public interest in publishing the stories.

The physical and mental toll that it takes to publish such accusations and handle the legal consequences that follow are clear. 'It has been very hard for our body and our minds. It's very scary,' they told us. Matilde said: 'I didn't anticipate how bad it would be—journalists being sued is portrayed as a brave and courageous thing, it feeds ego and, as a journalist, it's seen as brave; when I thought about the possibility of being sued, I didn't think it would be so traumatising and make me feel so economically unsafe and physically unsafe and that I would become so depressed that I couldn't work anymore.'

Guerra filed and obtained a ruling from a court in Colombia that *Volcánicas* had to correct its article by adding more information. The journalists responded by adding not only further information, but also more allegations against the director.

Despite intense pressure, they have maintained source anonymity; they know that if they revealed the names of the women who accused Guerra, the women would face an onslaught in the media. In many other countries, there are laws designed to protect the identity of these women and their anonymity. But in Colombia, there is no such protection: it is completely legal for other media outlets to plaster their names and faces across their front covers, opening these alleged victims up to personal attacks and to the possibility of more violence. By refusing to identify them—even to police—the journalists are protecting these women.

Media Defence, an NGO, has emphasised how *Volcánicas* is insisting on source protection and maintaining the confidentiality of its sources, as journalistic ethics require. It is an important aspect of the right to free speech that journalists are not forced to reveal their sources. Media Defence is supporting the journalists' legal defence to ensure that journalists reporting on matters of public interest don't face legal actions for defamation for reporting on these stories or suits that seek to force them to reveal their sources.

Talking to Catalina and Matilde, it's hard not to be struck by their passion for feminist journalism and their desire to make the world a more equal place. The David and Goliath nature of their legal fight is clear. Here are two young women, who can't afford legal fees, facing multiple legal actions—civil and criminal—for publishing allegations of misconduct by a powerful industry figure, who is using the law to protect his reputation. We see these competing legal interests time and time again in cases around the world: his right to privacy and reputation versus her right to free speech.

In 2021, the national Colombian weekly magazine *Semana* published a story under the headline 'Strategy of Intimidation and Abuse'. It detailed how the organisation FLIP (Fundación para la Libertad de Prensa), a leading free-speech organisation in Colombia, has argued that Guerra's civil demand for nearly US$1 million is so disproportionate that it amounts to judicial harassment of the *Volcánicas* journalists. FLIP explained that these types of cases against journalists chill publication on public-interest matters, leading to self-censorship. They also accused Guerra of trying to achieve censorship by not only suing for money, but also seeking an order that the journalists can never again print anything about Guerra, whatever the subject matter.

Catalina and Matilde's case is now going to the Constitutional Court in Colombia. It will ultimately decide whether their right to free speech has been violated. The journalists and their lawyers are hopeful, since Colombia's court has in recent years had some of the most advanced jurisprudence on free speech.

Ana Bejarano, one of Catalina and Matilde's lawyers, is one of Colombia's leading free-speech lawyers. She explained to us that while the Constitutional Court has not yet decided a case about journalists reporting on gender-based violence, it has decided a number of cases involving the rights of women to speak out about their own abuse. The court has considered the balance between her right to speak and his right to reputation and has decided in favour of free-speech rights, explicitly stating that a woman's right to live a life free from violence informs that right and outweighs his rights to honour and privacy. It remains to be seen whether the court will follow its previous reasoning in Catalina and Matilde's case.

Catalina and Matilde's battle underlines how it's not just the women who speak out about their own sexual abuse and gender-based violence who face risks—so do the journalists who report these facts. In May 2022, an international free speech organisation, Article 19, published a report that we wrote following interviews with leading free-speech and women's rights experts around the world. The picture for journalists and social media communicators is grim. They are frequently targeted and face a range of security risks, from murder, death threats and sexual violence to online targeting and hacking. Women journalists often face a specifically misogynistic form of online abuse. A similar pattern was observed in research in countries from Bangladesh, Sri Lanka and Nepal to Brazil, Chile and Paraguay. Women journalists require greater protection and enhanced security measures for the work that they do. And criminal and civil defamation laws are just one problem—increasingly, women are being targeted through the use of cyber-security and cyber-harassment laws. But they are also facing laws specifically designed to silence them.

In early 2022 we spoke with Galina Arapova, a leading Russian human rights lawyer and director of the Mass Media Defence Centre. She told us how the Russian government is using draconian laws designed to criminalise espionage, and a mechanism called 'foreign agent designation' to silence journalists and the lawyers representing them.

Journalistic freedom in Russia is facing massive issues generally, but this is a specific issue facing women who report on gender-based violence and sexual assault. Galina told us a chilling story about a young journalist, one of her clients, who fled the country after investigating and publishing a story accusing a teacher of sexual misconduct. The teacher had allegedly harassed and abused underage students for more than twenty years at an elite Moscow school. Yulia Lukyanova, a brilliant young Russian investigative journalist, published the story in news outlet *Proekt*, which was famous for reporting on high-level corruption in Russia, and the teacher was fired from the Kolmogorov Boarding School. In a familiar pattern we see around the world, Yulia was then sued in a civil court for defamation. She was also threatened with criminal defamation proceedings by the teacher's lawyer during the court proceedings. Yulia has since won this case at first instance, which Galina explained was a very important victory. But she is unsure if the case will be appealed. The story is still not over, she told us.

For Yulia, it got worse. On 15 July 2021, the Russian authorities suddenly banned *Proekt* and classified its staff, including Yulia, as foreign agents. That designation not only silences Yulia's reporting in Russia, but it makes it more difficult for Galina and her colleagues at the Mass Media Defence Center to defend her in the civil defamation case.

Galina told us that most of the journalists on the government's list of 'foreign agents' are women journalists, who are increasingly being pressured to keep silent. The *Proekt* website was blocked; dissemination of the information on it is now banned. There are 'different levels of silencing that operate in Russia', Galina explained, and this action against *Proekt* and Yulia was 'full silence'. Not only is Yulia having to fight the defamation case, she also now has to fight her designation as a foreign agent. That designation not only silences Yulia's reporting in Russia, but it is also now more difficult for Galina to defend Yulia in the defamation cases. It is a case of silencing upon silencing.

It would soon become worse for Galina too. Days after a Russian journalist was awarded the Nobel Peace Prize in 2021 for the risks he faced for doing his job, Galina became the first lawyer in Russia to be designated as a foreign agent. She explained to us that the designation means that before she gives a lecture or speaks in public, and even before she posts something on Facebook—whether it is work-related or personal, and even if it is as trivial as a post about a restaurant she has just been to—she has to state, in pro-forma language provided by the Russian government, that she has been designated as a foreign agent.

Galina has since lost her job as a lecturer and faces stigmatisation and discrimination. The designation also means she faces onerous reporting requirements and state surveillance of her expenses and bank accounts. It has hampered her ability to defend Yulia and her other journalist clients who are fighting the same designation. The government is silencing Galina for her work defending free speech. Her life and livelihood are in danger simply because she is standing up for human rights and journalistic freedoms.

We spoke to Galina in January 2022, just before Russia invaded Ukraine. She told us then that she was seriously worried for her own safety, and for the safety of others who were working for human rights, including free speech, in Russia. The outbreak of the war has undoubtedly made the situation for journalists in Russia even worse, with new laws having passed that criminalise journalists for reporting the truth about the war, about Russian opposition to the war, and about war crimes by the Russian forces. Not long after we spoke with Galina, she was forced into exile.

Our conversation with Galina Arapova was an important reminder of how free speech is the cornerstone of a democratic society, and just how central it is to all our rights, including the right to live a life free from violence. Reclaiming free speech— and reclaiming feminist politics on free speech—is therefore an essential aspect of holding governments to account, and of ensuring our right to live in peace and free from violence. As the writer and feminist Audre Lorde says, we have to be able to transform silence into action.

Silencing the silence-breakers

At the heart of the MeToo movement has been a willingness by women to break their silence. Silence is a powerful weapon that protects and enables abusers. But breaking silence still comes at a very real cost—which can include facing defamation lawsuits and public backlash and abuse. Both are powerful and effective ways of silencing women, which is why so many of us are fighting for change.

One story that has moved us both, and that shows how both these silencing methods play out, is that of Shiori Ito, a woman who is fighting for change in Japan. Shiori prefers to be known as a silence-breaker, rather than as a rape survivor or victim, and here we share her story.

Keina's perspective

Today, Shiori Ito is instantly recognisable in Japan; she was one of *Time* magazine's people of the year in 2020. But the first time I met her, back in 2018, it was not long after she had gone public about her allegation of rape. She was living in London, having been subjected to horrendous abuse in Japan after speaking out about her experiences.

When Jen and I discussed writing this book together, Shiori immediately came to mind as someone who has been changing the national conversation in Japan. I'm Japanese-Irish, and spent some of my childhood living in Tokyo. I go back to see my family there every year. I've always been fascinated at how the outside world views Japan as a progressive, techno-capitalist Asian country, full of Pikachus and *kawaii* or 'cute' culture. But the idea of Japan as a 'progressive' country should be more nuanced.

Japan still has the death penalty and carries out executions. According to the global Gender Equality Index 2021, Japan ranked 120th in the world, which makes it one of the lowest-ranked countries in the Asia-Pacific region (only ranking higher than Papua New Guinea and Vanuatu). By way of comparison, Ireland, my other country of nationality, ranks ninth; Spain, where I live now, ranks fourteenth; the United Kingdom, where Jen and I work, is 23rd; and Australia is 50th. In other words, Japan's track record on gender equality is abysmal. Of course, there is incredible activism and organising by feminists within Japan, and Japan has a surprisingly good record in appointing Japanese candidates to CEDAW. But Japanese women are subject to stereotyping and are more limited in their opportunities to participate in public life than women in most Western countries.

This is why Shiori Ito is such a hero of mine. She is breaking down barriers, fighting to change laws, and advocating for a society in which gender equality is discussed. By speaking out at a press conference about her own experiences of reporting her allegation of assault to the police, she forced open a conversation in a country where rape and violence against women often goes unreported in the media. There have been only a handful of cases in Japan where sexual violence has been discussed so widely in the media; one was the Waseda Super Free case in the early 2000s, when an elite university social club became known as a 'rape club' after members of the group were convicted of raping three women. But Shiori is the first woman I have seen come forward in Japan and speak on her own terms about the need for justice for her experiences of alleged abuse and assault. But for daring to speak out, she has paid a high cost.

I first met Shiori Ito at the offices of the Centre for Women's Justice in London, where we were gathered to discuss law reforms for sexual offences in Japan. The Centre for Women's Justice is led by the formidable human rights lawyer Harriet Wistrich. She founded Justice for Women, a law-reform group, and has specialised in fighting for justice for women who have killed their violent partners after years of abuse.

Harriet represented Sally Challen, who was convicted of murder for killing her controlling husband Richard; Challen later walked free after Harriet's intervention highlighted the impact of coercive and controlling behaviour. Harriet and I have worked together on Fiona Broadfoot's case. Fiona had been in local authority care when she was groomed, pimped and prostituted. Instead of being protected, she was prosecuted by the police and convicted by the courts for street prostitution. The law that was meant to protect her actually punished her, and then prevented her from getting jobs years later, so we fought to have her criminal record—which stated she was a 'common prostitute'—removed.

Harriet is a feminist lawyer who is tireless in making women's rights to live a life free from violence and misogyny a reality. So it's little wonder that people from around the world ask for her advice and her perspective on law reform. On this occasion, it was a group of Japanese lawyers, prosecutors, psychologists and journalists, who were on a study tour to learn from organisations in the United Kingdom about how to improve the law in Japan on sexual offences and how to provide better victim support. Shiori was among the expert Japanese group seeking to reform the law. I was invited along as a half-Japanese barrister working on issues of violence against women.

I remember Shiori clearly, as we were two of the younger members of the group squeezed into a small conference room. Shiori has a presence that I quickly warmed to. She speaks English with an American lilt and is the kind of person you want to be friends with. Her eyes sparkle with intelligence and she has a passion for justice. She handed me her business card after the meeting, a Japanese custom, and I apologised for having forgotten to bring mine.

In the years since I first met Shiori, a lot has happened. Shiori has since become a symbol of Japan's MeToo movement and has battled multiple defamation cases, both as a claimant and as a defendant.

In 2013, Shiori Ito was a young journalist trying to find her way into the news industry. She was ambitious and talented, and decided to study in New York. It was there that she met Noriyuki Yamaguchi, the Washington bureau chief for Tokyo Broadcasting System, a major media network. Yamaguchi was powerful and well connected, with close ties to the Japanese prime minister of the day, Shinzo Abe. Yamaguchi introduced her to colleagues and she got an internship.

In 2015, Shiori met up with Yamaguchi again at a restaurant in Tokyo to discuss a job opportunity that he had emailed her about. Five days after the meeting, Shiori Ito went to the police and reported that, after their dinner, she had allegedly been raped in a hotel room by Mr Yamaguchi while she was unconscious.

Shiori asked for a female police officer at the police station. But the only one available worked in the traffic department, so her case was handled by male officers. The police officers made her re-enact the alleged sexual assault, using a life-sized doll. They took pictures. She was asked again and again whether or not she was a virgin. It was not until two years later, in 2017, that prosecutors said there was not enough evidence to bring the case.

In Japan, the definition of rape requires evidence of force or violence—it's not enough to show that you didn't consent. Because Shiori told the prosecutors she was unconscious, her rape was considered, in law, a 'quasi-rape'. And the prosecutors said she did not have enough evidence to prosecute even for this lesser charge. Shiori has publicly stated that prosecutors in charge of her case told her that because the incident occurred behind closed doors, it was a 'black box'. They meant the 'truth' of what happened could never be known, so prosecuting the case was not worthwhile. (Shiori would later use this term as the title of a book about her experiences, *Black Box*. Yamaguchi would countersue following its publication and, according to newspaper reports, win.)

Her hopes for a trial—and for accountability—vanished. There was no way for her to get justice, or even to be heard. So she decided to go public. In May 2017, she held a press conference, calling upon the police to reopen the investigation, and bringing attention to the unjust laws and practices in the criminal justice system. Shiori's decision to speak out soon led to an avalanche of media reporting and internet speculation. She was called a North Korean spy, and many commented that her allegation was politically motivated, since Yamaguchi was by now close friends with former prime minister Shinzo Abe. The media also judged her for the way she dressed, questioning whether a 'real victim' would have had the top button of her shirt undone at a press conference—or given a press conference at all.

At the same time she faced this public backlash, Yamaguchi brought a defamation claim, for an amount so high it would have bankrupted Shiori. Instead of backing down and being silenced, Shiori decided to countersue him for calling her a liar, arguing it was defamatory for him to allege she was making the accusation up. This had never been attempted before in Japan: using defamation against the alleged offender.

In 2019, Shiori Ito won damages in her civil suit against Yamaguchi, with the court dismissing his 130 million yen defamation claim against her. The court found that she had been 'forced to have sex without contraception, while in a state of unconsciousness and severe inebriation'.

In July 2022, the Japanese Supreme Court dismissed Yamaguchi's appeal to the civil suit and finalised the lower court's ruling that he had sexually assaulted Shiori. Shiori was awarded 3.3 million yen in damages (US$24,000). The Supreme Court also made a separate ruling awarding Yamaguchi 550,000 yen in damages (US$4000) and ordered Shiori to pay this for claims made in her book that he might have drugged her. On 21 July 2022, Shiori gave a press conference following the Supreme Court ruling, stating that, while sexual assault victims are finally being heard, the burden of filing a lawsuit has been mentally and financially huge for her. The Supreme Court judgment brings an important end to a long-running lawsuit and vindicates Shiori's decision to speak out.

But Shiori's legal battles are not over. In Chapter 8, we will explain how she is using the law to fight back against the online harassment and trolling that she receives because she went public. She is campaigning to make the internet a safer space for women and girls, and to reform Japan's sexual offences laws to be based on consent—rather than requiring victims to prove the use of violence or intimidation, or that they were 'incapable of resistance'.

The trolling Shiori receives is so bad that she needs a team to go through her social media so that she does not have to see it and take on all of the trauma. It is so bad that she decided to live outside of Japan for a while. This is the other cost of speaking out: it's not just the legal battles, but the enormous personal and financial pressures that come from advocating for change and for women to be able to live lives free from violence.

As we were discussing the similarities of the arguments made about 'real victims' in court cases around the world, Shiori said simply, 'Different legal systems, same story.' That perfectly sums up the problem, and the pattern we are seeing around the world. Like us, Shiori wants to solve it by changing and improving the law.

Breaking the silence

The law as it stands is silencing the voices of victims and survivors. Some of these laws were designed to protect women, but in practice they have often ended up protecting perpetrators by silencing victims who want to speak out. Some of these laws censor or ban certain speech—or ban speech from certain individuals. Others result in a less direct form of silencing, but with similar effect, making journalists fearful of reporting allegations because of the risk of lawsuits, which are expensive and can result in bankruptcy or even prison.

This global picture of silencing—especially in how it undermines women's rights and the right to be free from violence—underlines why it is so important to defend free speech as a women's right and as an equality issue. We must ensure that journalists can do their work and report abuse, that domestic violence shelters can raise money and campaign, and that silence-breakers can speak out, inspire other women to come forward, and advocate for changes in the legal system. We need to free her speech and end gendered censorship.

Chapter 3

WHAT HAPPENS WHEN WOMEN SPEAK?

Women had been speaking about sexual assault and violence long before MeToo—it was just mostly behind closed doors or in whispers. They might pull a new colleague aside, whispering the names of men she should 'watch out' for. Maybe they would be waiting in line for the bathroom, quietly talking about what they'd heard about how a guy at the party treated one of their friends. Maybe it would be in the form of a joke—the kind of joke that has the sting of truth underneath.

Far from being rumours designed to ruin reputations, this 'whisper network' existed for one main reason: protection. It was a way women could protect themselves and other women. It was especially important when the men in question were in positions of power—when speaking in more than a whisper might have serious personal and professional consequences for her—and went far beyond not being believed. But it was imperfect and inefficient, and it did not address the root of the problem—or provide a meaningful mechanism of justice for survivors. That's where MeToo came in.

In a lot of ways, MeToo brought the whisper network into the public sphere. These whispers were no longer whispers, they were statements made out loud, and on the record. MeToo recognised that while whispering might have protected some women, it also protected the men and the institutions that sheltered them.

The MeToo movement took off in the United States and around the world. There was a clear message for men who were used to being protected by silence: women were speaking. And they were being heard. A new form of justice began to take shape. We saw how just one woman having the courage to speak out could encourage so many others to come forward. We saw even powerful men held accountable—and prosecuted. We saw how, together, women speaking out could spark protests, and legal and political change.

But in making violence against women more visible, the MeToo movement also made more visible the cultural and legal obstacles women face when they speak out. This is what had maintained the status quo of silence for so long. In the backlash, we saw these same cultural and legal tools being used to reassert that status quo—to silence the women who spoke out, and deter anyone else who might be thinking of speaking out in the future.

In this chapter, we look at the MeToo movement in Australia—how it started and what happened when women spoke out—as a case study to show the intersectional, cultural and legal issues that women come up against in their efforts to seek justice and create change.

When the movement kicked off in Australia in 2017, the legal backlash was swift: defamation claims and threats rained down on women and the media who reported their stories. Many mused about whether the law had killed the movement.

That oversimplification ignored the complex cultural reasons in Australia—established as a penal colony, with an ambivalent relationship to its own racism, and renowned for its sexism—that meant the MeToo movement didn't catch on in the same way as it did in other countries. But a few years later, a group of young women started to stand up and say—again—enough. Their stories came together to spark a national controversy and protest movement in 2021, which shifted public discourse and political space and started to force change.

MeToo and the Australian media

Soon after Hollywood adopted and amplified the MeToo movement, social media in Australia was set alight. And from the fire that was starting to burn, one Australian figure promised to bring the same reckoning as Weinstein faced to Australian shores: journalist Tracey Spicer. She called for women to come forward with their stories, promising to read and respond to every single one. Soon, she was overwhelmed. Spicer has said that more than 2500 women reached out to her with their stories of sexual abuse and harassment.

The first big MeToo story in Australia—prompted by disclosures made to Spicer, and published by *The Sydney Morning Herald* and the ABC in November 2017—reported multiple allegations of sexual harassment against the gardening TV personality Don Burke. Burke denied the allegations and called it a witch-hunt. But in a later case against him, which we discuss in Chapter 8, his denials were found to be 'implausible'.

Media organisations suddenly clamoured for more MeToo stories, and others soon followed: about former *Neighbours* star Craig McLachlan, and the Oscar-winning actor Geoffrey Rush.

Both men sued for defamation: McLachlan sued the media and Christie Whelan Browne, the woman who had made the allegations. He would withdraw his case in 2022, but only after the trial had started and $2–3 million in costs had been incurred. Rush sued Sydney newspaper *The Daily Telegraph* and won (we discuss both cases in Chapter 6).

Even women who hadn't wanted their story to be made public faced defamation cases and threats. A troubling aspect of the early days of MeToo in Australia was the number of women who became the subject of media reporting without their consent, including for the political objectives of men.

The *Daily Telegraph* story on Rush had itself been rushed: the matter was reported without ever seeking comment from the woman at the centre of it, Eryn Jean Norvill. She had made a confidential sexual harassment complaint at the Sydney Theatre Company and never intended for it to be public. But it ended up on the front page and in court.

Under the cover of parliamentary privilege, a NSW government minister outed his political opponent, opposition leader Luke Foley, alleging he had sexually harassed a journalist. That journalist, ABC reporter Ashleigh Raper, had chosen not to complain about the incident and never wanted it to become public. She said she had feared she might lose her job, and worried about the publicity and the pressure she and her family would face. But her choice was taken from her. After her story was 'outed' in parliament, she decided to tell it herself. Foley denied her allegations and threatened to sue the ABC for defamation for having published her story.

Catherine Marriott had made a confidential internal complaint to the National Party against the former party leader and deputy prime minister Barnaby Joyce over an incident of alleged sexual harassment at an official event. It was leaked and she became front-page news. She said the publicity was 'horrific'. Joyce said her allegations were 'spurious and defamatory' (i.e. she lied), questioned why it took her a year to report it and claimed 'it should have been dealt with immediately'; he said she should report it to the police so he could defend himself.

How many women will report sexual harassment—even confidentially—if it might end up on the front page of the newspaper and they are threatened with defamation? Incidents like these did not empower women to report or speak out, and only exacerbated mistrust. Women must be allowed full agency over whether or not they speak out about their experience—and the media should always seek their consent before reporting it and before naming them.

At the same time, all of these defamation threats fuelled commentary that Australia's defamation laws were stifling the movement, deterring women from speaking out and stopping the media from reporting on it. The backlash was not just legal—and it was directed at those speaking out and the journalists reporting on it: Spicer said she received death threats and vicious online abuse for her work exposing sexual misconduct. Christie Whelan Browne, who spoke out about McLachlan, received an avalanche of online abuse, including comments like 'hope she gets raped'.

Spicer spoke about being swamped and said she was, understandably, unable to handle all of the disclosures on her own. She co-founded NOW, an organisation which was meant to be the Australian answer to TimesUp. It promised a triage service to help women who wanted to speak out: it would direct survivors to journalists and the legal support and counselling they needed. She told BuzzFeed that she started NOW 'after it became clear our defamation laws were severely restricting the movement' and 'protect[ing] the rich and powerful'.

Then came the magazine cover. *Latte*, a women's business magazine, featured the headline 'Tracey Spicer and the women dismantling discrimination'. As Jess Hill writes, it showed 'Spicer, strong and defiant, at the centre of a circle of mostly white women in power suits'. This was the image that would come to define the movement in Australia but it also drew criticism. As Laura La Rosa, a Darug woman, feminist writer and critic, wrote, the movement was 'glaringly white and middle-class in its representation'.

Soon after the magazine cover incident, Spicer would step back from her work with NOW 'to allow more diverse voices into the space and to look after her mental health'. She was later awarded the Sydney Peace Prize in 2019, together with the US founder of MeToo, Tarana Burke, for her work spearheading award-winning investigations into sexual abuse and harassment. In accepting the prize, Spicer spoke of the privilege of bearing witness to the stories of survivors, and of the emotional burden of being entrusted with those stories.

But the criticism and legal issues continued.

When an ABC TV documentary about Spicer, *Silent No More*, was shared with journalists for media publicity prior to its broadcast in late 2019, an error was made: the program failed to blur out survivors' names and the details about their stories. Spicer drew criticism from survivors for identifying them without their consent, and many took to social media to complain about her handling of their personal information. Having criticised the use of defamation laws to silence survivors, Spicer herself threatened to sue survivors and others for criticising her over the privacy breach—an irony that did not go unnoticed after her earlier critique of defamation laws. The ABC issued an apology for its error and the breach of privacy in identifying survivors. By June 2020, NOW had been dissolved.

Around this time, many began to think the Australian MeToo movement was over. Dr Karen O'Connell of the University of Technology Sydney wrote that it 'seems to have gone quiet', and high-profile cases (such as those involving Burke, McLachlan, Joyce and Foley) had 'mostly faded from public view'. As O'Connell observed, while all were alleged sexual harassment cases, none of the women had claimed or received any remedy under sexual harassment laws. Instead, she wrote, 'what most of these cases have in common is that the men involved have sued or threatened to sue for defamation . . . [and] may lead someone who has experienced sexual harassment to think that the reputational interests of the accused are better protected by law than those alleging harassment'. And if not better protected by the law, they are certainly better remunerated for it: as she explained, damages for defamation claims over allegations of sexual harassment far exceed the amounts women would ever receive in damages in claims for suffering sexual harassment.

So what went wrong? Was it our defamation laws? As detailed by journalist Jess Hill in her *Quarterly Essay*, the problem with trying to reproduce the MeToo movement in a different context became apparent very quickly. The early days of MeToo in Australia were characterised by its spotlight on the experiences of white, middle-class women—which left women of colour, working-class women and queer folks out of the conversation altogether. This lack of intersectionality matters: in media coverage and the public conversation in Australia.

But the next wave of the movement was about to break. At the forefront was Dhanya Mani whose fight to be heard spurred her into action—for herself and for all women, including women of colour. But was Australia ready to listen?

Dhanya's story

I joined the Liberal Party when I was 17. When I began attending social events, I was given a list of the men I should avoid due to their lengthy records of sexual harassment. When I asked whether these serial offenders had ever been reprimanded, I was laughed off. I was told these men were 'good guys' but this was 'just how they were' and so I should be aware.

These are the words Dhanya Mani wrote in an essay for *Women's Agenda* in 2019. The child of first-generation migrants, a Liberal Party member and survivor-advocate, Dhanya told us that she experienced sexual harassment and assault by a fellow political staffer while working in the NSW Parliament in 2014, when she was just 21. For years, her internal complaints had gone nowhere. As a result, she left politics to pursue her career in law and landed a prestigious job as a judge's associate on the NSW Supreme Court. But while working there, she says she faced sexual harassment from one of the most powerful men in the legal profession: former High Court justice, Dyson Heydon AC KC. She said it happened several times and in the court building. It was 2018 and two years before the *Sydney Morning Herald*'s explosive 'Dirty Dyson' exposé about how a culture of silence had protected Heydon when he sexually harassed a succession of young women lawyers who worked for him on Australia's highest court. And it was two years before Australia's first woman Chief Justice, Susan Kiefel AC, apologised to six women after an independent inquiry found they had been sexually harassed by Heydon. (Heydon 'categorically' denied the allegations.) So Dhanya didn't know then that it had happened to others: the women were still in silos of silence. She reported it to the judge she was working for, but nothing was done. 'I felt there was nowhere else to go. I had left politics because of the sexual assault. I went into the law, then I faced sexual harassment from someone who was revered . . . I just thought, that's it, if I confront him, I am done, if I don't confront him, I am done. My boss idolises him, all the judges in the equity division are mates with him . . . This is why I reached out to [Spicer].' The MeToo movement gave her the confidence to speak out. Encouraged by Spicer's willingness to take on men in power and NOW's promised nonpartisan approach, she contacted the journalist.

Months passed and she received no reply.

'I felt like I was suffocating,' Dhanya told us. 'I had nothing left. It didn't matter how much I had overcome odds to be there [in the law] and it was all for nothing. I thought there must be some way to get justice . . . and it's speaking out. And then nothing . . . if Spicer didn't want my story, when she was asking for people to speak to her, who else would?'

After a lot of self-reflection, Dhanya chose to tell her own story—in her own words and on her own terms—or at least, part of it. 'I knew how to write it in a way where I couldn't be sued. I could achieve what mattered to me on an emotional level,' she told us. She wrote the essay for *Women's Agenda* about her experience of the culture within the Liberal Party and the failure to properly deal with her complaint about the sexual harassment and assault she had experienced in politics. Having been warned that her credibility would be attacked if she spoke out before the state election, she deliberately waited to publish on the day after the election—and the Liberal government was returned to power. Pre-empting predictable attacks, Dhanya didn't want her allegations to be dismissed as politically motivated to damage the government's re-election. In her essay, she explained the victim-blaming culture she saw, observing negative comments about women who had raised complaints, such as 'she was drunk', 'desperate', 'easy', 'ambitious' or 'asking for it'. When Dhanya raised her own complaint, it went nowhere and she was deemed a trouble-maker. Various MPs and political staffers asked her questions like, 'Oh, I feel sorry for him—why don't you just date him?' and 'Are you sure you didn't lead him on?' and 'You do realise you could ruin his life and he could lose his job, don't you?' Dhanya explained how she had come to understand, from her own experience, the gaps in legislative protection for women working in parliament and the inadequacies in processes within both parliament and the Liberal Party itself. Her essay advocated for engagement by the Australian Human Rights Commission on sexual harassment in parliaments and for better workplace protections in parliament.

It was brave to speak out about Liberal Party culture when no one else was. Dhanya said she knew that she was sacrificing opportunities that had been offered to her within the Liberal Party, but she felt she had 'a moral imperative' to speak out. Her courage would encourage more women to speak out.

But she didn't tell her story about Heydon. 'I was too scared,' she told us. Dhanya explained that she already felt marginalised in the law, as a woman of colour and one of only two ethnically diverse people working on the court. 'I didn't have any friends or mentors I could rely on to support me. My parents were poor migrants. If I had spoken about my experiences, I was going up against one of the strongest legal minds in the country—what chance did I have? Be sued for defamation and be bankrupted? It didn't feel like an option to me. I would be committing career suicide and exposing myself to bankruptcy.' She would tell her story about Heydon in 2020, inspired by the courage of the six women who had come forward before her and broken the silence.

After her essay was published, Dhanya was contacted by another woman who had her own story: Chelsey Potter. Chelsey had worked for the Liberal Party in federal parliament and, like Dhanya, says she was sexually assaulted by a fellow staffer. Together, they took their stories to a journalist. Reflecting on this, Dhanya said, 'I didn't think anyone would care about it if it was just me; I needed to do it with a white woman. I regret that I felt that way, and I regret that I was actually right.' Months after Dhanya had first spoken out about her story, Nine Media published an 'exclusive' story about sexual harassment in the Liberal Party, reporting her story (again) along with that of Chelsey. The story made clear that, '[f]or legal reasons, 9News has chosen not to identify the two men, who strongly deny the allegations'. It emphasised the fact that neither woman had chosen to report her allegations to the police or their MP at the time. Dhanya told us that, like many women, she didn't go to the police because she didn't want to relive the trauma again. She didn't speak out because she wanted to see him in prison; she spoke out because she wanted the culture and processes in parliament to change.

Suddenly, now she was not alone, there were headlines: 'Liberal Party rocked by allegations two young female staff were sexually assaulted'. Dhanya and Chelsey co-founded 'Changing Our Headline', a network for survivors of sexual assault and abuse that happened while they were working in Australian politics. They aimed to create a 'campaign and community for survivors and allies to come together for a better political future', and for laws, policies and complaint mechanisms to ensure a culture where survivors could speak out without fear—and be heard and supported.

Dhanya was the driving force behind the creation of the network and has continued with the work since Chelsey stepped away. Motivated by her experience with NOW, Dhanya told us she has made sure that every survivor who contacts the network receives a response. She also created clear policies on privacy and on how survivors' information could be used. Survivors who contacted her had options: they could share their story and seek support and advice, and even if they didn't want to speak out publicly, they could contribute their ideas about what needed to change to inform advocacy. 'It was important to me to include survivor input on necessary law reform . . . so they could be given a voice and their experience could be utilised. I created as many pathways as possible so I could afford them some agency, even if they didn't want to be public.'

Disclosures of assault and sexual misconduct poured in— this time, to Dhanya. She was contacted by women in both state and federal politics. She reached out to Prime Minister Morrison's office to try to seek support and informed Morrison's principal secretary of the 'overwhelming' number of complaints she had received, including about cabinet ministers. Dhanya says, 'I was vulnerable and desperately attempting to seek help for myself and other women,' but she said he seemed more concerned about political risk. She never heard back.

Among the many women who reached out to Dhanya for advice and support were two women whose stories would become public—and would send shockwaves through the halls of power and inspire more women around Australia to speak out. ██

██

██████████████████████████████ The second was a woman called Kate, whose allegations against the then federal attorney-general, Christian Porter, resulted in a national controversy about accountability and a controversial defamation case. Dhanya would later rename her campaign Kate's List to recognise and celebrate the life of her late friend Kate.

Kate's story

Kate reached out to Dhanya to tell her story, more than 30 years after her alleged rape. This is not uncommon: many women wait to come forward with their stories, especially if the person they are accusing is powerful. By the time Kate felt able to speak out and take action, the man she was accusing had become very powerful: Christian Porter was the chief law officer of Australia, and a federal cabinet minister.

The facts about her alleged rape are taken from Kate's statements, which are now public on the Federal Court of Australia website as part of documents in separate legal proceedings associated with the defamation case. They are all allegations that Porter denies vehemently.

Kate, as she was known by her friends and referred to by the ABC in the subsequent defamation proceedings, was a promising young Australian woman: at sixteen years old, she was intelligent, articulate, ambitious and one of 'the most brilliant debaters of her generation'. Her future looked bright, with friends suggesting she would one day take high office. But after a debating event in Sydney in 1988, Porter—a fellow debater—took her out drinking. She claimed that he gave her a date rape drug, escorted her home, forced her to have oral sex and then raped her after she fell asleep. Initially, she said, she didn't tell anyone because she was so ashamed.

Porter went on to have a brilliant career in law and politics—and was even tipped as a future prime minister. Meanwhile, the bright career Kate's friends had predicted for her had not yet come to be—though she still had plans and aspirations. Mental health issues surfaced. Kate was later diagnosed with bipolar disorder, and eventually sought counselling from a sexual assault counsellor in 2013. She had never told anyone about what happened to her, but after the counselling she decided to tell her friends, including those who had been on her debating team at the time of the alleged rape. They believed her.

Kate later reached out to Dhanya's organisation for support. They soon became friends and were in almost daily contact. Before getting into the story, Dhanya pauses to provide important context to Kate's story: 'One of the greatest failures of the MeToo discussion in Australia has been the singular focus on younger women.' She points out how older women, like Kate, 'have more to lose in speaking out' and 'the complexity of this has been completely left out of the narrative'. They are more advanced and established in their careers, which makes any forced pivot harder, they have families who will be affected, their perpetrators are also older and often in positions of power—'and yet, they are not a cultural priority'. For this reason, Dhanya admired Kate's courage in coming forward: 'It was heart-breaking to hear her say to me, "seeing you say these things helped me realise I could stand up to people in politics". I found it bizarre that I enabled her; I looked up to her, I was half her age. We don't really have approachable contactable figures for anyone in that demographic, so it was brave for her to reach out to me.'

Kate was very clear in her intentions. She wanted Porter to face trial. She did not want to be identified until after any criminal trial and conviction. Dhanya explains, 'She wanted it to be a story about abuse of power, about what survivors are put through, about the inadequacy of mental health care. She wanted to run for parliament. She wanted to be a voice for change.' But things took a tragic turn. 'Kate didn't want it to happen the way it did,' Dhanya says, in grief and anger.

Encouraged by her friends, and by Dhanya, Kate reported the rape to the police in November 2019. By June 2020 the police had still not taken her statement. Dhanya was dismayed by the police failures. Kate was encouraged by the specialist detective who was assigned to her case in Sydney, but repeated requests for them to travel to enable Kate's statement to be taken were refused. Kate had worked with a lawyer to prepare her statement and supporting documents—all that was left was for her to meet with police and sign it. 'There is no good reason why her statement wasn't signed. There were so many options to get it done,' says Dhanya. Dhanya told us how this had been the cause of further upset and anxiety for Kate. 'I kept saying "keep the faith, it will work out". But thinking about it all now, maybe I should have validated her complaints about the delay with the police—because clearly my faith was misplaced.'

In the interim period, Kate sought further psychiatric care. Dhanya said Kate was proactive about seeking help and encouraged Dhanya to look after her own mental health too. She was released from care but, while waiting for further treatment, she was isolated at home, kept apart from her family and friends by

Covid-19 restrictions. After a week of being isolated at home alone, on 23 June 2020 she sent an email to the police to say she could not continue with the complaint for medical and personal reasons because she couldn't take it anymore. The next day, she killed herself.

In the days leading up to Kate's death, Dhanya had been busy: she had just gone public with her story about being sexually harassed by Heydon. But she had noticed something strange: she hadn't heard from Kate after the news broke and Kate didn't respond to her messages about it. Kate had supported Dhanya in her decision to speak out about Heydon—she would have been the first to message or call her about it. Dhanya knew something was wrong. She was devastated when she was told of Kate's suicide. 'Kate had never wavered for a moment from her ultimate motivation to speak about what had happened to her and to hold power to account to give other women hope.' Dhanya believes Kate was failed by the police and by health services—and that this should be explored in a coronial inquest.

Kate had been believed by her friends, but the man she accused was powerful. The police let her down. And after Kate's death, what hope was there for accountability?

A few months later, in November 2020, the ABC's *Four Corners* program ran an episode titled 'Inside the Canberra Bubble' about the culture in parliament, featuring Porter. It painted a portrait of Porter as a man who had a long history of misogynistic behaviour and attitudes—even as far back as his law school days, he was 'tipped' as the most likely to become prime minister, and the most likely to be dismissed for inappropriate sexual misconduct. He had once argued in a debate that his opposition's arguments 'had more holes than Snow White's hymen'. A barrister who knew him at law school described him as 'deeply sexist', and said he had ridiculed women for how they looked. As a university law professor, he was accused of making sexualised comments to students. When he got to parliament, he was accused of making unwanted sexual advances towards staffers and even received a warning from then Prime Minister Malcolm Turnbull over his sexual relationship with a junior staffer—despite having a wife and toddler at home.

The program did not include Kate's allegations about Porter. Kate's friends say that the ABC had originally planned to include her story in the program—but it was cut out because of the defamation risk. Porter was protected from any public discussion about Kate or her allegations, for now.

After the program aired, Porter said he regretted things he had said in the past, but he denied (and continues to deny) all accusations of mistreating women. Maybe it's possible to look at each of the details the ABC had aired and say they were just examples of Porter 'joking', or the kind of childish sexist humour often seen from those who went to elite boys' schools. He wasn't a bad guy—he was just a bit of a larrikin. And a lot of men did think that way—including Prime Minister Scott Morrison. He said he thought Porter's conduct had passed 'the pub test', because 'Australians understand more about human frailty than perhaps you are giving them credit'. Boys will be boys, as they say. Porter remained attorney-general.

Months went by after the ABC's story about sexism and the culture of the federal parliament. But another brave young woman would soon capture the nation's attention: on 25 January 2021, Grace Tame was announced as the Australian of the Year, and gave a powerful speech about the silence that had protected her abuser. Her words reverberated around the nation. Grace was being recognised and celebrated for being a silence-breaker about child abuse, and for her #LetHerSpeak campaign, which helped break the silence for other survivors. She would encourage many more women to come forward, ███████████████████████.

Brittany's story

██████████████████████████████████████
██████████████████████████████████████
██████████████████████████████████████
██████████████████████████████████████
██████████████████████████████████████
██████████████████████████████████████
██████████████████████████████████████
████████████████████████████████████
█████████████████████████████████
██████████████████████████████████████
██████████████████████████████████████
██████████████████████████████████████
██████████████████████████████████████
██████████████████████████████████████
██████████████████████████████████████
██████████████████████████████████████
██████████████████████████████████████
██████████████████████████████████████
████████████████
█████████████████████████████████
██████████████████████████████████████
██████████████████████████████████████
██████████████████████████████████████
██████████████████████████████████████

[REDACTED]

Speaking out as a mobilising force

[REDACTED] Kate's friends decided to take action against Attorney-General Christian Porter. On 23 February 2021, they wrote to Prime Minister Morrison with a dossier of evidence, including a copy of the witness statement she had prepared to report Porter to the police. Since the police were not investigating the case after Kate's death, they said they wanted the matter pursued because that's what she had wanted. Her friends urged Morrison to undertake an inquiry:

> This is a difficult issue. Victims share information in confidence and sometimes do not want to pursue claims, at least initially. In this case, a victim shared her story with many and begged the people to help her seek justice. To date, defamation law and political inactivity have adversely impacted the ability of

[her] claim to be properly addressed. The Commonwealth Attorney-General has the right to protect his name. Given the facts of this case, we suggest that you could . . . conduct a discrete parliamentary investigation into the matter to see what facts could be established.

Having learned about this letter, a journalist decided it was time to tell Kate's story. ABC journalist Louise Milligan reported the story of how the prime minister, senators and the Australian Federal Police had been informed of the historical allegations made by Kate about a cabinet minister and that Kate's friends were calling for an inquiry into the allegations. Her stories did not name Porter. Social media was set alight with speculation—who was the minister being accused of rape? Off the back of Milligan's earlier, 'Inside the Canberra Bubble' story, many pointed the finger at Porter.

After widespread speculation and intense public pressure, Porter outed himself as the subject. In his press conference, Porter vehemently denied that the alleged rape ever happened, and said he had never been contacted by anyone—by Kate, by the police or by the ABC—before the allegation was published. 'It just didn't happen,' he said. Porter claimed that he was being placed in the position of having to 'disprove something that didn't happen 33 years ago'.

Prime Minister Morrison praised Porter's decision to identify himself as the subject of the rape allegations, and his decision to take mental health leave—'to get support to deal with what has obviously been a traumatic series of events'—and said he 'looked forward' to Porter returning to work. Treasurer Josh Frydenberg emphasised Porter's right to be presumed innocent and pledged his full support. Meanwhile, the new Minister for Defence, Peter Dutton, praised Porter as 'a first-class act' for naming himself. But what about the suffering and trauma of Kate and her friends and family? Where was the support for them? What about the trauma the news, and the response from the prime minister and senior ministers, triggered for survivors around the country?

Meanwhile, the media went hard on Kate's mental health history—even publishing her diaries. 'She was made to look crazy,' Dhanya said, arguing that she wasn't and that she had put together a credible case with her lawyer. In his later public statement, Porter would complain about his 'trial by media' and claim Kate's allegation lacked 'credibility' because she was 'unwell' and that it was based on 'repressed memory'—an allegation Kate's sexual assault counsellor had refuted. Dhanya raised concerns that because Kate had died, she couldn't be defamed—and couldn't defend herself or push back on the narrative built about her.

Women went to social media to share their stories and how triggered they were by the high-profile rape allegations and the lack of accountability—and support for #March4Justice swelled. The movement was started by Janine Hendry and quickly gained 27,000 followers on Facebook. Women across the country began to organise protests in other capital cities and regional towns. As one sexual assault survivor, Carol Shipard, said, the government's response to ███████████ ███████████ felt like 'a punch in the guts'; 'the closing of the ranks' by powerful men had to stop. Another organiser, Aoife McGreal, told *The Guardian*, 'I feel like every woman has a story. Whether it's workplace harassment, or abuse in the home, or on the street, even. It's time for women to speak up. I feel like it's a time of reckoning for Australia.'

Kate's family supported an inquiry into the allegations she had made, and public pressure grew. As attorney-general, Porter had ordered the inquiry into sexual harassment allegations against former High Court judge Dyson Heydon. Why shouldn't an inquiry be held into Porter, many asked. But the prime minister stood firm against any inquiry because, he said, it was a matter for the police. Instituting an inquiry 'would say the rule of law and our police are not competent to deal with these issues'. As Dhanya made clear, the police had already failed Kate. And worse: even before the prime minister asked the nation to leave it to the police, the police themselves had told the media that the investigation into the matter had been closed because of 'insufficient admissible evidence'. It would only emerge six months later, after an internal review, that the NSW Police had never even commenced an investigation. In fact, the police had asked to close the case the very same day they had received the dossier of evidence with Kate's witness statement.

There is a common refrain in rape and sexual assault cases: if it happened, why didn't she go to the police? The implication is that what this woman says cannot be true because if it were true, she would have gone to the police immediately. And the presumption is that, if she goes to the police, the police will do their job, and that all women must therefore take the criminal justice route.

In Kate's case, she had gone to the police—but she gave up in dismay after police delays. That's why it was so frustrating that the prime minister said he thought it should be a matter for the police: the police had already bungled it. And as Laura Tingle, the ABC's chief political correspondent, pointed out, Morrison's position that the Porter matter should be left to the police was 'disingenuous at best', because he knew full well that Kate's death 'made it virtually impossible for NSW Police to investigate the case'. Dhanya, on the other hand, rejected the proposition that Kate's death meant the case could not be prosecuted, pointing out that the Catholic Cardinal, George Pell, had been prosecuted for historic sex offences in relation to two men when they were aged thirteen, one of whom had since died (Pell's conviction was later overturned on appeal to the High Court). 'Why not Porter? It was police negligence that meant Kate's statement had not been signed,' Dhanya said.

At the same time, concern was raised about Porter's right to due process and the presumption of innocence—and that he should not face 'trial by media'. ABC journalist Annabel Crabb noted that while the media was the forum in which the allegations were being 'thrashed out', it was 'the only institution with current access to both sides of the story', given the incapacity of the criminal law to deal with the allegation for both people involved: 'In death the woman is forever denied her day in court. In life, Mr Porter will never get his either.'

As women across Australia were preparing to march, Porter and his lawyers were making preparations for him to get his day in court—but in a defamation lawsuit, rather than a criminal case. His defamation claim against the ABC and journalist Louise Milligan over Kate's rape allegations was filed the same day as the March4Justice protests (see Chapter 6 for further discussion of this case). The significance of the chief law officer of Australia filing his defamation case on the same day of protests fuelled by women's frustration over the government's failure to hold him and other alleged perpetrators to account was not lost on anyone.

If that wasn't enough, Prime Minister Morrison took to the floor of the House of Representatives to proclaim that it was a triumph of Australian democracy that the women protesters outside Parliament House were not 'met with bullets'.

The defamation claim Porter filed over the historic rape allegation—and not the rape allegation itself—cost him his job as attorney-general: he couldn't oversee Australia's defamation law reforms while suing the public broadcaster for defamation himself. But he remained in cabinet. And while the defamation claim cost him his job as chief law officer, it gave the prime minister an answer to calls for a public inquiry into Kate's allegations. The prime minister then started saying that her rape allegations would now be determined by a court in the defamation claim against the ABC, so it would not be appropriate to conduct a separate inquiry. When Porter later settled his defamation case before trial, so there would never be that day in court, the prime minister shifted again: there would still be no public inquiry over Kate's allegations—and no accountability for Kate.

The March4Justice protests ended up being the largest protests seen in Australia in years, with an estimated 110,000 people protesting in 40 different cities and regional centres to demand 'equality, justice, respect and an end to gendered violence'. Jen joined her local protest with her eleven-year-old half-sister and her 85-year-old grandmother. It was her little sister's first ever protest and one of many for her grandmother, who had protested for equal pay and funding for domestic violence refuges in the 1960s and '70s. She told Jen she was 'too old to still be out protesting about this shit'—but there she was, joining with thousands of other women in a massive inter-generational protest. Amid these protests, it was announced that Kate Jenkins, the Sex Discrimination Commissioner at the Australian Human Rights Commission, would lead an independent inquiry into the culture of Parliament House. It was the very action that Dhanya had called for two years earlier. The power of more women speaking out and of protest was clear: things had to change and reform recommendations were coming.

Look at Dhanya Mani and the other women who spoke out about Heydon, who have spoken of losing their passion for the law. How many women have left politics, law—or other careers—after having similar experiences? How many women have left careers they love after the institution in which they worked failed to protect them from abuse or harassment?

And how many women had to speak out and protest about this before it would change?

Even after the protests, Porter remained in cabinet and was later promoted to temporarily fill in as leader of the House of Representatives—a move by Morrison that Grace Tame would call 'a proverbial slap in the face of our entire nation' and 'an insult to all survivors' that would only embolden perpetrators. Tame wrote that Porter's were 'circumstances steeped in the protective privileges of a patriarchal parliament' and '[g]iven the seriousness of the allegations against Porter, the bare minimum test of his fitness to hold ministerial office would be an independent inquiry'. Only later, when it emerged that Porter had accepted $1 million in a 'blind trust' to fund his defamation case against the ABC, were questions raised about the integrity of that arrangement and whether he had complied with his code of conduct as a cabinet minister—or as an MP. Porter would later resign from cabinet and from politics: not over the historic rape allegation, but over the shady financial arrangement that had funded his defamation case. He is now back in legal practice. There would be no inquiry into him accepting funds from anonymous donors who funded his defamation case—or into Kate's allegations. If the man holding the highest legal office in the country would not face accountability, who else would?

Accountability for his party would come at the ballot box. Spurred by the events of 2021, a group of independent women, 'the teal independents', ran for federal parliament to knock off Liberal Party seats. Running on platforms of equality for women, accountability, transparency and climate, they were elected in record numbers in 2022. Julie Bishop, former long-time Liberal MP and foreign minister said, ██████████ ████████████████████████████████ that women 'didn't see [Morrison and the Liberal Party] as having any empathy for the concerns of women'. Simon Birmingham MP pointed out the obvious: 'What we can't do is abandon the space on listening to women . . . We can't have a situation where women are voting for us in lesser numbers than males.' The rest of his party seemed to have forgotten: women's votes count in a democracy.

Chanel's story: enabling speech to challenge rape culture

As Australia was grappling with the culture of parliament ████ ████████████████████████████ another young woman was spurred into action. Chanel Contos was motivated by her own experience—and that of too many of her friends—to start an initiative to help young women share their stories and to show up rape culture in Australia.

After the MeToo movement kicked off, Chanel had been away with friends from high school when they had a conversation—similar to the many other conversations that had quietly started in living rooms, bedrooms and around dinner tables, in an inversion of the old 'whisper network'. She and her friends were sharing their experiences of sexual assault. Like so many others, Chanel was horrified to learn that most of her friends had been sexually assaulted—and pretty much all of them had had a 'close call'. Chanel told her friends about her own assault by a guy they knew. It turned out he had done something similar to another woman a year later. Chanel started shaking, and became very upset. She would later learn that these are trigger symptoms—the body reliving the experience of assault.

Chanel felt it was time to do something. She started by disclosing her assault to her brother. Then she expanded the conversation she'd had with her close friends to others. A pattern emerged: she and many women she knew who, like her, had attended elite girls' schools in Sydney, had experienced sexual violence at the hands of young men from privileged private boys' schools.

It wasn't until Chanel left Australia that she could see this more clearly. She told us that her time living and studying in the United Kingdom, among students from around the world, helped her to understand the culture she'd grown up in at home. She said, she had 'never spoken to anyone who has experienced rape culture the way me and my friends had growing up in Sydney amongst private schools'. The problem suddenly seemed obvious to Chanel: it wasn't about any individual person. It was a problem of culture—a rape culture—and the general lack of understanding about consent.

In early 2021, Chanel decided it was time to act. She started an anonymous Instagram survey, whereby survivors would simply say the name of the school the perpetrator had attended. The point was not to 'name and shame' perpetrators, but to get a picture of the culture from which they came and put the onus on schools to better educate boys. She received thousands of testimonies. Overwhelmed by the response, Chanel decided to create a website for survivors to share their stories, so that people could understand just how big the problem was. The powerful and well-heeled of Sydney were glued to the screen, watching for a story that could be about their brother or son to appear.

Chanel's efforts showed just how pervasive sexual assault was, sparking a crisis meeting of 100 private schools.

Soon the threats started: letters from school principals, from lawyers, saying they would sue Chanel for defamation. It didn't matter that the boys (some now powerful men) were not named—they would claim they were identifiable from the anonymised details she had published. The letters and messages kept asking: didn't she know she might ruin the careers, and the reputations, of these men? 'But what about the trauma and impact on her life?' Chanel said, highlighting how society is often far more concerned about his reputation in facing an allegation than about women's suffering and their ability to speak about it.

Chanel told us that many dismissed her project and the value of the anonymous testimonies. She said that one prominent Australian figure had claimed that 'the testimonies are performative and made up'. If a woman speaks out and tells her story in the media, she is fame-hungry; if she does it anonymously, she is 'performative'. It doesn't seem to matter how women speak out—whichever way they do will be used to attack their credibility—which makes clear the problem isn't how they do it, but the fact they do it.

Meanwhile, the NSW Minister for Women, Bronnie Taylor, said the stories were 'extremely concerning' and experts mused on the reason for this 'worrying sexual assault trend in Australian schools'.

Chanel went on to start a petition calling for better consent education in schools, and within just three weeks it had 30,000 signatures. She founded an organisation, Teach Us Consent, which calls for earlier and ongoing holistic consent and sexuality education for children. Chanel wants all young people in Australia to receive comprehensive sexual education, to empower teenagers to identify sexual assault situations when they see them or experience them—and to stop it before it happens. In February 2022, the organisation achieved this goal: the federal and state governments have agreed to provide sexual consent education for schoolchildren from age five.

Chanel also helped NSW Police launch a campaign to inform survivors that there is an alternative reporting option that enables them to report their assault to police without the requirement for them to press charges immediately—or ever—so that the police have a contemporaneous report of the crime. Survivors can also consent to be contacted by police, or not, if the perpetrator is reported by another woman. And she can decide whether to pursue charges or whether she wants to support the other survivor. This—and the profile of Chanel's campaign about rape and sexual assault among teenagers—has resulted in an unprecedented 60 per cent increase in reports to police. Chanel explains that many women don't want to see their perpetrator in prison and just want to protect others from it happening again. She told us:

> Culture needs to change. We need to stop pretending that rapists aren't common and aren't all around us, our friends, people we know—we know the figures. Our society couldn't function if every rapist was sent to jail. It's hard for women to speak up about it, so we have to change the way we deal with that and make it easier.

Prompted by the success of Chanel's initiative in Australia, a young British woman, Soma Sara, reached out to Chanel. She had launched a similar initiative, 'Everyone's Invited', a movement in the United Kingdom focused on 'exposing rape culture through conversation, education and support'. Encouraged by the response to her campaign in Australia, Chanel told us that Soma began asking those posting their stories to start naming their schools and universities to ensure the institutions could be held accountable. By April 2021, she had 15,000 responses—a figure that has since risen to 55,000 and has since sparked an Ofsted review.

These two award-winning campaigns have made visible the extent of sexual violence among young people in a way that we have not seen before. Both women created innovative campaigns and spaces to enable women and girls to speak out about their sexual assault—without facing the legal risks they would if they did so on their own. Their aim was to raise awareness about rape culture in order to try to change it—and it's working. Their examples show the common problems, challenges and solutions that women encounter around the world, as well as the benefits of sharing insights and innovations across nations—and the importance of women being able to tell their stories—to tackle violence against women.

Australia and intersectionality

We first reached out to interview Dhanya Mani in early 2022, before Prime Minister Scott Morrison announced that he would make an 'apology' in the federal parliament to women who had suffered sexual harassment in parliament. At that time, she told us that very few journalists or commentators had contacted her to report on her story or her work. Dhanya feels very strongly that she has been left out of the media conversation. Dhanya was not invited to parliament for Morrison's speech or acknowledged alongside the other women who had spoken out about the culture of parliament, ██████████████ ████████████ women who came to prominence after seeking advice and support from Dhanya. Grace Tame and Chanel Contos were invited given their important work, which was unrelated to parliament workplace culture. 'Somehow I had disappeared,' Dhanya said.

On the day of Morrison's apology, Dhanya spoke out about her erasure—and that of all women of colour—and there was a flurry of media interest in her story. It started an important and much-needed conversation about the visibility and recognition of women of colour in Australia. A few days later, Greens senator Larissa Waters read Dhanya's words in her speech to the Senate: 'I will not stop until skin colour and minority status do not determine whether we are acknowledged, whether we are recognised by politicians and the media, and whether cultural and historic milestones built on our advocacy and labour belong to us.'

What we didn't realise until we met her was just how hard and how long Dhanya had been fighting to be heard and seen. She had been fighting for visibility—a fight that continues.

When Dhanya first raised her complaint in the NSW Parliament she said she was 'gaslit and ignored'. She was the first to speak out about her experience in the Liberal Party and the person who established an organisation that encouraged and supported so many other women to come forward and made recommendations for reform. It took years—and more white women—to speak out before anyone really listened.

████████████████████████████████████
████████████████████████████████████
████████████████████████████████████

██

██

Her work was not acknowledged in the federal apology either. Even after all the media controversy that followed, when the new NSW premier, Dominic Perrottet, apologised to Dhanya in state parliament this year, it barely got a mention in the Australian media.

'How many more women might have come forward earlier if I had only been white?' Dhanya asks. Even now, Dhanya says she hasn't been offered the support or opportunities offered to the other young women who came to prominence for speaking out, ██████████████████████████ the mentorship, institutional support, employment or funding opportunities. All three women have book deals; at the time of writing, Dhanya does not. The problem is structural. As Dhanya told us:

> The media landscape hasn't changed and the work of women of colour has not been recognised or credited . . . The absence of this has limited the conversation in Australia, and until and unless we have voices in the media acknowledge their bias and the mistakes that have been made, it will not open up space for conversations about how people of colour are treated . . . there is an empathy gap. There is a particular difficulty in finding resonance if you are not white or if you are First Nations. I think that is why it's hard for our stories to take off.

As author Sisonke Msimang wrote for *The Guardian* in 2022, people like Grace Tame represent the 'acceptable' white faces of Australian feminism. Msimang makes very clear how much she admires both women—and how she struggled to find a way to express in her critique about how Black women are not 'greeted with the same kind of public solidarity or sympathy' they receive. Msimang writes how, in Australia, 'a narrative emerge[d] of white women as fighters, as eloquent challengers of the status quo, as upholders of the feminist legacy with little to no reference to Black women who have been doing this for years.' Perhaps it is as simple as Scott Morrison said: these are the faces of the daughters of Australia's most powerful men.

Msimang rightly points out that Black women have always been at the forefront of struggles for equality and justice in Australia. 'There is no reckoning for Australian women if the media and the public aren't able to listen and relate to the stories of Aboriginal women, women in hijab, women whose skin is far "too" dark, and women who live on the wrong side of town; who can't go to university and who will never report from parliament or file stories in newsrooms.'

In an essay in 2018, Amy McQuire—a Darumbal and South Sea Islander journalist—wrote about how 'white liberal feminism . . . finds the loudest voice in mainstream media,' while the deaths of Aboriginal women are found in footnotes. Violence against First Nations women has not sparked nation-wide protests of women, but it should. As McQuire writes, the issue isn't that First Nations women are 'silent': 'Aboriginal women have been talking about violence for decades—the "silence" is not the issue. It is that no one listens unless it is spoken in a way that bypasses the role of white Australia, and places blame right back onto Aboriginal people themselves.'

A feminism rooted in racism, colonial violence and ableism is not really feminist at all. Activism rooted in a deep and mean-ingful appreciation of intersectionality is the work that needs to happen to bring about meaningful change, change that ensures the voices and stories of women of colour are not erased or silenced. 'There is so much injustice in this country,' said Dhanya. 'But we are where we are today . . . We need more white people talking about this and to showcase white women and women of colour working together and creating positive and mutually affirming relationships.'

Women are—and have been—speaking. We all need to ask: who will do the work of listening to and amplifying what they say to push for real change? All of us have a responsibility to ensure that all women are heard, and that we are not complicit in the silencing.

**When speaking out ▮▮▮▮▮▮▮▮▮▮
becomes contempt**

▮▮▮▮▮▮▮▮▮▮▮▮▮▮▮▮▮▮▮▮▮▮▮▮▮▮▮▮▮▮▮▮
▮▮▮▮▮▮▮▮▮▮▮▮▮▮▮▮▮▮▮▮▮▮▮▮▮▮▮▮▮▮▮▮
▮▮▮▮▮▮▮▮▮▮▮▮▮▮▮▮▮▮▮▮▮▮▮▮▮▮▮▮▮▮▮▮
▮▮▮▮▮▮▮▮▮▮▮▮▮▮▮▮▮▮▮▮▮▮▮▮▮▮▮▮▮▮▮▮
▮▮▮▮▮▮▮▮▮▮▮▮▮▮▮▮▮▮▮▮▮▮▮▮▮▮▮▮▮▮▮▮
▮▮▮▮▮▮▮▮▮▮▮▮▮▮▮▮▮▮▮▮▮▮▮▮▮▮▮▮▮▮▮▮
▮▮▮▮▮▮▮▮▮▮▮▮▮▮▮▮▮▮▮▮▮▮▮▮▮▮▮▮▮▮▮▮
▮▮▮▮▮▮▮▮▮▮▮▮▮▮▮▮▮▮▮▮▮▮▮▮▮▮▮▮▮▮▮▮
▮▮▮▮▮▮▮▮▮▮▮▮▮▮▮▮▮▮▮▮▮▮▮▮▮▮▮▮▮▮▮▮
▮▮▮▮▮▮▮▮▮▮▮▮▮▮▮▮▮▮▮▮▮▮▮▮▮▮▮▮▮▮▮▮
▮▮▮▮▮▮▮▮▮▮▮▮▮▮▮▮▮▮▮▮▮▮▮▮▮▮▮▮▮▮▮▮
▮▮▮▮▮▮▮▮▮▮▮▮▮▮▮▮▮▮▮▮▮▮▮▮▮▮▮▮▮▮▮▮
▮▮▮▮▮▮▮▮▮▮▮▮▮▮▮▮▮▮▮▮▮▮▮▮▮▮▮▮▮▮▮▮
▮▮▮▮▮▮▮▮▮▮▮▮▮▮▮▮▮▮▮▮▮▮▮▮▮▮
▮▮▮▮▮▮▮▮▮▮▮▮▮▮▮▮▮▮▮▮▮▮▮▮▮▮
▮▮▮▮▮▮▮▮▮▮▮▮▮▮▮▮▮▮▮▮▮▮▮▮▮▮▮▮▮

Turning silence into action for change

Women telling their stories is powerful. When the whisper network in Australia became public, it lit a fire that burned all the way through the halls of power.

One woman speaking helps give others the courage to speak. But we also need to acknowledge the extreme personal and professional costs each of these women accrue for their courage—and the legal risks they face. And while women should speak if they want to, the burden placed on them to enter the spotlight is not fair—and must change.

It has been encouraging to see the law reform, activism and change that has been sparked by these stories. It could only happen once women were given a platform to speak. And there is still a long way to go.

These stories show how cultural and legal obstacles come up when women speak—and can have the effect of silencing. We need to acknowledge the role of the law in silencing women and maintaining cultures of silence. And we need to think about how these laws might need to change if we are serious about allowing women to speak. And it's not just about protecting women: it's about creating a system of justice that puts survivors at the centre—and recognises their right to speak.

Chapter 4

HER GUIDEBOOK
TO HIS PLAYBOOK

On 27 March 2022, *The Sunday Times* published an explosive piece about Charlie Elphicke, the former Tory government minister who was jailed for sex offences in the United Kingdom. 'Elphicke had spent four years suing *The Sunday Times* for revealing a woman accused him of rape [and] used British libel law to silence her and prolong her pain,' explained Gabriel Pogrund, the journalist who broke the story.

In 2017, a young parliamentary worker in her twenties went to the police to report that she had been raped by her then boss, Elphicke—an MP, former government minister, lawyer and married father of two. She was scared and worried that she would not be believed. According to the newspaper, this woman, to whom it referred as 'Jane', approached *The Sunday Times* in 2018 after the police failed to carry out an investigation. By then, Elphicke was already under investigation for allegations of sexual assault by two other women, a nanny and a parliamentary staffer. But *The Sunday Times* published another story: Jane had accused him of rape and the police had failed to investigate.

Elphicke sued, alleging *The Sunday Times* had published 'serious untruths'. The disgraced former MP was able to use libel and privacy laws to suppress any further reporting of the allegations. It wasn't until 2022, after Elphicke was convicted of sex offences and withdrew his legal claims, that *The Sunday Times* revealed for the first time the long and expensive legal battle it had faced for publishing Jane's story. In Elphicke's criminal trial, the sentencing judge had described him as 'a sexual predator who used . . . success and respectability as a cover'. But *The Sunday Times*' story showed how he had also 'used his power, and the law, to protect himself'.

According to *The Sunday Times*, Elphicke hired Carter-Ruck, a law firm it described as being 'notorious for aggressively defending oligarch clients'. *The Sunday Times*' journalist explained that Jane's story 'never entered public discourse' because other media outlets were too scared to print the allegations in case they were also sued. Pia Sarma, the head of legal for Times Newspapers Limited later explained that it spent an estimated £600,000 defending the publication: defending Jane's truth and the public interest in reporting her story.

The *Sunday Times* exposé came amid public outcry in the United Kingdom about a slew of high-profile defamation claims, including those brought by Russian oligarchs against journalists and authors, and sparked a nationwide debate about how the rich and powerful are using and abusing libel law to suppress free speech and avoid scrutiny for wrongdoing. When we spoke to Pia she explained that stories about sexual misconduct are particularly vulnerable to libel suits and notoriously difficult to print:

It takes courage on part of the complainant and warmth and tenacity on part of the journalists, and commitment and resources on part of the newspaper. The organisations that have the time and commitment usually don't have resources and they are vulnerable to libel actions. The knock-on effect is chilling free speech and the right of women's voices to be heard. Women are coming to the media instead of the police so that other women are warned.

In this chapter, we explain the set of strategies used by rich and powerful men to silence women and the media. We know this story: we have seen it play out, over and over again, with our clients and with the women and journalists with whom we have spoken. We also explore what women go through in order to speak out, and the legal risks they face. We understand what she might come up against, and what journalists face when trying to report on these issues. Think of this as her guidebook to his playbook. And as we will explain, it is a playbook enabled by the law.

The sheer scale of allegations of misconduct against the rich and powerful might make it seem like publishing these stories is easy. But the fact is that publishing allegations of violence against women takes a lot of hard work—and resources—behind the scenes. Perhaps his celebrity or power has protected him so far. The journalist wants to tell your story, which, let's face it, will be damaging to his professional and personal life. Then lawyers get involved. The financial risks for speaking out are huge. Even before you enter the courtroom, hundreds and thousands of pounds of legal costs start to ratchet up. He is litigious and will probably threaten to sue. Even where the allegations are well known in certain circles or where rumours are already circulating, publishing them for the world to read is another matter entirely.

This is the story behind the stories you see in the papers. It's the story of what it takes to get a story over the line and into print. It's a practical illustration of how the different laws play out and how the rich and powerful don't always—in the words of Gill Phillips, head of legal at *The Guardian*—'fight fair'.

We tell this story of silencing through what we know from our work with survivors, journalists and media organisations. We tell it through the example of what has been reported about the experiences of those silence-breakers and survivors who chose to go to the media about their abuse at the hands of Jeffrey Epstein and Ghislaine Maxwell.

Speaking out

Before a newspaper prints a story with accusations of sexual or domestic violence, there will be a woman (or several women) at the heart of that story who has made the very difficult decision to speak out.

In our experience, women take this decision for a range of reasons. They may have no faith in the police, or they may have had faith in the police but been failed by them—if their allegations weren't taken seriously or weren't properly investigated. In some cases, they have no interest in sending their perpetrator to prison: perhaps they still love him, have children with him or are related to him. But in our experience, the overwhelming reason that women decide to speak out is to warn other women and prevent the man from abusing anyone else. They want to highlight police or employer failures in the hope it will help others in future. Some consider this to be part of their own healing process.

It is a woman's right to speak out if she chooses. But there are many legal rules and risks that come into play.

If she has gone to the police to report a crime, this will have an impact on how and when the media can report her story, and will affect what she can say and when. During an active police investigation in the United Kingdom, the media will be nervous about reporting the suspect's name because of his privacy rights. Most newspapers, at least in the United Kingdom because of ever-expanding privacy laws, are unlikely to print a story about him until an arrest is made. And even then, what they will print is very limited because the rules on contempt of court make it a criminal offence to report on the proceedings in any way that might prejudice his jury trial.

'Don't speak about it.' This will be one of the first things police and prosecutors will advise her. 'Don't speak about it to other potential witnesses', they will be warned because they will be cross-examined in court about it and be accused of colluding or having contaminated their own or others' evidence. 'Don't speak about it to the media: it could prejudice the trial or provide more material for his defence counsel to use to undermine you in cross-examination at trial,' they will say. If she has her own lawyers, they will also warn her not to speak about it outside of court because of the risk of being sued for defamation. If a woman is sued for defamation, the case will be stayed, pending the outcome of his criminal trial. (And it's much easier for her to be sued successfully for defamation than it is for him to be convicted of rape.)

While the police investigate, she can't tell her story because his privacy rights will protect him from any media reporting (at least in the United Kingdom). If the police decide not to investigate or don't charge him, this will then also probably make journalists wary of reporting her story—because they might think there isn't anything to it, or because of the risk they will be sued for defamation too. It could also prejudice her in any future defamation case. If the authorities didn't prosecute him, then her allegations mustn't be true, it will be said.

If the matter goes to trial, journalists can report what happens there without being sued, but it must be a 'fair and accurate report' of the proceedings. In practice, as we have seen, this often means that the reporting of the criminal trial is dominated by his narrative, not hers. She has no control over what is said in court because she is not a party to the proceedings— she is a witness for the state prosecutor—and she does not have the ability to respond to or rebut the narrative his lawyers are building in his defence. She often isn't even allowed in the courtroom except when she gives her evidence, so she might not even hear what he says about her until she sees it in the media. All she can do is answer the questions put to her when she is on the stand.

Many women report feeling silenced and disempowered by the situation they are placed in by the criminal law: they cannot rebut his claims in court (including baseless allegations like 'she wanted it' or 'she was into rough sex'), which are then dutifully reported by the media. This ensures the media is protected by the law—it is providing a 'fair and accurate report' of proceedings—while she remains liable to a defamation claim if she rebuts them outside of court. In the 1 per cent of rape cases in the United Kingdom that result in conviction, she will be free to speak about her case. If he is acquitted—i.e. if this is one of the other 99 per cent of cases that don't result in a conviction—then many will claim she lied (even though it just means it couldn't be proved 'beyond reasonable doubt'—a very difficult evidential standard—or worse, he might have been acquitted because of juror prejudice and the harmful myths we explained in Chapter 1).

Journalists will be even more wary of reporting her claims and she is at even greater risk of being sued for defamation if she speaks out. We can't report that he is a rapist if a jury has acquitted him, it will be said. Women face different forms of silencing throughout the criminal justice process—and after it.

Given the extremely low level of prosecution and conviction in cases of domestic violence and rape, many women decide not to go to the police. Some women don't want to be retraumatised by going through the criminal justice system. Some women feel they cannot go to the police, as we explained in Chapter 2, for fear that they will be arrested for immigration offences or under other morality laws. Some women don't want to see their former partner or boss in prison. You need only look up the hashtag #WhyIDidntReport to get a sense of why only 14 per cent of women in Australia, Canada, the United Kingdom and the United States ever report their abusers to the police.

Whatever their reason for not reporting to the police, women and other victims and survivors of violence should not be criticised or penalised for choosing not to do so—but, as we show later in this chapter, too often they are, in public and in the defamation claims brought against them. 'You're damned if you do go to the police, and you're damned if you don't,' one woman told us. Justice comes in many forms and, for women, the criminal justice system is but one forum, and a deeply flawed one at that. While there is a certain kind of silencing of women in the criminal justice system, there are different legal risks and associated forms of silencing when women choose to speak out.

As Pia Sarma explained to us when we interviewed her in early 2022, many women decide to approach journalists to tell their story to obtain a different type of justice and to warn other women. As Pia explained, 'MeToo triggered an enormous wave of women coming forward', with women choosing to go to the media instead of the police, or resorting to the media after the police failed them.

This is what motivated Maria and Annie Farmer to speak out about Jeffrey Epstein back in 2002. They decided to tell a journalist at *Vanity Fair*, Vicky Ward, about their 1996 abuse by Epstein and Ghislaine Maxwell—and to go on the record about it—because telling the FBI, 'did not lead to either of them being held accountable'. When the Farmers approached *Vanity Fair*, rumours were already circulating. Ward had heard these whispers about Epstein and young women, and that Maria Farmer had had 'a bad experience' with him. Indeed, future US president Donald Trump had told *New York Magazine*, 'It is even said that [Epstein] likes beautiful women as much as I do, and many of them are on the younger side.'

But it would take more than a decade for the full story of Epstein's abuse to be told—and it was not told by *Vanity Fair*, which decided against publishing the Farmers' allegations for legal reasons. It was only in 2006—three years after *Vanity Fair* spiked their stories—that Epstein was arrested for the first time. It would take many more years to understand the sheer extent of his abuse: more than 150 women have since accused him of sexual abuse, including many who were underage.

It is also what motivated Virginia Giuffre to speak out to ABC News in the United States in 2015. But ABC didn't air her interview either—again, for legal reasons. It was not until 2019, after reporting by Julie Brown at *The Miami Herald*, that Epstein was arrested for sex trafficking of minors—but he committed suicide in prison before he could be put on trial. Maxwell was convicted in late 2021 for her role in Epstein's sex trafficking of underage girls.

As David Folkenflik has written for National Public Radio (NPR), until 2018 Epstein's abuse largely escaped media scrutiny. Why was it that Epstein's victims' stories were silenced for so long? And how many women could have been warned and protected if the Farmers' story had been published in 2003 and Epstein was exposed then as the criminal he was?

Going to a journalist

Some women decide to take their stories to the media. But once you speak to a journalist, it is not up to you whether the story will be published: it will be up to them, their editors and their lawyers to decide whether or not to investigate your claims, to determine whether there is enough evidence for them to publish your story, and to decide if and when your story will be told. Those investigations can take weeks, months and sometimes even years.

When speaking to the media, survivors need to consider whether they want to be named or not—and an ethical journalist will discuss your options and the risks of identification with you. In some countries, you will automatically be entitled to anonymity. Some, like 'Jane' in the *Sunday Times* story, choose to remain anonymous. But some women decide to waive their legal right to anonymity in order to more effectively tell their personal story to fight for justice and change. But with that comes the scrutiny, the online trolling and the sadly inevitable attacks on your reputation and credibility—and even death and rape threats.

If you don't want to be named, how can your identity be protected? The journalist will have to be careful about the details they report to protect you from the risk of 'jigsaw identification'—that is, where there is enough information in the article and elsewhere in the public domain for people to piece together the story (like a jigsaw puzzle) and identify you. It's important to be clear with journalists about whether you want to protect your identity. It's also important to be clear about how much of your story, and of the information you give them, is on the record (which they can publish) or off the record (for their background knowledge but not for publication). Some women don't want all the graphic details of their assault reported—and it's often not necessary to tell the story—so don't be afraid to be clear about what you're comfortable with being reported.

One of the first things a journalist will ask is if a woman has gone to the police. For the reasons we explained earlier in this chapter, this can affect what they can report and when—and it may even affect whether they investigate the matter at all.

Alongside the 'has she gone to the police?' flow-chart of legal considerations, the journalist has to carefully consider all the circumstances. The journalist knows that allegations of this kind are serious. Jeffrey Epstein was reportedly one of the richest and most powerful men in New York in the early 2000s—and had a lot of powerful friends. Allegations of violence against women can seriously harm a person's reputation and have consequences for his work and his family life. Any story that includes them comes with significant legal and cost risk, and could also have serious consequences for the journalist's reputation—and their publication's—if they get it wrong. Each investigation and each story is its own legal adventure.

Is there a non-disclosure agreement, or NDA? If there is—whether from an earlier settlement of her legal claims against him or as part of her employment contract—things are legally very tricky (see Chapter 5). She has been contracted to silence. An NDA cannot stop her reporting him to the police, but it will likely be a breach of her NDA for her to speak to a journalist, and even for the journalist or their lawyer to look at the terms of her NDA to know what they are dealing with. She would need to seek independent legal advice on her NDA before any investigation could progress. He could—based on the NDA—get an injunction to stop publication, and sue her and the newspaper for damages if the story is published. The courts will typically uphold her contractual obligation to him to remain silent. Most people can't afford to bring proceedings to try to get out of an NDA: the fees can run into the thousands; if he fights it, maybe the millions. That could be the end of the road for the story.

While it was reported that some Epstein victims had signed NDAs, Maria and Annie Farmer had not—so their story could go ahead.

If the investigation proceeds, it will often take months of detailed investigation before the story ever makes it into the newspaper. It will involve interview after interview with the woman, or women, about what happened—both to assess their credibility and test the facts. Who is the perpetrator? Where did it happen? Are there witnesses? Did you tell anyone else? If not, why not? If so, who and when? Why didn't you go to the police? Do you have any documentary evidence to confirm what you say? Her motivations will be questioned. It will also involve gathering as much contemporaneous evidence as possible to corroborate her truth: text messages, emails, medical records and evidence from friends, family, colleagues or anyone she might have told about it. Some media organisations require the women to give a formal witness statement or make a statutory declaration to affirm the truth before they will publish her story.

Some survivors can feel demoralised by the barrage of questions they face from journalists and their lawyers. Even if a journalist believes you, they have to conduct a rigorous investigation of the facts and they have to get it past their lawyers and editors. A good journalist should explain this to you, and the legal reasons for which they have to question everything you tell them. Journalists aren't prosecutors, but reporting these stories should (but doesn't always) involve a rigorous process of building a strong case, with the mindset that it may well one day end up in court.

The difference between a prosecutor and a journalist is that the latter needs to be able to prove your case to the civil (rather than criminal) standard of proof: the truth, on the balance of probabilities. They have to be able to show their editors and counsel that, if they were ever sued for printing your story, they could prove in court that what they have written is true—or at least that their investigation met the standards required of public interest journalism. That's what the law and the courts require. It is in your interests for journalists to do their job properly, as their aim is to protect themselves and you from the stress and cost of legal claims.

If it is one woman accusing him, then it's her word against his. For some journalists, this is too legally risky: some say they would need to gather testimonies from multiple women before they feel confident to approach their editor with it, let alone before they will print a story. One woman's account is too easily attacked as lacking credibility, they say. One in-house legal counsel told us the same thing.

Years of feminist advocacy has meant that, in criminal cases, a woman's own account is enough evidence on its own to convict an accused offender. Juries are now specifically reminded that her testimony is enough. But when it comes to libel, it seems that for some journalists, lawyers and courts, one woman's evidence often isn't enough: it must be corroborated by other evidence, or by other women. How many women must accuse a man before a story about his abuse can be published?

One media lawyer we spoke with raised the importance of ensuring that the allegation is a matter of public interest. Is the figure against whom the allegation is being made a public figure? Is there something that makes it a public interest story? She suggested that these questions are important, and that printing a story that includes an accusation or allegation of sexual assault or domestic violence of an unknown individual might not make it over that hurdle, whereas allegations against industry leaders or other public figures likely would. Recall the case of Andrew Griffiths (see Chapter 2), where public interest arguments were made in relation to allegations and civil findings of abuse against a man who had been an incumbent MP.

In Epstein's case, reporting about his abuse was clearly in the public interest. Maria and Annie Farmer both went on the record and had agreed to be named as part of the story. Both women said they were sexually assaulted and exploited by Epstein, with Maxwell's help. They had told their mother and friends, and their mother also went on the record. But when it came to it, *Vanity Fair* did not publish their story. Vicky Ward's profile, entitled 'The Talented Mr Epstein', merely spoke of his tendency to surround himself with young women.

In the years since, and particularly since Epstein's death, there has been a heated debate about why the women's story was spiked. Ward has since claimed she was determined to expose Epstein as a sexual abuser, but that Epstein convinced her editor, Graydon Carter, not to publish the story. 'It came down to my sources' word against Epstein's,' she told *The New Yorker*, 'and at the time Graydon believed Epstein.' It has been reported that Epstein threatened and pressured Carter not to publish the story, but Carter disputes the suggestion that this affected his editorial judgement. Instead, he says, the abuse story was pulled for legal reasons: it would not have withstood a libel claim. Carter told *The Hollywood Reporter* that Ward did not have three sources on the record, which he said he considered necessary for the story—but he later clarified that Ward did not have three sources that met the magazine's 'legal threshold'.

How many women had to accuse Epstein before the story could be published? Two or more, according to *Vanity Fair*.

Whatever the truth about why *Vanity Fair* spiked the story, there is a lesson for women wanting to speak out: it is important to think carefully about the journalist you choose to speak to, and the publication's track record in reporting stories of violence against women.

The situation can sometimes be 'chicken and egg'. It often takes one allegation to be reported for more people to come forward—reporting the story about him will 'shake the tree'. That is to say, reporting one story about him can encourage more women or more witnesses to come forward about him. The important public interest role played by the media is recognised by police, who often make statements to the media appealing to the public to come forward with evidence to assist their investigations. As cases from Harvey Weinstein to Bill Cosby show, it usually takes that first woman to come forward—and the first journalist or media organisation to bear the initial cost risk to publish—to break the dam. As we saw in those cases, more and more women coming forward to the media finally prompted police action and criminal prosecutions. Indeed, when federal prosecutors finally charged Epstein with sex trafficking in 2019, the then US Attorney for the Southern District of New York said, 'We were assisted by some excellent investigative journalism.' This kind of public interest reporting is incredibly important, and can also be relevant in some jurisdictions when it comes to defending defamation claims.

Even where there are multiple accusations, the story might not get over the line. It is often said that if the women's stories are similar—as they were with Weinstein—it shows his modus operandi and it's more likely they are all telling the truth. But it can cut both ways: if their stories are too similar, have they colluded? Journalists have to assess their credibility, because the women will inevitably be accused of lying and/or colluding out of revenge. Did the women know each other? Have they spoken to one another about their allegations? For Pia Sarma at Times Newspapers Limited, one woman's story can be enough, but in practice the media organisation must always have in mind how a judge might respond to the claimant lawyers who still 'churn out those lines about women being devious and manipulative', and the sometimes sexist arguments that we still see being run by what are largely all-male legal teams before mostly male judges.

The fact is that the media's assessment of the credibility of certain women's claims can silence stories. The Weinstein story broke after powerful, high-profile women in the entertainment industry spoke out on the record. Why did it take so long for Epstein's victims' stories to be reported? 'Some critics of the press's performance say ruefully there may have been a class element at play . . . Epstein and his associates recruited young women from working-class backgrounds and disrupted families,' writes David Folkenflik for NPR.

Journalist Jim DeRogatis investigated abuse claims against the musician and producer R Kelly for twenty years before Kelly was finally prosecuted and sent to prison. He is reported to have harmed as many as 48 women and girls. 'Everyone failed these young Black girls,' he said.

Despite many young Black women coming forward, DeRogatis struggled to place his stories in the media. His dogged reporting is now credited with helping to end Kelly's abuse, but DeRogatis said his conviction was 'too little, too late' for the women whose stories he reported. 'It was very difficult for any of them to take satisfaction out of the fact it took two decades to stop it,' he said. Throughout his reporting, the most common comment he heard from women was: 'Nobody cares about young Black girls. Nobody is going to believe us.'

Then there is the question of what the journalist will report about the allegation and how it will be reported. Survivors often want their truth told, and they want journalists to publish it in definitive terms: she was raped and he is a rapist. But for legal reasons, in any story about rape or gender-based violence, you will read the words 'alleged', 'claimed' or 'reported' before the words 'abuser' or 'rapist'. You will find, somewhere in the story, 'she said' and 'he said': a denial from him or words to the effect of 'all claims are strongly denied'. Survivors can sometimes feel betrayed by this, but it is the work of the newspaper's legal counsel, who is trying to ensure that the paper, the journalist and the person making the accusation in the news story don't get sued. It is easier for the newspaper to defend in court an allegation that there were grounds to suspect he had raped her, rather than a statement that he is guilty of rape. Language matters—and it really matters in the law.

Similarly, publishing an allegation of a specific crime like attempted rape or strangulation is risky: could he allege that he didn't intend to rape her? Could he allege that he didn't intend to kill her? We need only look back at Nicola Stocker's case ('he tried to strangle me') in the Prologue to see why language matters. This is why the language is often softened by the newspaper's lawyers: the newspaper might use wording such as 'sexual misconduct' or some form of words which is not defined in criminal law. Again, this is to make it easier to defend a lawsuit later, if they are sued. We've seen time and time again the media's tendency to minimise violence against women. But there are also legal pressures that contribute to this.

The story is carefully reviewed and checked by the legal department—but there is one very important stage left: the journalist has to go to him for comment. By this time, the investigation could have taken weeks, if not months. The journalist will have spoken to the woman or women making the allegation multiple times, and obtained any corroborating evidence there might be. The story will have cleared the internal steps to prepare it for publication. Journalists are supposed to contact the subject of any story who is accused of wrongdoing to give him notice of the story and allow him time to respond (it is required by broadcasting rules in the United Kingdom and for journalists who want to later rely on a public interest defence in any defamation claim).

This is called the 'right to reply' and it allows the subject of the story to ensure their version of the facts are included. In MeToo type situations, the reply is often simple and predictable: it's all lies, and all wrongdoing is denied. But what it also means is that he is put on notice—if he didn't otherwise already know—that she is speaking out.

What's the first thing he does? Make a call to his lawyer (or team of lawyers)—and his PR team. This is where his playbook begins.

Play 1: The legal threat letter

His first strategy is simple: send a letter. But not just any letter. This letter will threaten costly legal proceedings: it might threaten the journalist that he will go to court for an injunction if they don't undertake to stop publication, or he might claim the allegations are 'false and defamatory' and threaten to sue if they go ahead and publish. This is what reportedly happened when *The Sun* tried to publish abuse allegations about Jimmy Savile, the former BBC television presenter, in 2009, while he was still alive. The stories were only reported by the media after Savile's death in 2011, by which time there was no risk in doing so because you can't defame the dead. A Met Police report in 2013 later found that Savile had committed sex offences against 450 people, including 328 minors. How many women and children could have been warned and protected if the story was published earlier?

The legal threat letter is an effective tactic because legal proceedings are extremely expensive—even if the defamation claim never gets to trial, masses of costs can be racked up. Pia Sarma told us that if you get a story about rape wrong and later have to pull it and apologise, it could cost hundreds of thousands in legal fees and damages. Even if you get it right but you're forced to defend it at trial, it will cost hundreds of thousands—or even millions—more. For many journalists and newspapers, the cost risk is simply too great. For every defamation trial you see, there is an avalanche of legal letters and threats that have stopped stories from reaching the public domain: the threat of legal action has prevented publication. No one knows how many women's stories have been silenced, because these letters are confidential and marked 'not for publication'. No one knows about it except the journalist, their legal team and his lawyers. In this way, the rich and the powerful have ensured—in some cases for decades—that allegations of abuse and harassment, even if widely rumoured, have not been reported in the media.

For journalists, it is much easier to report on allegations of rape or abuse where there is a prosecution. As we have seen, journalists cannot be sued for defamation for fairly reporting on what is said in court. Where there is no criminal prosecution or any other civil claim where the facts are heard in court, though, they are at legal risk. In some countries, especially in Latin America, journalists will only report a case after a trial has commenced, or even wait to be sure and report only after it has concluded with a conviction. The problem is that most rape cases don't go to trial, and 99 per cent don't result in a conviction—so for a media organisation to require a conviction before it publishes an allegation is to effectively refuse to report on 99 per cent of rape cases.

After the receipt of a legal threat letter, it takes deep pockets, determined journalists, and editors and lawyers who have an appetite for risk to follow through and print the story. As Gill Phillips explained to us, the lawyers at a newspaper advise on the legal risks but the choice to publish ultimately rests with the editor. While it might be possible for large media organisations with large legal budgets and experienced in-house counsel to assess the risk and deal with these letters, for freelance journalists or small media houses, it is much harder—seeking external legal advice is expensive, and legal action could mean they face bankruptcy and are shut down.

When Professor Julie Macfarlane decided to go public about her abuse by an Anglican priest (see Chapter 1), she went to the *Church Times*. In her book *Going Public* (2022), she explains how the journalists were threatened with an injunction by the diocese and had to have a barrister on call. The journalists admitted to her that they wouldn't normally have the legal budget to contest an injunction. Happily for Julie, they were able to publish. The resulting publicity led other survivors to reach out to her—and the church suddenly became interested in settling her case.

For some small publications, though, the legal threat letter can force self-censorship: smaller media organisations often just can't afford to take a risk on stories about violence against women. Rich and powerful men, and their lawyers, know this. They know that one warning shot can be enough to shut the story down, and silence the victim and the journalists who want to tell her story. The legal threat is not about winning the case at trial, but about pressuring her or the journalist into self-censoring. The result can be a silencing of stories about a particular man for years, even decades. If no one in the media reports on it, then other women who might have come forward never find out that they were not alone. Women remain in their silos of silence. That's often why these letters are so aggressive: their aim is to shut the story down before it starts rolling, and before other women (if there are any) come forward.

Vanity Fair's decision to pull the Farmers' Epstein abuse story because of the defamation risk is just one example— there are others. In 2006, the allegations of almost three dozen more women led to Epstein being charged. But his lawyers struck a controversial plea deal so he could plead guilty to reduced state charges of 'soliciting prostitution from a teenager', instead of the more serious charge of sexual assault of minors. Epstein spent fifteen months in jail, with much of it on 'work release'. Afterwards, Epstein was quickly accepted back into society: he hosted a dinner to honour Prince Andrew at his Manhattan home, and donated large sums to scientists and institutions for art and music.

Years passed and the story seemed to be over. But in 2015, another survivor, Virginia Giuffre decided to tell her story about Epstein and the powerful people around him, including Prince Andrew. She decided to speak out because 'Epstein was walking around a free man, comparing his criminal behavior to stealing a bagel,' as she wrote in an email to NPR. 'I really wanted a spotlight shone on him and the others who acted with him and enabled his vile and shameless conduct against young girls and young women.' Giuffre went to ABC News; she later told NPR that she saw an opportunity to call out the government 'for basically looking the other way' and she wanted 'to describe the anger and the betrayal victims felt'. But the story never aired, and she was never told why.

According to NPR, the story was pulled after Epstein's powerful lawyer, Alan Dershowitz, called ABC to speak with the producers and their lawyer. ABC told NPR their decision not to broadcast the interview 'reflected proper journalistic care', but refused to detail its editorial choices. Giuffre has said: 'I was defeated, once again, by the very people I spoke out against and once again, my voice was silenced.'

After ABC pulled Giuffre's interview, it would be another journalist's work that would result in more of the Epstein story finally being told. Julie Brown at *The Miami Herald* continued to dig and investigate Epstein after the government allowed him to plead to lesser charges—and later revealed the extent of his abuse. As *The New Yorker* reports, her persistent reporting and the role of investigative journalism in helping to hold Epstein accountable was praised by Attorney General William Barr after Epstein's arrest in July 2019. Journalistic inquiry and reporting can assist the criminal justice authorities. But, as Brown has said, she—and all journalists reporting on Epstein— lived in constant fear of being sued for defamation.

Even now, at the time of writing—after Epstein's suicide and Maxwell's conviction—we haven't yet heard Giuffre's full story for legal reasons. In 2022, Prince Andrew settled the civil claim brought against him by Giuffre for sexual assault and battery during her time working for Epstein and Maxwell for a reported US$12–15 million. The settlement came with a limited NDA: she couldn't tell her story until after the Queen's Platinum Jubilee. Amber Melville-Brown, a media lawyer, said Giuffre's time-limited silence under the settlement would be 'worth its weight in gold to the Queen'. Prince Andrew denies all wrongdoing.

The Epstein story shows that even large media outlets will silence stories because of legal risks. *Vanity Fair* and ABC News silenced Epstein stories. Journalist Ronan Farrow reportedly left NBC and went to *The New Yorker* after NBC refused to run his reporting on Weinstein. It can be seriously upsetting for the journalists who work with women for months—sometimes years—to build trust to enable them to come forward and tell their story, only to have the story spiked by an editor or their legal team, often at the last minute.

According to Vicky Ward, it was an editor at *Vanity Fair* who informed her that the magazine had decided not to include the Farmer sisters' allegations against Epstein in her story. 'I must have gone into the office, because I do remember being there and just crying . . . They had been so brave, and we just let them down,' Ward later recalled.

For the women who have trusted journalists to tell their story, it can feel like a brutal betrayal of trust. In a statement to NPR, the Farmer sisters said: 'It was terribly painful. We hoped the story would put people on notice and [Epstein and Maxwell] would be stopped from abusing other young girls and young women. That didn't happen. In the end, the story that ran erased our voices.'

Their lawyer, David Boies, claimed that *Vanity Fair*'s omission made it more difficult for other victims and witnesses to speak out. 'I think it helped create the impression among many of the victims that the media was under Epstein's control, that Epstein had all this power.'

The fact is that women's stories are often silenced for legal reasons. For every story you read in the paper, many more have been spiked—thanks to Play 1.

Play 2: The privacy injunction

His lawyers have written to vehemently deny the allegations. And to threaten legal action (Play 1). But the media organisation's in-house counsel nevertheless signs off to publish the story—provided, of course, that the journalist includes the accused man's denial in the story. The next move from the playbook will now be made.

His lawyers might rush to court to obtain an injunction or suppression order from a judge to stop the publication. A letter then arrives to inform the journalist that they cannot publish because there is an interim injunction or suppression order. There are different types of injunctions, but usually it means a journalist can't report certain details of the story, either because it affects his private life or because she was silenced by a contract (an NDA). The newspaper cannot legally publish her story, and will have to apply—at great expense—to challenge the injunction or let the matter go to trial. They will have to prove to the court that there is some legal justification for publishing the story, or that the public interest in publishing the story outweighs his private interest in keeping it quiet.

We want to make it clear here that injunctions aren't all bad: they can protect individuals against unlawful intrusion by the media, and the publication of private information, such as threats to sell or publish intimate photographs, a sex tape or other sensitive information. Injunctions can also be obtained by victims of sexual offences to protect their anonymity where they are concerned that publication would lead to their 'jigsaw identification'. In this way, injunctions can provide important protections.

But the playbook injunction is one that seeks to suppress legitimate and public interest reporting on allegations of sexual harassment, rape, sexual abuse or domestic abuse, and misconduct. They are sought by those who have the money to get them, in order to prevent criticism and silence women and force newspapers into expensive legal battles before they can tell important, public interest stories. They are increasingly sought in the United Kingdom—but in places like the United States and Australia there aren't the same privacy laws.

In 2008 Max Mosley famously sued *The News of the World* over a front-page article entitled 'F1 boss has sick Nazi orgy with 5 hookers' and a video that accompanied it. The court held that the newspaper had breached Mosley's privacy, confirming that we are all entitled to have a reasonable expectation of privacy in relation to consensual sexual activity in private—even if the sex was 'unconventional'—but not where it amounted to criminal conduct. The question is one of balance: does the free speech and public interest in publication outweigh his right to privacy? In this case, the sex had involved some 'spanking', but it was consensual and no offences had been committed. On this basis, the court found there was not sufficient public interest to justify publication, and ordered the newspaper to pay Mosley £60,000 in damages for violation of his right to privacy. The problem for Mosley was that the cat was already out of the bag: he was only able to sue for damages after publication. He complained to the European Court of Human Rights that the newspaper had not given him advance notice for him to have the opportunity to obtain an injunction to stop the story before it ran—and that the law should require the media to give advance notice. Jen intervened for the media in that case with Geoffrey Robertson KC, arguing it was too strict a rule and would chill public interest reporting, and Mosley lost. As confirmed by the European Court, and the following Leveson Inquiry—the British public inquiry into the culture and ethics of the British press after the *News of the World* phone-hacking scandal—prior notification is 'good practice but not a legal requirement'.

Privacy rights have been developed in cases like this to protect individuals from excessive intrusion by the press and by the state. It was in fact model Naomi Campbell who played a leading role in ensuring that everyone, including celebrities, has their right to privacy protected in the era of tabloid journalism.

That's a good thing. Privacy is an important right, and has since developed to stop people from posting or sharing intimate information, naked images or sex tapes. But there are concerns that privacy injunctions are being used by rich and powerful men to cover up misconduct—and, more recently, even to cover up abusive and potentially criminal conduct.

In the United Kingdom, there have been heated debates about the availability of super-injunctions to cover up alleged sexual misconduct. A 'super-injunction' is an order that prohibits any reporting of the matter, but with an added extra: not only can you not report on the matter, you cannot even report the fact that an injunction against reporting the information exists. Celebrities and footballers used them to prevent what were once known as 'kiss and tell stories'. For example, in 2011 the Manchester United footballer Ryan Giggs got a super-injunction against Imogen Thomas and *The Sun* newspaper to stop any reporting on his extramarital affair with her. We only know about it because an MP later named him in parliament under parliamentary privilege.

Gill Phillips, the in-house legal counsel at *The Guardian*, has written about these injunctions, and how 'courts are allowing men to treat women like chattels'. Back in 2010, Gill argued: 'The real harm of these orders is not that they gag the press—it is that they stop the wives, partners and families from finding out about the bit on the side.' She questioned whether the courts were confusing private information with public image or commercial reputation.

Famous people have obtained injunctions to stop reporting about hiring prostitutes, with the courts holding that 'sexual encounters in private with a prostitute' should also be protected under privacy rights. These privacy injunctions are often brought by male barristers on behalf of male celebrity clients, and are granted by male judges. As Gill points out, 'little or no regard appears to be given to the rights of women in these cases'. Indeed, privacy rights have developed to a point where, when it comes to sexual secrets, 'his asserted entitlement to autonomous control of information about his sexual life' seems to countervail other rights, including a sex worker's right or potentially even his mistress's right to talk about her own sexual life. The problem Gill highlighted is that privacy injunctions have been granted in a way that privileges his rights over hers.

We caught up with Gill in 2022 to talk about recent developments in the law on privacy. As she explained, the MeToo movement in 2017 has shifted the cultural debate. Allegations which perhaps would not have been reported back in the 1970s or '80s are now fearlessly investigated by journalists around the world. Story after story has emerged since Weinstein's downfall. Gill pointed to the reporting on the allegations against Prince Andrew, a member of the British royal family, which would have been unthinkable in the 1970s. But Gill also explained that, in parallel to this cultural shift and understanding, the law has also been subtly moving. The debates no longer centre on super-injunctions, which are increasingly rare. Now, there is a creeping shift and expansion in the circumstances in which injunctions are being made available to protect privacy rights, including to protect a person's identity when they are under investigation and the allegation against them would damage their reputation.

On 14 August 2014, Sir Cliff Richard's home was due to be searched by the South Yorkshire Police. The BBC was tipped off about the search, and to the fact that he was under investigation in relation to allegations of a historical sexual offence (which he strenuously denied, and no charges were ever brought). Sir Cliff's case established a new precedent in UK law: that a suspect has a reasonable expectation of privacy in relation to a police investigation. The High Court held:

> If the presumption of innocence were perfectly understood and given effect to, and if the general public was universally capable of adopting a completely open- and broad-minded view of the fact of an investigation so that there was no risk of taint either during the investigation or afterwards (assuming no charge) then the position might be different. But neither of those things is true. The fact of an investigation, as a general rule, will of itself carry some stigma, no matter how often one says it should not.

In 2022, in a case brought against Bloomberg News, the Supreme Court of the United Kingdom confirmed that, as a starting point, when a person is under investigation for a criminal offence, they have the right to privacy in relation to the fact that they are being investigated until they are charged. The Supreme Court ruled that Bloomberg had been wrong to seek to name a businessman, 'Mr ZXC', as facing a criminal investigation into his work activities—and upheld the injunction that he had obtained to stop publication. It held that reporting this information before the authorities had made the decision to charge him would cause unfair reputational damage to Mr ZXC, violating both his rights to reputation and other aspects of his private and family life. The lower courts in the case had explained that it is a 'human characteristic to assume the worst (that there is no smoke without fire)' and that people tend to overlook the legal principle that an accused person is innocent until proven guilty. The Supreme Court explained that, as a legitimate starting point, until someone is charged with an offence the information relating to a criminal investigation is private.

The Supreme Court's finding has raised numerous questions for the media: can a newspaper name a person who has not yet been charged with a criminal offence but who is under criminal investigation? Does a person have a right to privacy to prevent publication of the fact that they are suspected of criminal activity? Can a privacy injunction be used to stop newspapers printing allegations of gender-based violence if there is a police investigation? When do the circumstances tip towards reporting and when do the scales tip towards privacy?

'It's a legal minefield,' Pia Sarma told us. She explained that these decisions have made publishing stories about gender-based violence even more difficult. It could also potentially thwart investigations and reporting—for example, if a newspaper has been investigating and gathering sources for months, and a police investigation then commences, the journalists will be deterred from publishing what they have learned.

Another big concern for the media is what this decision means where the person accused of sexual offences is not yet under criminal investigation. What happens when the press report allegations of serious criminal wrongdoing, such as sexual assault or rape, but there is not (or not yet) a police report, investigation or conviction? At present, these allegations will be published and the accused's legal remedy is to protect his reputation by suing for defamation. But the *ZXC* decision has led media lawyers to question whether a man might now be able to obtain a pre-publication injunction for libel as well as for breach of privacy—the very possibility Jen and Geoffrey Robertson KC had warned the European Court of Human Rights about in the Mosley case over a decade ago.

Serious concerns exist that the expansion of privacy rights and the use of pre-publication injunctions will be used to stifle free speech and public interest reporting about domestic and sexual violence. And there are indications that this is already happening.

For example, in the United Kingdom in 2018, *The Daily Telegraph* stated that it had been gagged from reporting MeToo allegations, running with the headline 'British #MeToo claims which cannot be revealed'. The newspaper reported that it couldn't publish this MeToo story because a 'wealthy businessman' had obtained an injunction based on the non-disclosure agreements (NDA) his employees had signed. This resulted in litigation in which the courts upheld his NDA over the public interest in reporting the sexual harassment claims against him. After widespread concern about the courts' decisions and speculation about the identity of the business-man at the centre of the scandal—as we explain in Chapter 5—Lord Peter Hain, a member of the House of Lords, used his parliamentary privilege to name Sir Philip Green as the businessman. Sir Philip, a high-profile British businessman and billionaire known for owning high street fashion stores such as Topshop, was able to get an injunction to stop the alle-gations of sexual harrassment and bullying from being printed because of the NDAs the women had signed when they settled their employment claims against him.

In 2019, a multi-millionaire businessman applied for 'secrecy orders' to prevent reporting that he was accused of serious sexual harassment and assault. Sean O'Neill, a leading journal-ist, reported on how a rich and powerful figure was preventing *The Times* from naming him as the person facing serious allegations. They referred to him only as 'Mr X'. Six months later, *The Times* reported that Mr X was continuing to try to censor newspaper reporting, and that Mr X was 'at the centre of a police investigation over sexual assault allegations'. *The Times* detailed how he had 'enlisted defamation lawyers and a reputation management firm to further restrict coverage by *The Times* of the police inquiry into allegations made by a former employee'. Mr X strenuously denied the allegations. His identity has never been publicly revealed, but a different story was: how the most wealthy and powerful use the law to suppress and silence reporting on their alleged assaults.

But if there's no injunction forthcoming—or if the media organisation can afford to fight it, the public interest wins the day and the injunction is overturned—publication can go ahead. But they can still be sued.

Play 3: Non-legal and unethical silencing techniques

A whole range of other techniques are used to suppress and silence women's stories—these represent the darker side of his playbook. We have seen these techniques deployed both before and after publication. Some techniques suddenly became more visible after 2017, when the tactics of powerful men such as Harvey Weinstein were revealed to the public. They include threats, online attacks, spying and PR campaigns—all with the aim of undermining and silencing both women and the journalists who are trying to tell their stories.

Undermine the accuser

Along with letters threatening legal action, those who make accusations of misconduct have found themselves personally attacked or spied on by the accused's lawyers or by an investigative firm. Sometimes this is done to gather material to attack the complainant's credibility, with the aim of deterring the journalists and editors from reporting the story. Sometimes it aims to damage the woman's reputation in the media or later in court so the public and juries won't believe her, or it may be done to deter other women from coming forward (in countries without anonymity protection for women making accusations of sexual violence).

Women have told us how they have been spied on, how their friends, colleagues or landlords have been approached, how they feel unable to go out for dinner or speak about certain things in public, and how they have even moved countries in a bid to escape prying eyes—and worse. Women report facing immense attacks online, and apparently coordinated inauthentic online activity, as well as rape and death threats. Women have told us—and we have seen it happen to our own clients—how every detail of their life is scrutinised and turned over to try to frame them as harlots or liars. This includes the use of the harmful myths we explained in Chapter 1 and all kinds of sexist tropes that sometimes mesh with specific cultural ones.

For example, Shiori Ito, whose story we told in Chapter 2, told us how she had to leave Japan because of the scrutiny and attacks she faced after she accused a powerful man of rape.

The use of spies and private investigators to undermine and silence women received widespread international attention back in 2017. That was when Ronan Farrow broke a sensational story, 'Harvey Weinstein's Army of Spies', in *The New Yorker*, detailing how Harvey Weinstein had allegedly set out to suppress allegations that he had sexually harassed or assaulted women by hiring private security agencies to collect information and spy on those who were trying to expose him. The company Weinstein hired was Black Cube, an Israeli private intelligence agency that employs former members of Mossad and other military organisations.

Personal information about each of the women, including their sexual histories, was collected. Farrow reported that these investigations were run past Weinstein's lawyer, David Boies, the lawyer we mentioned earlier for Virginia Giuffre, who 'personally signed the contract directing Black Cube to attempt to uncover information that would stop the publication of a *Times* story about Weinstein's abuses'. The key point was that the law firm had contracted and paid private investigators to 'dig up dirt' on women and journalists to avoid scrutiny of and publication of allegations of sexual violence. Farrow continues:

> Techniques like the ones used by the agencies on Weinstein's behalf are almost always kept secret, and, because such relationships are often run through law firms, the investigations are theoretically protected by attorney–client privilege, which could prevent them from being disclosed in court. The documents and sources reveal the tools and tactics available to powerful individuals to suppress negative stories and, in some cases, forestall criminal investigations.

Writing in 2019, Farrow explained that Black Cube was only one of the agencies hired by Weinstein to prevent the disclosure of sexual abuse claims. Dossiers were created on journalists and accusers. One of the people placed on a 'list of targets' was Rose McGowan. In her 2018 book *Brave*, the actor explained her experiences leading up to the publication of her allegations against Weinstein. With Jen's assistance, Rose also made a submission to the Women and Equalities Committee of the UK Parliament in 2019, outlining her experiences. In the latter, she said:

> I was later to learn that he and his powerful lawyers had another strategy to silence me: they hired Black Cube, a London-based private security firm who sent out former Mossad agents using false identities to infiltrate my life, extract information from me about my book, *Brave* (which I was then writing and has now been published), and about the journalists I was speaking to, so they could stop the story coming out. Their aim was to silence me and the other brave women who wanted to speak out. They now have PR people, lawyers and pliant journalists who troll my every public statement and appearance to make sure I am always to be harassed and targeted. They first wanted to silence me and, when they couldn't silence me, they are now doing everything in their power to discredit me.

McGowan told the committee how she was approached by a woman who gave the name Diana Filip, who said she wanted to invest in McGowan's production company. Rose later discovered that she was a Black Cube agent, sent to 'silence and steal' her story:

> 'Diana Filip' was an alias for a former officer in the Israeli Defence Forces working for Black Cube. According to their

$600,000 contract, their goal was to stop the publication of any stories about the man who assaulted me and '*obtain additional content of a book which is currently being written and includes harmful negative information on and about the Client*': that is, my book, *Brave*. The documents (obtained by *The New Yorker*) show that Black Cube delivered more than a hundred pages of transcripts and descriptions of my book, based on tens of hours of recorded conversations between me and 'Diana Filip'. The contract had provided for them to get a bonus $50,000 if Black Cube secured '*the other half*' of my book '*in readable book and legally admissible format.*'

The *New Yorker* investigation, led by Ronan Farrow, also uncovered a million-dollar bounty on my book, *Brave*. Apparently, it was not enough to have assaulted me and ruined my career in film—he then intruded into my life to silence me and steal my story. Ultimately, Weinstein succeeded in getting 125 pages of my book before its publication. I felt violated all over again. I was pursued in the manner authoritarian governments pursue journalists or human rights defenders; when all I am is a woman speaking out about sexual abuse to stop an international predator.

McGowan wasn't alone. Zelda Perkins, Weinstein's assistant who went public about her NDA (see Chapter 5), told us that she too was a target on this list. Zelda told us that, over the years before she went public, she had been approached by a number of people posing as journalists: she now believes these were attempts by Weinstein to sound out whether she was going to tell her story.

Undermine the journalist

This is another strategy straight from his playbook: undermine the personal and professional credibility of those working to tell her story—go for the journalist, the editor or the publication itself. Since Trump, it often starts with a narrative that the journalism, based on her account, is 'fake news'.

Two former *Vanity Fair* journalists claim that Epstein personally threatened them and their editor in order to silence the stories of the Farmer sisters and other survivors. According to Vicky Ward, Epstein claimed he could have her then husband, a venture capitalist, fired. Another *Vanity Fair* journalist who investigated Epstein, John Connolly, claimed that Epstein 'was torturing' their editor, Graydon Carter—calling him, berating him and turning up at his office to pressure him not to tell the women's stories. Connolly said a bullet was left at Carter's Manhattan home, which they had viewed as a threat from Epstein. In 2006, when Connolly was investigating the story about the charges against Epstein, a dead cat's head was left on Carter's doorstep. Connolly claimed that Carter was concerned about his children's safety, and so Connolly decided to drop the story. Carter acknowledged the threats he faced, but disputed whether they were, in fact, from Epstein; he denied that it ever affected his editorial approach.

In 2015, when ABC was going to air its interview with Virginia Giuffre, the ABC journalist received phone calls from Epstein's lawyer, Alan Dershowitz, which resulted in ABC pulling the story because the story hadn't 'reflected proper journalistic care'—essentially, an allegation that the journalist hadn't done their job properly.

We have spoken to journalists who have told us about how their integrity and judgement has been called into question because of their attempts to publish allegations of misconduct and violence against women. Women journalists, including Catalina and Matilde from *Volcánicas*, told us how colleagues have called them naive or questioned their nous for reporting stories when the allegation had not been reported to the police. Ronan Farrow and other experienced journalists have spoken out about how this is not the journalistic standard required for the publication of stories about violence against women, and not the standard to hold women to: their stories can be reported even if police don't investigate or prosecute—or indeed if they have chosen not to go to police.

Build up his reputation to undermine both accuser and journalist

Reputation management and crisis management firms—sometimes working on retainer, sometimes hired anew—go into overdrive to build up his reputation and trash hers. There are PR campaigns to create 'himpathy', as Kate Manne has termed it: that is, to generate sympathy for the man through the media.

Wives, ex-wives, female colleagues and other survivors of sexual assault are called upon to defend the accused. Industry figures often come out to express their support for him and attest to his character, while colleagues and friends give positive quotes and interviews. The man is a loving father, brother, lover, husband or friend, they say, or a great boss or colleague. A nice guy. He can't possibly be an abuser or a bully. Former partners or women friends might say he has never been abusive to them, which will be used to undermine and isolate the woman or women making the allegations and question their credibility. If he didn't hurt them, then he musn't have done it, or so it goes.

This is obviously irrelevant to whether or not he did it: just because you can't imagine him doing it or because he hasn't tried it on with you doesn't mean he didn't do it to her. This argument also ignores the reality of power dynamics: just because a man we know has never harassed us, that doesn't mean he didn't harass or abuse other women—or this one particular woman—because of his position of privilege and power in relation to her, by virtue of her class, her race or her disability. As the Academy Award–winning film *Promising Young Woman* depicts: even men who are considered (or consider themselves) 'nice guys' can be predators—or apologists for predators.

Nevertheless, the himpathy spectacle has well and truly begun—fuelled by the gender bias in the media and in society, and by the prejudices, preconceptions and gendered stereotypes that tell us that women are unreliable and not to be believed.

Unleash the trolls

Often the tactic of burnishing a man's reputation in the media goes hand in hand with online trolling and attacks on the woman and/or the journalist who reported the story—social media campaigns, leaking to the media and spreading stories about her, her previous relationships, making out she lies or is mentally unwell or is motivated by politics or money. Journalists are accused of spreading gossip, of being duped by an unreliable source or of having their own agendas. Victims who have a legal right to anonymity have their names exposed, despite it being a criminal offence to do so.

Whether it's directed and curated or spontaneous and organic, we see this response time and time again, and across cultural contexts: journalists, women and their friends and support networks face vicious online trolling.

Play 4: Post-publication legal action

If a newspaper or media organisation decides to publish and the allegations go public—there was no injunction and the other strategies failed—a whole new raft of legal options opens up.

In some cases, the men just say sorry and disappear for a while, only to reappear later as 'a changed person' to get on with their lives and careers. Criminal investigations into the allegations remain rare. When media coverage results in criminal prosecution, it is often only after a cascade of allegations, lots of media reporting and significant public pressure.

This can create a double bind for women who want justice in the courts. Proving that there is something worth prosecuting or that the police messed up the first time around often requires a high level of media attention and public concern. But the widespread media reporting of her allegations can also be used by him later to argue that he cannot get a fair trial because he has undergone 'trial by media'.

Defamation claims may be filed—against her or the journalist and media organisation, or both. He will claim she lied and it is defamatory. She is liable for what she has said to the newspaper and is published, and the journalist and newspaper are liable for what they have published about him.

Defamation cases are incredibly expensive, which explains why wealthy, powerful men are over-represented as plaintiffs. And the damages and legal costs can be staggering. As in a criminal trial, she will face retraumatisation when cross-examined by his lawyers. But this is a civil claim brought at his behest, so she may also face bankruptcy in defending her truth, and will not have the financial support of the state.

Women we have spoken to in different parts of the world have had to reach out for financial support and rely on pro bono legal support in defending defamation suits. There is no legal aid available. One woman we spoke to feared losing her house. Another feared losing her job because of the adverse publicity. It's little wonder most defamation claims settle before they get to court—and the rich and powerful know that the cost pressure can be used to censor. These men don't face the same cost pressures for bringing action; in the United Kingdom and some other jurisdictions, men bringing claims can even get insurance against the costs if they lose. So there is no cost risk for them.

If he sues only the media organisation, and not her, she has no cost risk—but she also has no agency in the proceedings, and will have no say in how the defamation suit is defended. All she can do is volunteer to be a witness to help prove her truth in court (unless there is an NDA, in which case she will have to be subpoenaed: see Chapter 5).

'Don't speak.' Whether he sues her personally or the journalist, once he sues, she will be told not to speak about the matter. The journalist will be warned not to write anything further, for fear of aggravating the damage to his reputation and increasing the damages to be paid later, if they lose. This silences the woman, the media, her friends and any advocacy groups that might want to support her by campaigning for justice, who will also usually be advised not to repeat or comment on the allegations.

Once women are sued, they can become isolated from their support networks. It limits what they can say about their own life experience. Women have used the words 'my alleged rapist' instead of 'my rapist', even in private, because they are scared that they will be overheard or because they have been conditioned by how the law requires them to speak about their perpetrator in public. Women have told us how they became scared to speak. Women have told us how the silencing stopped their healing process: they could not speak about their own lives, the abuse they suffered, even to their friends. And women have told us how they were retraumatised by having to have contact with his lawyers and being forced to revisit what he did to them.

Defamation proceedings can take years to resolve, and there is nothing to stop a rich and powerful man from suing in multiple jurisdictions. Some women we spoke to were tied up in libel proceedings for years. By suing, he stops people talking about it and he stops further reporting on it—at least until the matter goes to trial. But not all defamation claims get to trial.

Some women have to settle the claims brought against them for financial reasons, and can be permanently silenced: it is often a condition of the settlement that she cannot repeat the allegation or she will face fresh legal action. In some cases, she is even required to apologise to him. Some settlement contracts contain a non-disparagement clause, which means she cannot speak ill of him. Settlements like this can have a chilling effect on the media too—reporting on the matter now carries the risk of aggravated damages, because the media company knows about the settlement and her apology.

When a newspaper settles, it also has the effect of silencing the media generally—and her. The newspaper might have called his bluff, believing that he wouldn't actually sue, and publish anyway. When he follows through with his threat and sues the newspaper, he will claim that she lied. The newspaper might choose to settle for commercial reasons: proceedings are too expensive, their legal budget is under pressure, or maybe they just want to move on to the next story. But when the organ-isation decides to settle, it implicitly says that her allegations are not true and she lied—or that's what he will say—which warns off any other journalist who might report it. In fact, what it often actually means is not that she lied, but that lawyers have adjudged that her allegations couldn't be substantiated to the level of evidence required in court or they couldn't afford to fight it. But that will not stop him from claiming that it means she lied. Sometimes the settlement requires a public apology, which you will see printed in the newspaper. Where does this leave her? She will be silenced too—she won't be given another platform to tell her story, and risks being sued herself if she finds one.

Once the matter goes to trial, the problem in media coverage arises that we are familiar with in criminal cases: the media is protected from being sued by providing a 'fair and accurate report' of proceedings. This means they'll be reporting both sides of the story, giving his legal team the opportunity to spin all kinds of narratives and attack her credibility. The report-ing shifts from allegations of sexual assault, domestic violence or misconduct to become a sensationalised drama in the media, which repeats and perpetuates many of the harmful myths, sexist tropes and stereotypes raised in court in his defence.

Women we spoke to explained the costs that speaking out had had on their private lives. Domestic violence allegations made in a family court context are often private and confi-dential; in the criminal courts, she will have anonymity if she wants it and may seek additional protections while she gives her evidence. But once a woman is sued in libel her identity— along with the allegations—will usually be openly reported. That was the case for Nicola Stocker: newpapers reported on the libel proceedings, including the intimate details of their marriage, and journalists doorstopped her and her family. Newspapers will print her name and her picture, and report on the allegations made, and the libel trial becomes a form of entertainment.

Amber Heard's testimony in the US defamation trial—including about domestic and sexual assault—was broadcast live on TV and online, published around the world millions of times and mocked on social media. Women have told us how the publicity associated with defamation cases is particularly difficult for their children. In Nicola Stocker's case, fewer than ten people had seen her original Facebook post about the alleged assault. Once the libel trial was underway, the allegation and details about her marriage were reported in the national press.

If he wins, then the silence will continue—and potentially be permanent. In jurisdictions like Australia and the United Kingdom, he will also ask for an injunction, to prevent the allegations from being repeated, and if she or anyone else does say it again, they will be in contempt of court.

If he loses the libel claim—she will be free to speak, finally. He will have to pay her legal costs or those of the newspaper (not in the United States, but in the United Kingdom, Australia and other 'adverse costs' jurisdictions). This is only fair, since he brought the proceedings in the first place, but there are no reparations available to her. No damages will be awarded to her for the suffering he put her through in suing her for defamation or for her silencing. He can use the law to silence her for years—for the cost of paying her legal fees. She can only claim damages against him if she can countersue him for defamation.

In some jurisdictions, the publication can lead to a criminal defamation prosecution against her and/or the journalist who published her story. A charge of criminal defamation—which exists in Colombia, India, Japan, Uganda and many countries around the world—means that women and journalists not only face the risk of having to pay damages, but could also face police investigation and jail time. In Japan, for example, there is no truth defence to a charge of criminal defamation: you could face prison for publishing a truthful allegation that harms the honour of the accused perpetrator. These antiquated laws are being used to target journalists and women, criminalising those who speak out instead of the perpetrator of the abuse.

Bizarrely—or perhaps predictably—in some cases, journalists reporting on MeToo stories have told us that the criminal investigations in their defamation cases moved incredibly quickly, with police calling them in to be interrogated just weeks after an online publication. This is in stark contrast with how police treat allegations of domestic and sexual violence, where investigations are slow and (in most jurisdictions) prosecutions are rare. Instead of prioritising investigations into the claims of sexual harassment or abuse, police are targeting those who have spoken out about it or reported on it.

International human rights courts and tribunals have advised countries to repeal criminal defamation laws for their chilling effect on free speech. But one media law expert told us how civil proceedings can have an equally chilling effect. Based on our clients' experience and what women have told us, we agree: civil proceedings can ruin your life. This expert commented that many clients would almost prefer to be sued abroad for criminal defamation and end up with a €3000 administrative fine, rather than face half a million pounds in costs and damages in the United Kingdom. The sheer cost of the proceedings is 'life-changing', he told us. He explained how people embroiled in civil defamation proceedings can lose their house, while the proceedings themselves take over their lives.

Whatever form of defamation claim women and journalists face, it is terrifying—and him bringing or even threatening a claim can have the effect of silencing and chilling speech—and stopping the story.

Understanding is the first step towards winning the game

These are the playbook strategies we see being used all over the world to stop women and journalists speaking out or publishing claims against powerful and wealthy men. The law is being weaponised. Too often women have no idea of what they are getting into when they decide to speak out, and as a result they are not prepared for the challenges they face when they do. We want every woman and every journalist to know his playbook—so that when they do decide to speak out, they are informed.

Chapter 5

CONTRACTED TO SILENCE

Why did it take decades for allegations against Harvey Weinstein, Jeffrey Epstein and Bill Cosby to become public?

A culture of victim-blaming, shame and silence? Sure.

Power? Definitely.

Being influential figures who could make or break careers, particularly of the women they targeted? Absolutely.

But there was another reason—a specifically legal one. These men had got the women they employed, harassed and/or abused to sign contracts, promising—usually in return for a sum of money—to remain silent. This is an NDA, or non-disclosure agreement, and it has been used to protect men for decades.

Before MeToo, most people didn't know what NDAs were, let alone about the widespread practice of powerful men and corporations using them to silence women who have suffered sexual abuse and harassment. NDAs have been used to devastating effect, prohibiting women from speaking about their experiences, isolating victims in silos of silence, preventing them from warning other women and enabling their perpetrators to continue their abuse.

In this chapter, we share what we have learned—from both our legal practice and from our interviews for this book—about the many ways in which NDAs are used and abused. We've talked to women who have been contracted to silence to show how NDAs work, how power imbalances come into play and what the impact is on survivors who feel forced by circumstance—if not by pressure from the perpetrator—to sell and sign away their freedom of speech. We explain what happens when NDAs end up in court, and the arguments that can and should be used to protect women's right to free speech.

What is an NDA?

A non-disclosure agreement (sometimes known as a confidentiality agreement) is a legal contract in which a person agrees to keep information a secret. They were typically used to protect trade secrets, intellectual property and other commercially sensitive information—so that an employee or contractor wouldn't share information with competitors and the world at large. For example, the recipe for Coca-Cola has been protected by an NDA for over 100 years. Things like patents, which also protect intellectual property, go on a public register. But an NDA is a private document. Once it has been signed, no one except the parties involved or their lawyers are allowed to access the document. Some NDAs even include clauses stipulating that you aren't allowed to talk about the fact that you've signed one—and some women haven't even been allowed to keep a copy of the agreement itself.

NDAs aren't all bad: they have been, and continue to be, used for good reasons. For example, NDAs are used in national security contracts to protect sensitive information necessary to ensure public safety. In journalism, they have been used to protect sources and sensitive information, including on big data projects where journalistic material is being shared among people working for different newspapers. But there is also ample evidence of their abuse in keeping information secret that is in the public interest.

For years, NDAs were used in the settlement of child sex abuse cases against various religious institutions, which kept the victims and their allegations quiet, ensured silence about the perpetrating priests and enabled them to move parishes and molest children with impunity. An NDA—part of a research grant contract between the asbestos industry and a leading research laboratory—was used to force the man who discovered that asbestos caused cancer to keep his research quiet for decades. How many children and lives could have been saved if we'd known these facts earlier?

Our own legal practice and the controversies that have erupted since MeToo have shown us that NDAs have become the go-to solution for organisations, corporations, individuals and public bodies to settle cases of sexual misconduct, rape and abuse, and gender discrimination. NDAs are included in all kinds of employment contracts, divorce agreements and settlement agreements resolving all kinds of legal claims, and have been used to cover up domestic and sexual abuse, as well as sexual harassment and abuse in workplaces, schools, universities and religious institutions. But how do they work? And where are the problems?

It is important to note that every contract is different, and the terms of each NDA must be read carefully to understand their implications. But here is an overview of the sorts of terms you can expect to see in NDAs.

Contracting yourself (and the world) to silence

When a woman is asked to sign an NDA as part of a settlement over sexual assault or abuse allegations, it doesn't just stop her speaking to the media—she is also unable to talk about her experience with her family, friends and sometimes even her therapist. Some NDAs require secrecy about the existence of the NDA itself: so a woman who signs one can't talk about what happened, or about the fact she has signed an NDA. It is also common that the agreement includes a denial by the accused person of all allegations and that they are permitted to publicly deny the allegations if asked about them, while the woman is prevented from speaking about the matter or responding to his public denials.

Non-disparagement clauses prohibit the survivor from ever publicly criticising her perpetrator, sometimes going so far as to require the survivor to deny what happened to her if she is ever asked about it, and even to disparage her own friends if they speak out about what they know about her abuse.

Even more controversially, some NDAs have included non-cooperation clauses, which prohibit or limit the survivor from cooperating with law enforcement in criminal investigations into the perpetrator. This kind of term is unenforceable: no contract can prevent a woman from reporting to the police; no court will enforce it and it is unethical for a lawyer to include terms that purport to prevent or limit cooperation with police. But unfortunately we know that some women have signed contracts like this and believed that they were bound by them.

However, there are other clauses that don't prevent a woman from going to the police but require her to give notice if she intends to cooperate with law enforcement over her allegations, or to give notice before she goes to the police. It doesn't limit cooperation with police, but it does require her to give him a heads up. For example, the confidentiality agreement in Johnny Depp's divorce settlement with Amber Heard—now public thanks to the defamation proceedings—required her to give his lawyers 48 hours' notice if she decided to go to the police with her domestic violence allegations.

NDAs keep settlements and the misconduct secret, buying the silence of those who have suffered the abuse and holding them to that silence by contract. Having such contracts, as Weinstein, Epstein, Cosby and others discovered, can be very effective in keeping the story of their misconduct under wraps. Once signed, the NDA financially incentivises silence and deters women from ever going public by increasing the consequences for them if they do. As if the existing societal and cultural pressure were not enough to keep women silent, an NDA renders her story confidential by way of contract.

Later, if the woman changes her mind and wants to speak out, and/or if a journalist intends to report her story, an injunction can be obtained from a court to prevent publication of her story. If she speaks out anyway, she is in breach of contract and might be pursued for damages and legal costs. 'Clawback' clauses can mean that the woman is required to pay back her settlement sum—the amount paid in damages to compensate her for the abuse or harassment she suffered—and she might also be liable for the perpetrators' legal costs, which can run into hundreds of thousands—or, as we explain later, millions. Some NDAs have also specified an additional financial penalty for any breach of the NDA, which can be significant: one Weinstein contract reportedly included a penalty specified at US$1 million, which was far more than the women silenced were paid in settlement in damages for what they had experienced. Her silence was clearly worth more than the damage he had done to her. In the NDA put in place by USA Gymnastics in order to keep quiet the abuse by former national team doctor Larry Nassar, the penalty was US$100,000, which is a lot of money for professional gymnasts. (Chrissy Teigen offered to pay it to release gymnast McKayla Maroney from her silence.)

Journalists and newspapers who are not even party to the contract can be sued, and so can be silenced by the contract she signed. It is no answer for a journalist (or, indeed, any person) to say they are not party to the contract and therefore not bound by it: if there is an NDA, they know that the information is to be treated as confidential in law and they can face legal proceedings if they publish that information. Before publication, journalists might face an injunction to stop publication. After publication, they might face a legal claim for damages for publishing the confidential information. All they can do is argue for the public interest in disclosure—and, as we will explain, the courts have consistently found in favour of upholding the contract.

Whether you need to contest an injunction application before publication to enable her freedom of speech, or defend breach of confidence or contract proceedings after publication, it is an expensive business. In the United Kingdom, Australia and most places around the world, for reasons we will explain, there's a very good chance you'll lose. Whether you are an individual woman wanting to speak out or a media organisation with your own in-house legal team and large legal budget, the cost risk is significant—often prohibitively so—which means staying silent.

The main reason NDAs are used in this context is to silence. NDAs silence the person who has made the allegations—and anyone else who might talk about them. NDAs are often deployed when a woman is traumatised—by the abuse and/or harassment she has faced, and by the fact that, in many cases, she has been forced to leave a job she otherwise loves. NDAs are also often deployed in the context of stressful and expensive legal proceedings. So for the many women who just want to move on, or for those who are simply unwilling or unable to go through lengthy and costly legal proceedings, settlement might be her preferred outcome but often comes on the condition that she never speak about it again. The point is that the pressure to sign can be immense and, once signed, NDAs can be very difficult and expensive to get out of.

The tip of the iceberg

We may never know how many women have been kept silent by NDAs—or how much evidence of abuse will remain hidden, while perpetrators carry on with their lives and careers.

NDAs are common in divorce agreements, including where a spouse has alleged domestic or sexual violence, and in employment contracts and settlement agreements. NDAs have been used to cover up alleged sexual misconduct by media figures—from both the right (Roger Ailes and Bill O'Reilly at Fox News) and the left and liberal (Charlie Rose at NBC and Matt Lauer from *Today*)—and by political figures including Donald Trump and the former New York mayor and presidential candidate Michael Bloomberg.

It is now the norm for celebrities and prominent people to put in place NDAs with consensual sexual partners to prevent them from later selling their story to the tabloids. So pervasive is their use that Billie Eilish sings a song about making a 'pretty boy' sign an NDA after he stays overnight, which a music review in

Nylon described as 'a weird act of power'. Eilish says her song was about the dark side of fame—the fact that NDAs are required at all—but what about the dark side of NDAs? What happens if the encounter turns non-consensual? If it is considered 'a weird act of power' to have a consensual partner sign an NDA, then what should we say about the powerful men and corporations requiring women to sign contracts to ensure that they never speak about the abuse they have suffered?

And it's not just celebrities and public figures: NDAs are also being used in parliaments, in universities and in other public institutions. Around the world—from Australia to Canada to the United Kingdom, Ireland and beyond—religious institutions from Hillsong to the Church of England have included NDAs in settlement agreements with women and child sexual abuse survivors, prohibiting them from speaking about their experiences.

In the United States, Congresswoman Jackie Speier revealed that the US House of Representatives had paid more than US$17 million to settle 260 claims of harassment over the twenty years before 2017 (a figure that included sexual offences as well as harassment based on race, age or other factors). In the United Kingdom, between just 2017 and 2019, British universities had spent more than £90 million on settlements that included an NDA related to sexual assault. The House of Commons has also used NDAs in settlements with former staff. The *Guardian* reports that NDAs have been widely used to silence women in cases of pregnancy-related discrimination at work.

In Australia in 2020, Senator Deborah O'Neill used parliamentary privilege to air testimony from a whistleblower and former employee of AMP, a large financial services company in Australia and New Zealand, after a sexual harassment scandal.

The young woman reported that, after reporting sexual harassment by several senior male executives, one was promoted while she faced retribution and was told she would lose her job if she did not sign an NDA. In a clear articulation of the pressure women face, she explained: 'I had run out of funds to pay my lawyers and I was physically and psychologically destroyed, so I signed.'

More and more stories about NDAs are being reported—many of them anonymously, because of the legal risks for women who speak out in violation of their agreement.

Rich man's justice

From Weinstein to Epstein to Cosby to R Kelly, secret settlements including NDAs have been used to resolve allegations of rape, sexual assault and harassment, which kept the matters secret and enabled the men's conduct to continue, sometimes for decades, before they faced any criminal consequences. NDAs have allowed men who have behaved abusively—and potentially criminally—to remain in their jobs or move to other workplaces without any information about what they had done being revealed, placing others at risk and enabling them to do it again (and sometimes again and again).

'It is a classic case of rich man's justice,' said prominent US lawyer David Boies, himself a notorious go-to lawyer for the rich and powerful. Boies acted for Weinstein but also represented Virginia Giuffre in her legal claim against Prince Andrew. He also represents two survivors who signed NDAs with Epstein. Boies has claimed that as many as eight dozen women had signed NDAs as part of secret settlements after being groomed and abused by Epstein.

However, lawyers for some of Epstein's other victims have made clear that they 'refused to allow Epstein to buy control over his victims' by not allowing their clients to sign NDAs as part of the settlement of their civil claims. These women can talk about what happened to them if they choose to, and are prevented only from revealing the amount they were paid. This underscores the fact that NDAs do not have to be accepted by default—and that survivors should get robust, independent legal advice. However, some of Boies' clients are so bound—and many of Epstein's staff are bound by NDAs in their employment contracts, and so are prevented from speaking about what they saw while working for him. Despite what many have claimed, Epstein's death in prison did not release anyone from their NDA obligations and it is reported that the attorney general of the Virgin Islands has declined to release them from those contracts.

Bill Cosby used NDAs as well. Andrea Constand was friends with Cosby and visited his home one evening in 2004 to discuss a possible career move. Cosby gave her what he told her were some herbal remedy pills. She passed out and says that she came in and out of consciousness, unable to resist him as he raped and assaulted her. Constand says it took months for her to make sense of what happened, but she eventually went to the police in 2005. Montgomery district attorney Bruce Castor declined to prosecute, saying there was not enough 'credible and admissible' evidence to merit criminal charges: her word was not enough. Constand then sued Cosby, and in his deposition in her civil case he admitted to drugging and assaulting her. They reached an out-of-court settlement of US$3.38 million, but she also had to sign an NDA and the court documents were sealed—and remained secret for eleven years. For over a decade, she remained silent.

It wasn't until women began speaking out in 2014 and 2015 that Constand learned that she wasn't alone: as NBC reported, 60 women spoke out, accusing Cosby of committing a variety of offences over the past 50 years, including sexual assault and rape. Only through their coming forward, and the efforts of lawyers and Associated Press journalists, were the court documents—and Cosby's admission in Constand's case—eventually unsealed in 2015.

In releasing the documents, the court found that Cosby's right to privacy was outweighed by the public interest in disclosure, given the number of allegations made against him, and by his public denials and his public profile. As CNN reported, Constand's case was the only one—out of the 60 known cases against Cosby—that wasn't time-barred by the statute of limitations. So hers was the first and only criminal prosecution that could take place. If all those women hadn't spoken out and the media hadn't pursued the documents, the evidence would have remained sealed and Cosby would not have been prosecuted.

Cosby was convicted by a jury in 2018 and sent to prison for ten years. However, Cosby walked free after serving only three years. He successfully appealed the conviction, arguing that his due process rights were violated because his admission was made only after an earlier prosecutor had told him he wouldn't face criminal prosecution.

Among the many headlines related to Cosby's trial, conviction and release from prison, one story was almost lost. Just before his trial went ahead, Cosby sued Constand, her lawyers and media organisations for violating her NDA. Constand and her lawyers were accused of breaching her NDA by voluntarily cooperating with the criminal investigation. Constand was also accused of violating her NDA because of a media interview she gave to *The Toronto Sun* about her case, because of statements by her and her lawyers criticising the 2005 decision not to prosecute Cosby, and because of two tweets she posted in 2014, in which she said: 'I won't go away, there is a lot more I will say,' and 'It's not that everybody just forgot about it, truth is nobody cared.' Cosby sought damages and 'disgorgement of profits': that is, the entire amount he had paid her in settlement of her civil claim over the assault.

In motions to dismiss filed by Constand, her lawyers and the media outlets, the judge ruled that she and her lawyers could not be sued for cooperating with a criminal investigation, even if their cooperation was voluntary—that part of the NDA was unenforceable because it was against public policy to inhibit women from reporting assaults and assisting police and prosecutors. Importantly, however, the claims against her for speaking to the media and for her tweets, even though they did not reference Cosby, were allowed to go ahead. Cosby later withdrew those claims, perhaps because of the adverse publicity of suing her for publicly criticising the earlier decision not to prosecute him while he was facing trial for sexually abusing her. But we don't know why Cosby withdrew the case—or whether the court would have upheld Cosby's NDA contract or found that her speech was protected and in the public interest.

Constand has now written a book, *The Moment: Standing up to Bill Cosby, speaking up for women* (2021). In her book and in interviews, she has explained her ordeal, the pain she felt at being silenced by the NDA and how important it was for her to hear from a jury that they believed her. She is donating a portion of the proceeds from her book to sexual violence survivors and has vowed to work to 'close the legal loopholes' that enabled Cosby to walk free. Here, we are more interested in the legal agreements that enabled Cosby to keep his offences quiet for so long.

This is not all old news—more and more stories are emerging. In 2021, when the footballer Cristiano Ronaldo returned to play for Manchester United, Level Up—a feminist group—organised a protest at his first match. A plane flew over the pitch with a banner reading 'Believe Kathryn Mayorga'. Level Up said it wished to send 'a message to football that rape allegations can't be kicked off the pitch'. Mayorga claims she was raped by Ronaldo in Las Vegas in 2009. When her allegation became public in 2017, Ronaldo said he 'firmly' denied it. But the Level Up protest was not just about the rape allegation—it was also about the NDA that was used to cover it up, and 'the culture of silence around abuse from the football community'.

Mayorga told *Der Spiegel* that she reported her rape to the Las Vegas police at the time. *Der Spiegel* also reported that her medical examination after the incident showed injuries consistent with the assault she described. She also told *Der Spiegel* that she was too scared to name Ronaldo to the police because of the publicity that she knew would follow. After Mayorga asked the police not to move forward with her statement, the police did not lay charges. She later accepted a civil settlement of US$375,000 from Ronaldo and signed an NDA. As *Der Spiegel* would later write, 'She was supposed to be invisible, damned to silence. Forever.' But it was not Mayorga who would make her story public.

Years later, in 2017, the agreement and other documents related to her case leaked to the media as part of the 'Football Leaks' disclosures, which revealed tax evasion and murky financial transactions among football's biggest stars. *Der Spiegel* published the initial story about Mayorga's rape allegation and the NDA, giving her a pseudonym, 'Susan K'. When the *Der Spiegel* journalist first contacted her for comment, she said, 'No comment.' Later, when journalists showed up at her house, she ran away from them. She couldn't speak about it because she was bound by the NDA.

When *Der Spiegel* first reported the story, Ronaldo's management agency, GestiFute, claimed it was 'journalistic fiction'. The GestiFute statement also discredited Mayorga, saying she 'refuses to come forward and confirm the veracity of the accusation'. What they didn't say was that she was prevented from doing so by her NDA. Ronaldo's lawyers threatened *Der Spiegel* with legal action and demanded it 'desist from reporting'. Ronaldo said it was 'fake news' and that 'they want to promote [themselves] by [using] my name'. But within the leaked material, according to *Der Spiegel*, was a document in which Ronaldo appeared to acknowledge Mayorga's account of the night—'She said no and stop several times' . . . 'She complained that I forced her'—and that he had apologised to her afterwards. His lawyers claimed the document was fake and the sex was consensual. His lawyers did, however, confirm the existence of the settlement and the NDA, stating that Ronaldo had only signed it on legal advice to protect his reputation: it was 'by no means an admission of guilt'.

After the controversy broke, and inspired by MeToo, Mayorga decided to waive her anonymity in 2018 to tell her story to *Der Spiegel*. She told *Der Spiegel* she signed the NDA for fear of retaliation and to avoid the public humiliation she was now facing since the story became public. As a result of the leaks, she explained that she had faced immense media scrutiny and online hate, with comments like 'as if Ronaldo needs to rape a woman'. Commentators remarked on how sexism and stereotypes about rape meant Mayorga 'became the accused' because of her allegation against the 'unimaginable rapist' Ronaldo.

Armed with more information thanks to the leaks, Mayorga reported Ronaldo again to the Las Vegas police, filed a new civil claim against him, spoke out about her experience of the NDA and challenged its validity. For a contract to be binding, it must be a bargain reached between two parties, exercising their freedom—which presumes competence—to enter the contract. *Der Spiegel* reported that her lawyer claimed she was 'not competent to enter into the agreement because of the psychological injury she sustained from the sexual assault'. But the police did not lay charges. Her challenge to the NDA failed in court.

Mayorga's lawyers say she has considered suicide and has suffered severe emotional and mental damage as a result of everything that has happened. Ronaldo vehemently denies any wrongdoing, and his career continues. But the story isn't going away. The Level Up protest in 2021 raised concern that Manchester United had given Ronaldo a 'hero's welcome' despite the 'unresolved rape allegations'. 'As a society, we can't let a woman's story of rape be silenced,' they said. 'We're sending a message of solidarity to all survivors who refuse to be silenced.'

Silos of silence: isolating survivors

Like Andrea Constand, many women feel traumatised and isolated by the NDAs they have signed. In our experience, this is common. We have seen how victims have been gagged, preventing them from speaking to family and friends about what happened, from warning others about the perpetrator, and from seeking solace and solidarity with other women who have suffered at the same workplace or at the hands of the same man, or with others who have been silenced by NDAs. We have also seen how NDAs have had a chilling effect on those wishing to speak up about wrongdoing, and how victims live in fear of the consequences of breaking the agreement.

To explain the problem, here is a hypothetical example that draws upon the kinds of cases we have been asked to advise upon in our practice, but which have never become public.

Katie worked at a large financial services firm in London, in a job she felt lucky to get in a highly competitive industry. Her boss, Max, was a big figure in the finance world. He seemed to take a special interest in Katie's career, giving her guidance and inviting her to meetings with big clients, meetings her peers were left out of. He occasionally made jokes about her coming back to his hotel room, which Katie laughed off. But then he started buying her expensive gifts. This included a set of lingerie, which made Katie feel uncomfortable.

They travelled a lot for work. On one business trip, Max insisted she come to his hotel room before a work meeting. There, he pulled her in for a kiss. Even though she said out loud 'stop' and 'I don't want this', he continued, and started to grope at her until she was able to push him off.

On her return to London, Katie went to HR to tell them what had happened. They immediately offered her a settlement package, including a confidentiality agreement. In retrospect, she said, she felt like she was on a conveyer belt, in a process that felt like a 'well-oiled machine'. But she wasn't in a position to know anything more—or whether it had happened to other women—and she accepted the settlement so she could get out of there as fast as possible and get on with her life and her career.

A year later, Katie ran into her former assistant and learned that her successor, a woman, had already left the firm. Katie's former assistant told her that she'd overheard an office secretary say, 'Apparently Max did something.' Later, another former colleague who had left the firm in hushed circumstances, Anna, confidentially admitted to Katie—in breach of her own NDA—that she had left the firm after Max harassed her, and that she had heard that Katie's predecessor had left for the same reasons.

Katie was horrified: she realised that when she was hired, the firm already knew what Max was doing. Without any warning, she had walked into what the firm knew was an unsafe workplace. And after Katie had experienced sexual assault, she had left and, like the women before her, signed an NDA and kept silent about it. She now realised that this had enabled Max to do it again to the women coming after her.

This was the reason Katie came to us for advice about what she could do: she didn't want to go public, but she wanted to make sure Max was held accountable. It was clear that the silo of silence that each of these women had been kept in was enabling him to continue to harass women with impunity because of his power within the company.

Provisions in NDAs that limit what survivors can say to their friends, family and therapists have the effect of isolating them from their support networks and even from accessing medical assistance. In our example, the silos of silence enabled by NDAs meant not only that Max was getting away with his assaults, but also that the victims were kept isolated from each other, prospective victims had no idea what they were walking into, and Max's company was getting away with it cheaply. Settlement in circumstances where one woman has experienced abuse is one thing, but repeated settlements where the company knowingly places women at risk is quite another. NDAs meant the women did not know there was a pattern, or that they had knowingly been put at risk.

Katie might have had an interesting claim, but in our experience, women in Katie's position often don't want to come forward and reopen the painful experience or begin a legal battle. The old trope that women somehow benefit from going public with their allegations is nonsense: we see time and time again that women who have legitimate claims, which could potentially force the courts to look differently at NDAs, don't go through with it because they don't want to become publicly and permanently associated with the name of their perpetrator and what he has done to them—and understandably so. Most also can't afford it, even if they wanted to challenge the validity of their NDA. Each of them had every right to accept their settlement and move on, with the confidentiality that protected them and their privacy just as much as it protected him.

But how is Max's company able to get away with it? As a private company without public disclosure obligations, what consequences are there for men like Max and the companies they control? What are they telling their shareholders about the repeated payouts to these women? What are they telling the tax office, and how are these expenses accounted for? Are they allowed as tax deducations, to reduce what the company pays into the public purse? We don't know.

Placing survivors in silos of silence under NDAs creates a culture of impunity that enables further abuse. How can we as a society tackle gender-based violence and workplace harassment if those affected by it can't talk about it? In this way, NDAs raise public interest and policy concerns, and potentially impede governments in their obligations to protect women and girls.

A parliamentary inquiry in the United Kingdom looked into NDAs in 2018. Jen, together with leading women barristers, made a joint submission to the Women and Equalities Committee setting out the problem and why governments need to better regulate the use of NDAs:

> [R]evelations of repeated allegations of rape, sexual assault and harassment against Harvey Weinstein, which it appears were effectively suppressed over decades through the use of NDAs, have brought to the fore legitimate concerns about the ways in which these agreements may be misused so as to gag individuals who have either suffered or witnessed serious sexual assaults and harassment. The issues raised include not only the concealment of the original wrongdoing but also the ways in which the misuse of NDAs may contribute to a culture of silence and otherwise foster an environment in which wrongdoers feel that they can continue to act with complete impunity. The result is that serious and criminal wrongdoing may go undetected over many years, increasing the pool of victims and otherwise putting individuals unnecessarily at risk. Importantly, the misuse of NDAs can not only serve to conceal very serious abuses of power, but can also constitute a powerful incidence of such abusive behaviour. Put shortly, the misuse of NDAs is substantially contrary to the public interest and is a serious social vice.

Fortunately, there have been women who have been willing to lift the veil of secrecy on this 'serious social vice', so that the public and our parliamentarians can understand the problem. Let's hear their stories.

Silence-breakers

> I want to publicly break my non-disclosure agreement.
> Unless somebody does this there won't be a debate about how
> egregious these agreements are and the amount of duress
> that victims are put under. My entire world fell in because
> I thought the law was there to protect those who abided by
> it. I discovered that it had nothing to do with right and
> wrong and everything to do with money and power.

These are the words of Zelda Perkins, quoted in *The Financial Times* on 14 October 2017. It was the first time her story about her NDA with Harvey Weinstein, which had covered up his sexual harassment and assault during her time working for him at Miramax, was reported. It was also the first time anyone subjected to a Weinstein NDA had spoken publicly about the legal tool that had protected him for so long—and how he had used them.

Back in 1998, Zelda Perkins was just 24 years old. She had a great job at Miramax Films in London, working in an all-woman team. She had never aspired to work in the film industry, and she now says that her lack of ambition in the industry is probably what protected her. But she loved her job, being paid to read scripts in what she told us was 'a cool Soho office in London surrounded by bright, but mostly young, women'. Everything changed when Weinstein flew in from the United States and she started working for him directly—but it would take twenty years for her to be able to tell her story.

In the years that Zelda had worked for Weinstein, she says, he sexually harassed her and pressured her for sexual favours while at work. But it wasn't until the 1998 Venice Film Festival, when her even more junior assistant told Zelda that Weinstein had sexually assaulted her, that she resigned and resolved to hold him accountable. Outgunned by his lawyers, overwhelmed by the power imbalance and dismayed by her available legal options, she and her assistant ended up settling their claims and signed NDAs.

As the MeToo movement kicked off in 2017 and allegations about Weinstein swirled, back in London, Zelda took the decision to speak out, deliberately breaching the oppressive NDA she had felt forced to sign, to highlight how NDAs had allowed Weinstein to abuse women with impunity—and in the hope that her disclosure would encourage others to come forward.

It certainly did.

Zelda's story

When Zelda jumps onto our Zoom call, she is flustered. Behind her are chickens, in the yard of her house in the English countryside—peaceful green hills and winding roads, her place to return to after campaigning in the public eye. She has been fighting for laws to reform how NDAs are used, and for better protection for survivors. It is not always easy, and her name and face mean she is recognisable—tied, always, to the downfall of Harvey Weinstein.

We are here to ask her to tell us what happened, in her own words. She tells us what happened and that the versions she tells to the media are intentionally sanitised, she says, as she doesn't want the details to distract from her message. (Out of respect to Zelda, we are only including the facts we consider to be relevant to show how NDAs function to perpetuate a culture of silence and enable impunity, and to show the impact they have on survivors.)

Before Zelda started working for Weinstein, she was given a warning of sorts. When she was offered the promotion to work directly for Weinstein, she was told that she really needed to think about whether she wanted the job. 'I had been given a light-hearted, jokey warning,' she explains. 'Never sit next to him on the couch . . . Don't turn your back on him.' The only explicit warning she got was about his temper. 'We all knew he was a monster temper-wise, but not any other-wise.'

What Zelda wasn't told was that sexual harassment and pressure for sexual favours in the workplace would be common and normalised—Weinstein would appear naked, grab her and request massages and oral sex. This was not something that was openly discussed among the women working for him. 'We were all isolated. We were all young women. We were culturally silenced,' Zelda says. 'We didn't want to look weak, or make a fuss, or look like we couldn't handle him. But later when [our silence] became contractual, it was even more powerful.'

Zelda did her best to warn others she interviewed to work with Weinstein. 'No one warned me about Harvey. I didn't know [beforehand that] he was a habitual abuser, but by then I knew what he did to me.' So she began telling young women that he would be inappropriate and they needed to be robust to be able to deal with him. Years later, after she broke her NDA and more details of Weinstein's conduct became public, two young women wrote to her to thank her: both had declined the job offer after her warning at their interviews.

For years, Zelda put up with and managed Weinstein's harassment. She thwarted his physical advances, developing a variety of avoidance strategies to do so. In some strange way, she said, she felt she was beating him at his own power game. But then her junior assistant, Rowena Chiu, came to her at the

1998 Venice Film Festival, upset, hysterical and in shock: she told Zelda that Weinstein had sexually assaulted her.

'It was very clear to me that something had happened,' Zelda explains. 'I was so horrified that I had put her in that position. She was my responsibility.'

This was the first time Zelda knew of Weinstein physically assaulting anyone. Rowena, who has since told her story to the media, was scared to lose what was her dream job. She chose not to report him to the Italian police. Zelda confronted Weinstein, but he denied it.

Zelda and Rowena both resigned. 'He has left us with no choice,' Zelda said she told Rowena. They both loved their work but they were forced to leave it behind.

But Zelda wanted to make sure Weinstein was exposed and stopped. She was told she would need a lawyer. She didn't know where to start: she was 'so naive', she tells us, that she called the Citizens Advice Bureau for help. In the end, she looked up lawyers in the Yellow Pages and found Simons Muirhead Burton (SMB), a respected, boutique law firm that was just a few streets away in Soho. It was after her first meeting with a young woman lawyer at the firm that she realised how bad her harassment had been and how normalised it had become. When Zelda told her about what happened with Weinstein, she says the lawyer 'was shocked, and I was shocked at how shocked she was'. Zelda again felt naive, and embarrassed that she had put up with it.

Her next shock was at the lack of legal options available to her and Rowena. 'I genuinely thought if we could go to court, it would all be fine,' she said. Zelda wanted to expose Weinstein and see him prosecuted in court. But it wasn't going to be that easy—the assault had happened in Italy, a different jurisdiction, and they hadn't gone to the police. Weinstein, with his almost infinite resources, wasn't going to go down easily.

'I was told that he and his lawyers would try to destroy us and our families, attack you upways, sideways and backways, find every skeleton in your closets, bankrupt you and anyone near you, and your legal costs will be beyond anything you can afford,' Zelda explains. The women were advised to seek damages through a mediation process.

Zelda was upset at the time, thinking it was the wrong decision. But she also took it as a lesson about the law and how it works for rich men. As she told us, she realised after frank discussions with her own lawyers that it would be futile for her and Rowena to take him on: she felt it would be 'just two silly girls' word' against Harvey Weinstein, his power and his immense resources.

Still, Zelda held out hope. She thought the negotiation process would be a chance to hold him accountable within Miramax, and stop him from doing this to anyone else. She wrote out a list of demands, including a new complaints procedure and that Weinstein go to therapy, and make a big donation to a rape charity. She was told she should just seek a year's pay (£20,000 at that time). At this stage, she had no idea that the matter would ultimately all be kept secret.

Zelda decided to ask for a huge sum, so that anyone who dug up the papers (which she had presumed would be on the public record) would see the money and see it as a big red flag, and in her words 'indicative of the crime'. She asked for £250,000. Her lawyers said she was crazy for asking that much. Within hours of their making the offer, though, Weinstein's team accepted it. When Weinstein's personal lawyer flew out from the United States to negotiate the details, it reiterated for Zelda just how serious the situation was.

However overwhelming and unfair the process felt, and however great the power disparity, Zelda did claim some wins: the contract included a requirement that Weinstein attend therapy for a minimum of three years, and Miramax promised a complaints procedure, as well as a provision requiring that if there was another complaint against Weinstein within two years of the contract and it resulted in a settlement of either £35,000 or six months' salary, Miramax agreed to report the matter to Weinstein's bosses at Disney—or to dismiss him. Zelda doesn't know whether Miramax ever complied with those requirements.

Zelda says she honestly did not know, going into the negotiations, that she would be required to sign a confidentiality agreement—it only came up in the closing parts of the negotiation, by which time she was too exhausted to fight. She also didn't know it was going to be so invasive, or the obligations so extensive. After a long week of late-night negotiations in Weinstein's lawyers' offices with her lawyer, she and Rowena were split into separate rooms, isolated from each other, and were asked to write down every single person they had told about the matter. Zelda refused to name anyone, and instead spoke in general terms. 'I felt like we were dealing with the mafia,' she recalls. 'I was really scared of these lawyers and thought that if I named any of my friends or family, these people would go after them.'

In the end, each NDA included a short schedule describing friends and family she had told. Both women had to call the people included in the schedule and say they were never to discuss the story again, not even with each other. If the women wanted to go to a therapist, they'd have to sign an NDA. The same if they saw a lawyer, the police or the tax authorities. Everyone around these women were now also bound to

Weinstein—legally required to maintain the silence that would protect him for years.

Once the NDA was signed, Zelda and Rowena had one last meeting: with Weinstein himself. They were led into a room, to sit face to face with the man who had sexually assaulted one of them. He apologised, but Zelda and her lawyer were not permitted to take or keep any notes of what he said. But as reported by *Tortoise* and as she told us, she did keep a record, in secret: 'Sometimes [I] don't know when its consensual,' Weinstein said.

By the end of the process, Zelda told us she was devastated and felt she was pressured into receiving what she now describes as 'blood money'. She chased Miramax afterwards to find out if Weinstein was in therapy and to make sure the complaints process was in place, but said they stalled, refusing to give her any information, and eventually she gave up. She also had trouble getting work because of the stories circulating in the industry about what had happened. To get away from it all, she moved to Central America.

Yet Zelda was deeply troubled by what had happened, and she found that the matter followed her. Over the years, journalists contacted her to corroborate allegations against Weinstein, but she kept quiet. That was until 2013, when she felt she could not stay silent any longer.

A journalist from *The New Yorker* told her that Weinstein was done for: Italian model Ambra Gutierrez had been assaulted by him, and had gone to the New York Police Department to report it. She agreed to be part of a sting operation aimed at getting Weinstein to admit to what he had done. She wore a wire, and caught him admitting it on tape. 'Finally,' Zelda thought. 'He is going down.'

Zelda decided to break her NDA to speak to the journalist to back up Gutierrez's story. But Weinstein's lawyers went into overdrive, hiring private investigators to dig up information on Gutierrez and discredit her. They launched a smear campaign, accusing her of being a prostitute and saying she was enacting revenge. Upsettingly, it worked. No charges were laid. Dragged through the mud, Gutierrez agreed to settle, and joined the many other women in their terrible little club: people who signed Weinstein's NDAs.

Weinstein's team suspected that Zelda had talked, and she started getting a lot of calls from 'journalists'—who it turned out were actually Weinstein's investigators, and former Israeli spies. Zelda would later discover that Weinstein's lawyer, David Boies, had hired the firm Black Cube to keep watch on Zelda and others who might break their NDAs. The actor Rose McGowan and other women were also contacted and harassed in this way.

When women started coming forward to journalists with their stories about Weinstein in 2017, Zelda was first contacted by journalists Jodi Kantor and Megan Twohey. Ronan Farrow also later reached out to her and told her that he was going to report more stories, including rape allegations. Zelda was floored: this was the first time she had heard Weinstein had been accused of rape. She knew what Rowena had accused him of back in 1998, but that hadn't gone as far as rape.

This revelation really affected Zelda, and she told us that she started to understand that her silence had enabled Weinstein to continue to act with impunity—and to go on to do worse. It was then, she said, that she realised 'this piece of paper is protecting a rapist'. She decided then and there that she was going to speak out: she was willing to break her NDA if she had to. She wanted to show the secretive legal processes that were being used by the rich and powerful to silence women about abuse and harassment.

Zelda wanted to take legal advice, but she had a problem: she did not have a copy of her own NDA, which she needed if she was to figure out a way she could talk to the media. It is Kafkaesque, but it's important to know that this was not unusual. All Zelda had was a document summarising her obligations under the contract. She called up her former law firm to get a copy of the agreement, but she was told she was not permitted to have it. She asked around for recommendations for lawyers, but she told us she was 'stonewalled' and that she wasn't allowed to show it to another lawyer. Zelda said a lawyer friend made some inquiries for her and was told, 'You've got to be fucking joking—we wouldn't touch that with a ten-foot pole—we get these signed all the time for our clients.' Firm after firm said that they wouldn't act for her. Zelda realised there and then that 'this is a stitch-up—and it's not just a Weinstein problem; this is a law problem'.

It was a huge decision for Zelda to speak out. In doing so, she had to calculate the risk: would Weinstein go for her in the midst of the unfolding scandal as more and more women came out against him? 'The people at [*The Financial Times*] basically told me, "You're fucked if you break this and we can't protect you, except in the court of public opinion,"' Zelda tells us. She thought, 'Well, fuck it, I've got to do it and this is all I've got.' *The Financial Times* put the story to Weinstein and his lawyers. According to Zelda, they threatened to get an injunction and sue for defamation. The newspaper considered the risk and published anyway.

And it was the right call, because Weinstein didn't sue. But what if she had spoken out earlier, before the MeToo scandal engulfed Weinstein? Would his lawyers have made a different calculation and sought that injunction, which would have prevented Zelda, *The Financial Times* and any other media organisation from reporting her allegations?

After Zelda's story was published, Weinstein could have sued Zelda for breach of contract for speaking to the media—and he might have won. He also could have sued her for defamation for the accusations she publicly made about the reason for the NDA—Rowena's allegations that he sexually assaulted her—and she would have faced immense legal costs and the usual evidential difficulties to prove her allegations about him in court. But by then his credibility was shot by the sheer number of women coming forward, the weight of evidence and the similarities of the women's accounts—and by then, as *The Financial Times* had rightly noted, public opinion was on her side. The situation had changed drastically since 1998, when Zelda and Rowena had signed their NDAs and been advised not to take him on: in a battle of credibility in 2017, the women would win. Rowena would later take the decision to speak out about her experience too. While the situation had changed, legally nothing had changed.

After Zelda spoke out, it emerged through the reporting of *The New York Times* and *The New Yorker* that Weinstein had used NDAs to keep all kinds of sexual misconduct quiet, and that employees from Miramax had felt silenced from speaking out about other wrongdoing at the company.

For Zelda, the process of going public with her experiences has been cathartic: 'Once I started speaking out, I found my voice . . . I found myself.' And she began campaigning to end the abuse of NDAs—a campaign that continues to this day.

Undercover reporting to reveal NDA abuse

Soon after Zelda spoke out, another NDA scandal would break, after which Prime Minister Theresa May announced a parliamentary inquiry into the use of NDAs in the United Kingdom (the inquiry in which Zelda's evidence and Jen's legal submissions would later play a key part). The story hit the headlines thanks to the work of two women undercover reporters, Madison Marriage and an unnamed colleague, again from *The Financial Times*.

Marriage replied to an advertisement for waitresses for the annual Presidents Club dinner. The men-only charity dinner, attended by 360 figures from the British business, politics, finance and entertainment worlds, had been running for 33 years and had raised £20 million for children's charities. FTSE 500 companies sponsored tables and sent their male executives. The dinner held in January 2018, hosted at the Dorchester Hotel, would raise £2 million. But charities would soon reject the funds the Presidents Club had raised.

The advertisement sought 'tall, thin and pretty' women to serve as hostesses at the event. Marriage wrote for *The Financial Times* that she was warned after her initial interview for the job that the women might have to put up with 'annoying men', who will try to get them 'pissed'. Two days before the event, Marriage and the other women were informed their phones would be 'safely locked away' at the event and that their boyfriends and girlfriends were not welcome at the venue. They were advised to bring black 'sexy shoes', black underwear, and do their hair and make-up as they would to go to a 'smart sexy place'. Upon arrival at the event, dresses and belts were supplied, which were short and tight, resembling corsets. The women were being paid £150, as well as

£25 for a taxi home, to work from 4 p.m. until the early hours of the morning. Most of the women were students working their way towards careers in law or finance, while others were part-time actresses, dancers, models and performers who did hostess work to pay the bills and get by. All were contract workers.

But before the women were handed their skimpy uniforms and had their hair and make-up done, they were handed a five-page document to sign: an NDA. They were forced to sign this contract before the event started as a condition of work. They were not given time to read or consider the terms—let alone to seek independent advice on those terms—and they were not allowed to keep a copy of what they had signed.

Given who was in attendance and what went down at the event, it is no wonder the event organisers wanted the women contracted to silence. As *The Financial Times* reported, the attendees and supporters of the event was like 'a roll call of British wealth and business influence'. Hosting the event was the comedian and author David Walliams, and attendees included businessman Sir Philip Green, cabinet minister Nadhim Zahawi (at the time the Under-Secretary of State for Children and Families), and Lord Mendelsohn, a Labour peer.

In a later piece for *Marie Claire,* Marriage provides a vivid description of what it was like to work at the event, which she describes as 'grotesque'. The MC opened the event by welcoming the men 'to the most un-PC event of the year'. Women were told to line up and then parade across a stage in front of 360 'braying' men, as they played the song 'Power' by Little Mix, a song choice Marriage described as a 'cruel irony', given the immense power imbalance between the young women and the powerful men in attendance.

The funds for charity were raised by an auction that included items such as lunch with Boris Johnson (then the foreign secretary). Marriage also explained that it included items like 'a night at Soho's Windmill strip club, and a course of plastic surgery with the invitation to "add spice to your wife".'

While the accompanying brochure included 'a full-page warning that no attendees or staff should be sexually harassed', it is clear from Marriage's reporting that numerous men either failed to read the instructions or simply ignored them. She writes 'many of the hostesses were subjected to groping, lewd comments and repeated requests to join diners in bedrooms' in the hotel—by men considered to be pillars of society. Hostesses reported men forcefully pulling them onto their laps and 'repeatedly putting hands up their skirts' and that one attendee had even 'exposed his penis' during the evening. At the after party, one of the hostesses was grabbed, poured a drink and told, 'I want you to down that glass, rip off your knickers and dance for me.'

Marriage's story was published in January 2018 and resulted in national headlines off the back of the controversy from Zelda speaking out about Weinstein's NDAs. It wasn't just Weinstein using NDAs to cover up misconduct; this was happening in the United Kingdom. Marriage has since written that the impact of her reporting went further than she ever could have imagined. Within days, the Presidents Club Charitable Trust was closed, its trustees stepped down from a number of government roles and directorships, the Charities Commission announced an investigation, charities refused to accept the promised funds, and those which had already received funds promised to improve their due diligence procedures. The story was debated in parliament, and Prime Minister May said she was 'appalled' by the behaviour of the attendees. Another prominent woman MP, Jo Swinson, declared the event to be 'stomach-churning' and evidence of the 'sexist culture still alive and kicking in parts of the business community'.

Marriage wrote about her desire that change would follow her reporting: that men in positions of power would change how they treat women and that they would be held accountable for their actions. But her story would also spark a national conversation about the use of NDAs and the need for better protections for contract workers who face sexual harassment. A public petition to reform the law to give greater legal rights to workers who experience sexual harassment in the workplace followed—and gained more than 100,000 signatures. And, as we noted above, Prime Minister May announced a parliamentary inquiry into the use of NDAs.

Jen's perspective

The allegations against Harvey Weinstein in 2017 were no surprise to me—the only surprising thing was that it took so long for them to reach the public domain. It was an open secret, and one so widely known that I'd even been warned by friends at the Cannes Film Festival before we headed into parties: 'Watch out for Weinstein—never be in a room alone with him.'

Yet Zelda's story was something new: it wasn't just about the sexual harassment and abuse, but the legal tools Weinstein had used to keep this 'open secret' a secret. In telling her story, Zelda gave the public an unprecedented look into the negotiations that lay behind Weinstein's NDAs. I remember reading the *Financial Times* story and being struck by two things: Zelda's bravery in speaking out in breach of her NDA, and the risk appetite of the newspaper in publishing her story. Both Zelda and *The Financial Times* faced the possibility that Weinstein would sue, with potentially serious cost implications. I respected the newspaper's in-house counsel and editor for the decision they took to publish.

It was the right one: by then, Weinstein faced numerous allegations, and the pattern they created was buttressing the credibility of each woman speaking out. It was clear that the NDA was the tool by which Weinstein had kept his misconduct from the public, and from the prosecuting authorities for decades. There was a public interest case to be made. Weinstein threatened to seek an injunction, but ultimately he didn't—which meant the newspaper could publish—and afterwards he did not sue. But hindsight is a wonderful thing. More risk-averse editors and lawyers would have made the call not to publish. Indeed, many before them had known of but not published the story.

The next time I had cause to turn my mind to Zelda's case was a few months later, at a Christmas party in North London. The indomitable Mark Stephens, with whom I had started out working in media law in London some years before, asked me over to a quiet corner. He had a new client: Zelda Perkins. He wanted to know what I thought.

Zelda had not found a lawyer willing to take on her case—until Geoffrey Robertson KC referred her to Mark, who is not the type to back down from rich and powerful men and their teams of lawyers. We shared our outrage at how she had been treated and the contract she had felt forced to sign. At this stage, there hadn't been much legal analysis of her situation, nor had Weinstein sued—but would he? We mused that, on basic contractual principles, the agreement could be deemed to be unenforceable for public policy reasons: from what we knew of it, the contract had covered up a potential crime or crimes, and enabled ongoing abuse. And wasn't there a higher free speech principle at play here? It was an argument Geoffrey had raised. The public interest in women being able to exercise their freedom to speak about their abuse, and the public good of preventing perpetrators from continuing to abuse with impunity, should surely trump any contract.

But, at that time, no court in the United Kingdom had considered this argument. It is one that academics—such as Dr Jeffrey Gordon of the University of Sydney, in his article, 'Silence for Sale' (2020)—are now making, and an argument that is increasingly being accepted by courts in the United Kindgom, the United States and elsewhere. But the most pressing question at that time was this: how could Mark properly advise Zelda when she was not even permitted to have access to the contract she was bound by?

Sometime later, Mark invited me and a group of leading women barristers to meet Zelda, hear her story and consider an independent submission into the UK Parliament's Women and Equalities Committee's investigation into NDAs. I had seen Zelda's powerful interviews on television, but when I walked into the room, there she was, even shorter than I am, swamped by Mark's large conference room and framed by sweeping views of the Thames and St Paul's Cathedral. She is fierce, and fiercely intelligent. I went away inspired by her courage and her commitment to create change for other women.

Later, we filed a submission setting out what Zelda already instinctively knew: how the law is failing women when it comes to NDAs. Zelda addressed the committee in Westminster, and I watched online as she told her story, peppered by questions from feminist MPs. I knew how nervous she had been, so I wrote to her to congratulate her: she had nailed it. I continue to marvel at her indefatigable campaign for law reform, so it is a privilege to be able to include her story in this book.

A sorry story: Public inquiries and calls for reform

After these women spoke out and reported on NDAs, and exposed the misconduct and abuse they were covering up, various parliamentary and regulatory inquiries were conducted (and are ongoing) in the United Kingdom, the United States, Australia and elsewhere around the world. But in Australia and the United Kingdom, despite recommendations, no legislative changes have been made.

The Women and Equalities Committee of the UK Parliament first looked at NDAs as part of its inquiry into sexual harassment at work in 2018, and it then conducted a second, follow-up inquiry specifically into NDAs; its findings were published in 2019. Zelda gave evidence before the committee, telling her story, and Jen, together with Anya Proops KC, Aileen McColgan KC and Natalie Connor, made a written submission to assist the inquiry, setting out how NDAs are used and misused, explaining the legal issues arising with respect to NDAs in the United Kingdom, and suggesting a range of reforms the committee could consider.

In its final report, the committee raised concerns that NDAs had been used unethically by some employers and lawyers to silence victims of sexual harassment, and that there was insufficient oversight and supervision of their use. In highlighting the chilling effect of NDAs in silencing victims, the committee cited Jen's joint submission on the main risks of the unethical use of NDAs: 'individuals will not report serious wrongdoing to the police; will feel compelled not to assist with relevant law enforcement investigations or prosecutions; and will feel unable to speak openly and in the public interest about serious wrong-doing, thus inhibiting public awareness and debate'.

However, the committee also recognised the value of NDAs for some victims. As Jen and her colleagues had emphasised, 'there may be times when a victim makes the judgment that signing an NDA is genuinely in their own best interests, perhaps because it provides a route to resolution that they feel would entail less trauma than going to court, or because they value the guarantee of privacy'.

Banning NDAs altogether is clearly not the way forward: any protective regime must protect all victims, so it would be problematic if confidentiality is not available as an option for those who want to choose to be protected by the confidentiality NDAs afford. Removing the option of confidentiality could, in fact, deter some women from reporting. But confidentiality can be achieved by specifying it in contracts—or by requiring it in legislation ensuring women in these circumstances anonymity. The committee challenged the status quo of considering NDAs as intrinsic to settlement agreements or employment contracts, and made clear that it was unacceptable that sexual harassment and abuse were being covered up by NDAs. But it stopped short of recommending that they should not be used at all.

A lot of NDAs include clauses that would be unenforceable if they were brought before the courts—including, as we have mentioned, any clause that purports to prevent or limit reporting to the police. But how many women who signed one are aware of this? Zelda did not properly understand her rights—and remained silent for years for fear of the consequences.

How many more women were in Zelda's position? How many women felt pressured into signing an NDA? The committee concluded that the effect of the clauses was that women were afraid to speak out—even if, legally, they were allowed to. Irrespective of the legal position, the committee found that many women feared criminal and civil sanctions if they reported to police, sought legal advice or spoke out.

Who are NDAs being used for? The committee raised concern about NDAs being used to protect 'rainmakers', or people in key positions of financial influence. Their behaviour is being excused: companies are using NDAs to settle and silence allegations rather than properly investigate them, and using their power and resources to draw out legal disputes to pressure women to settle and sign NDAs.

The committee did make a number of recommendations, including public education about NDAs to ensure people better understand their rights, and it demanded that legal professional regulators take action against lawyers if they misuse NDAs, especially where they are trying to prevent or deter victims from going to the police. The committee also recommended providing clarity on permitted terms, ensuring that NDAs do not prevent discussion of sexual harassment and abuse while keeping protections for victims who wish to protect their privacy, ensuring adequate financial support for employees to take independent legal advice on NDAs, and improving corporate governance and accountability on sexual harassment. This is important: what the committee had to say about NDAs matters, and has since been cited in an important court case about NDAs and free speech—*ABC v. Telegraph* in 2018—a case about the enforceability of Sir Philip Green's NDAs and whether the media could report the story.

But it isn't enough. As Jen and her colleagues told the committee, 'There is no doubt but that the misuse of NDAs is a serious social evil, and one that requires a robust legal response.' No legislative changes have been made to date and, as we explain, the case law has developed since Zelda spoke out in 2017, but it remains problematic.

In response to the controversy after Zelda went public, the Solicitors Regulation Authority in the United Kingdom published new guidance and 'warning notice'. It made clear that a lawyer was violating their professional ethical duties by improperly pressuring parties to sign NDAs. But the warning extended beyond clients—they also had to warn the lawyers who were using NDAs to cover up their own sexual misconduct.

Meanwhile, Weinstein's solicitor, Mark Mansell from Allen & Overy, was required to give evidence to the parliamentary inquiry about the terms of the NDA Zelda had been required to sign; Zelda later made a professional complaint against him. However, in January 2021, the *Law Gazette* reported that proceedings were stayed on the basis of Mansell's ill health. The Solicitors Disciplinary Tribunal reportedly said it was of concern that Mansell continued to practise law but could not appear before a disciplinary hearing over allegations of his misconduct.

In Australia, it was much the same story. In 2021, there was a Human Rights Commission investigation into sexual harassment in the workplace and the use of NDAs. As part of this, the commission asked for large employers to temporarily waive NDAs so survivors could come forward anonymously for the inquiry. Only 39 companies did so. This secrecy is a problem. The Human Rights Commission report *Respect@Work* noted— as we saw in the United Kingdom—the benefits of NDAs in protecting the confidentiality and privacy of victims and in helping to provide closure, but also the concerns that NDAs contribute to a culture of silence. However, the commission merely recommended the development of guidelines identifying best practice principles on the use of NDAs in workplace sexual harassment matters. Glaringly missing from any of the various official inquiries and their recommendations was what should happen for women who have signed NDAs but now wish to speak publicly about their harassment or abuse. It appears to be accepted that women can sell—and contract away—their right to freedom of speech.

For those who have signed an NDA and now want to speak out, there are few—if any—protections. In some jurisdictions, including the United Kingdom, there is whistleblowing legislation that can, in some exceptional circumstances, permit an employee to make 'protected disclosures' (including about sexual misconduct) to the media. But as Jen and her colleagues pointed out to the Women and Equalities Committee, these protections are very limited. While the committee recommended extending the regulators to whom disclosures could be made without violating an NDA, this did not extend the rights of women to speak out publicly to the media or on social media.

Various recommendations were made in public submissions to limit the use of NDAs in cases of gender-based violence altogether. For example, in the United Kingdom, the Centre for Women's Justice argued that NDAs should only be allowed to protect women's identities, and should not be permitted to prevent discussion of the facts about the harassment or abuse. In Australia, the Women Lawyers Association of NSW recommended that NDAs should not be permitted at all in respect of sexual abuse or harassment. Neither of these proposed recommendations was adopted.

This means that for women who have signed an NDA and wish to speak out about their experience of gender-based violence, we must consider how the courts will treat their cases if they are sued. If you've signed an NDA and later want to speak out, all you can do is argue that your disclosure is in the public interest, and more important than the public interest in upholding the contract. Will the court protect your freedom of speech?

The answer is the infuriating answer clients so often receive from lawyers: well, it depends.

Sue me: NDAs in the courts

A disappointing recent decision from the UK courts has made the situation more difficult for women and for journalists. The Court of Appeal found that, once an NDA is signed, the public interest in upholding the contract generally outweighs the public interest in women speaking out.

This was the case brought by Sir Philip Green, the billionaire and former owner of Topshop. In October 2018, *The Daily Telegraph* reported that it had been gagged by a leading businessman from reporting MeToo allegations, running with the headline 'British #MeToo claims which cannot be revealed'. They could not be revealed because of an NDA.

Sir Philip sought an interim injunction to prevent publication. Because of the NDA, there was both an 'open' judgment and a 'closed' judgment. The open judgment was light on details: it merely explained that on 16 July 2018, a journalist working for the *Telegraph* emailed the claimants (who we now know to be

Sir Philip and his company) saying that she intended to report 'certain matters'. On 18 July 2018, lawyers for 'the claimants' sent a letter threatening an injunction, and asked for an undertaking that the article would not be published. A rapid hearing was arranged for 23 July 2018. The judge concluded—in a great decision for the media and women wanting to speak out—that 'the public interest in publication outweighs any confidentiality attaching to the information', and denied the injunction. The claimant appealed, which meant his identity and the allegations of misconduct against him remained a secret, for now. All the identifying, and important, details were in the closed judgment. But the interest of the media was piqued, and speculation began on who exactly had sought the injunction—and what he was seeking to cover up.

And on appeal, he won. The Court of Appeal made clear the importance of protecting and upholding contracts and duties of confidence, emphasising the public interest in enforcing NDAs so that others entering such contracts can 'be confident that they can disclose, without risk of wider publication, information that it is legitimate for them to wish to keep confidential'. Freedom of speech can be limited in ways 'necessary in a democratic society'. Where a woman has signed an NDA, the court will generally put more weight on protecting the contract over protecting her right to freedom of speech. The rationale is that she can choose to sell her right to speak—and if she does, she must be held to it. But here comes the infuriating 'it depends'. The question the court must ask themselves in each case is 'whether, having regard to the nature of the information and all the circumstances, it is legitimate for the owner of the information to seek to keep it confidential or whether it is in the public interest that the information should be made public'.

In Sir Philip Green's case, it was on this question—and the balancing of the public interest between the right to contract and the right to speak—that the High Court and the Court of Appeal differed. The trial judge had placed emphasis on the controversies related to NDAs and the concerns raised by the Women and Equalities Committee about the misuse of NDAs to cover up sexual harassment. The Court of Appeal, however, emphasised the fact that the committee had also recognised the legitimate role of NDAs, including to protect complainants' privacy. Despite the *Telegraph*'s undertaking that the individuals involved would be anonymised in its reporting, the court was concerned about their privacy: one of the complainants did not want their story reported. The court therefore found in favour of upholding the NDAs over the freedom of speech of the newspaper and the two people who did want their story told.

In reaching its decision, the Court of Appeal made a strong statement about the enforceability of NDAs and upholding contracts—provided they were not procured by bullying, harassment or undue pressure, the person signing had independent legal advice and the NDA permitted disclosure to regulatory or statutory bodies. The court upheld the interim injunction and set the matter down for trial, where it would hear evidence to determine the validity of the NDAs and whether the public interest, in this case, meant the women could speak out and the story could be published.

Then, before a full trial could take place, a member of the House of Lords took matters into his own hands. Using the protection of parliamentary privilege, Lord Peter Hain named the businessman in parliament—rendering the injunction, and further litigation, moot. 'My motive was to stand up for ordinary employees against a very powerful and wealthy boss who, as described to me, seemed to think he was above the rules of decent respectful behaviour,' he said. Lord Hain claimed the women had told him that they had only settled and signed NDAs after being worn down by the spiralling legal costs of the proceedings against Green.

We don't know whether, on a full trial of the facts of the case, the trial judge may have come down in favour of disclosure or made any further statements of principle that may have assisted in future cases.

What we do know is that the precedent set in this case has already been used to suppress discussion about alleged mistreatment of women at work. For example, in 2019, the top tier commercial law firm Linklaters obtained an injunction against a former senior employee, who had said he intended to give media interviews about 'the ongoing struggle Linklaters has with women in the workplace'. In that case, the injunction was granted on the basis of a confidentiality clause in the former employee's employment contract. The court cited Sir Philip's case, reiterating the importance of upholding contracts and that this will generally triumph over the right to free speech, even if the issue is the mistreatment of women. However, the court did note that the public interest would be satisfied in a Weinstein-like situation: where the matters sought to be published were 'serious enough' and 'create a compelling picture of persistent or habitual wrongdoing', or if the disclosure involved 'correcting misleading public statements'. But the court found that nothing of that kind emerged from the evidence in this case and, taken together with concerns about protecting the privacy of the women employees who were involved in the relevant incidents of concern, the injunction was granted.

This case law in the United Kingdom is similar to a trend of cases in the United States, where the enforceability of NDAs is under challenge in relation to public safety and student safety, in particular where the NDA is covering up repeated misconduct and enabling further abuse and harassment. As Professor Julie Macfarlane, author of *Going Public*, explains, this law is developing alongside a growing body of case law where students have sued their university for failing to protect them from professors who engaged in repeated sexual harassment. In one case, which was settled for US$14 million, the students argued that the university failed to protect them from sexual harassment despite being aware of the professors' conduct for sixteen years. In short, institutions need to think more carefully about using NDAs—and how and when they use them, and what they are covering up.

So what would have happened if Weinstein had sued Zelda and *The Financial Times* back in 2017? Zelda's lawyer, Mark Stephens, told us that 'based on what the law is or at least as it was back then, he might have won'. In Zelda's case, she could have argued—as Mark and Jen had discussed back then—that, given the number of women coming forward with historical allegations, it was in the public interest for her and Rowena to tell their stories and to show how Weinstein had used the law to silence women for so long. Given that the courts now recognise that showing 'persistent and habitual wrongdoing' will tip the public interest balance in favour of allowing the woman to speak, she might have won.

But how many women have to have been harassed or abused before the public interest will allow them to speak?

This also creates a 'chicken and egg' problem: how do women know there was persistent wrongdoing if they are all in silos of silence? If all the women have signed NDAs, they will need to break their NDAs in order to talk to each other about what happened just to be in a position to know whether the court might find in their favour if and when they do speak out. Or at least one of the women would need to take the cost risk of breaking her NDA—as Zelda did—without knowing she had protection, in the hope others might come forward and support her. But what if, by virtue of her NDA, she isn't in a position to know there was persistent wrongdoing? And in what circumstances will an individual case of wrongdoing meet this public interest test? The law places the women—and the journalists who want to report on their experiences—in the position of having to take a risk. It is for this reason that most women don't speak out, and, if they obtain legal advice on their NDA, they will be advised to remain silent.

We think this is wrong. We think that there should be better protection for women who have signed NDAs to be able to speak out, especially when circumstances change. We agree with Mark Stephens, who believes that the legalistic approach to NDAs—looking at the issue purely from a contract law perspective—does not properly allow for the lived realities of women or the power dynamics at play: the cost risks, the serious inequality of bargaining power and the inequality of arms. What does 'the freedom to enter contract' mean when women—often traumatised by their experience—face the prospect of costly, stressful litigation? 'There is a clear risk that more powerful perpetrators will seek to exploit the victim's vulnerability to procure an NDA in the knowledge that, once it's in place, most are unwilling or unable to take the risk of breaking it,' he told us.

We think it should, with some narrow exceptions, be considered in the public interest per se for women to be able to speak about their experience of gender-based violence—and that the courts and parliament need to make this clear.

In the meantime, how do we get more cases before the courts to challenge these precedents and set better ones? Many women are frustrated by the injustice but do not want to go public or just can't afford it. If a woman chooses to speak out in violation of an NDA to test the law and then is sued, the costs to her are huge. When Sir Philip withdrew the proceedings against *The Daily Telegraph* because his name was already public, he was ordered to pay the bulk of their legal costs, which reportedly ran to £3 million. For most women—and most media organisations—running these cases will be cost-prohibitive. Whatever their legal rights are or whatever the legal possibilities might be, the cost risk will stifle women's ability to speak out.

The interaction of NDAs with defamation cases

Women who are considering signing NDAs should also be aware of the issue they can cause when it comes to any future legal proceedings. Many women don't realise that signing an NDA means that it can effectively turn them into hostile witnesses in any future defamation claim in which the truth of their allegations might be tested. For example, where an alleged perpetrator, having contracted a woman to silence, then sues a media outlet for publishing that he abused that woman (or another), the NDA may mean she cannot assist the newspaper to defend the case unless she is subpoenaed. This gives him a clear litigation advantage.

For example, in Johnny Depp's case against *The Sun* (News Group Newspapers, or NGN), issues arose about whether Amber Heard could give evidence to support the newspaper's case.

Her US lawyers said that she wanted to give evidence but was prevented from assisting the UK newspaper because of the NDA in her US divorce agreement with Depp. Amber's US lawyers were concerned that if she gave evidence in the UK court, she would be in breach of the terms of her NDA in the United States, which could result in Depp suing her for breach of contract and damages in that country and threaten their divorce settlement. Despite Depp bringing the claim—and asserting he wanted the truth to out—he refused to release her from the NDA for the purposes of giving evidence against him.

In a part of the *Depp v. NGN* defamation proceedings that has escaped much reporting, NGN filed an abuse of process application against Depp. Its argument was simple: it was an abuse of process to sue NGN in the United Kingdom with the claim it was defamatory that he was a 'wife beater'—that is, that Amber lied—while simultaneously refusing to release Amber from an NDA that would allow her to help them prove it was true. Amber, like other women who have signed NDAs, could be summonsed, or subpoenaed, to give evidence in court, and have witness immunity for the evidence she gave.

There are obvious public policy concerns about private contracts that prevent people from giving evidence in court. The courts strike a balance between the public interest in upholding contracts (including NDAs) and ensuring the court has the evidence it needs to determine disputes in a fair and just manner. However, Amber would not have been able to discuss the matter with NGN before giving her evidence in court. In effect, the existence of an NDA turns a witness—however willing they are and however much they want to assist the party in the case—into a hostile witness by virtue of the contracted confidentiality.

But there was an additional complication in Amber's case: her US counsel stated that Amber could only respond if she was subpoenaed for the purposes of legal proceedings in the United States: her NDA was silent on her participation in foreign proceedings. Despite her requests, Depp refused to release her to assist NGN to defend her truth.

There was evidence before the court that it would cost Amber between US$20,000 and $40,000 to use the arbitration mechanism under their divorce agreement to obtain an order from a judge in California to allow her to give evidence in the United Kingdom. There was also evidence that Amber had previously sought to use the same mechanism to seek remedy in relation to Depp's defamatory statements to the media claiming she was lying, but the process had gone nowhere after four months. Depp's refusal to release her would cause her costs and significant delay: NGN could not obtain evidence from its key witness until this process was completed.

NGN argued that it was within Depp's gift to release Amber to be able to give evidence so that it could properly test his claim that she lied, and that, since he had brought the proceedings, he should do so, and his failure to do so amounted to an abuse of process. As Adam Wolanski KC made clear for NGN, Depp's refusal to release her meant Amber's 'hands are tied . . . but she remains ready to assist the court if [Depp] stipulated her giving evidence would not put her at risk of legal action in the US'. NGN argued that there could not be a fair trial if Amber was not able to participate, give her side of the story and help NGN prepare their defence.

The threshold test in an abuse of process application is high: judges are, quite rightly, reluctant to deny a claimant the opportunity to vindicate their legal rights. In the Depp case, the judge found that Depp's refusal to release Amber was not enough to justify his claim being thrown out or stayed, because she had a mechanism available to enable her participation and she should go to the expense of going through that process to seek to release herself from the NDA. The judge indicated that he would entertain another abuse application if she were unable to obtain the order she needed from a US judge.

The Depp case is not the only defamation case where this has been an issue. In Australia, an NDA created issues in the Ben Roberts-Smith's case against Nine Entertainment and several journalists over claims he committed war crimes and physically abused a woman he had an affair with. The defence wanted to call Roberts-Smith's ex-wife, Emma, to testify—but she had signed an NDA as part of their divorce settlement. Roberts-Smith refused to release her from the NDA, and even threatened her with legal proceedings if she assisted the newspaper—threatening the financial settlement from their divorce. But Nine Entertainment subpoenaed her to the stand—which no NDA can stop.

Roberts-Smith denied hitting her. He claimed she had been drunk and fallen down the stairs at an event, and that this caused her the injury and the black eye—a fact that was later supported by witness evidence at trial. Person 17 did not contest that she had the fall and was injured by it. She maintained that Roberts-Smith had punched her when they got back to their hotel after expressing his anger about her conduct at the event and his concern that she had exposed their affair. In her affidavit, she said she didn't go to the police after the alleged incident because she was scared for herself and her children. Roberts-Smith said that her allegations were 'completely false' and a 'fabrication', and that he abhors domestic violence. It also emerged from evidence in court that Roberts-Smith had hired a private investigator to follow Person 17 to an abortion clinic.

Emma Roberts-Smith gave evidence that her former husband had asked her to lie to the media and make a false statement to his lawyers about his affair with Person 17 in order to keep custody of her children. She said that Roberts-Smith had threatened her, saying 'if you don't lie you will lose them'. She also contradicted several other aspects of Roberts-Smith's evidence. Her evidence was challenged on the basis of text messages which his lawyers suggest show that she is seeking revenge against her ex-husband. The case closed, with lawyers for the newspaper urging the court to reject 'outdated and discredited stereotypes' about domestic violence. Judgment is expected late in 2022.

Reputation protection or reputation risk?

Just months after Zelda spoke out, The Weinstein Company said it had released all its former employees from their NDAs, stating this was 'an important step toward justice for any victims who have been silenced by Harvey Weinstein'. But that change only came after Zelda spoke out, and after the company was sued by the New York attorney general.

Thanks to this and other controversies after women started speaking out, lawyers are now advising clients that NDAs may be more trouble than they are worth. We spoke with Rebekah Giles—one of Australia's leading reputation management lawyers—who told us that, since MeToo, NDAs can create more reputational problems than they resolve. 'I am now suggesting to some clients that they should not enter into an NDA if the alleged conduct is disputed,' she said, because 'down the track they can be accused of silencing or covering up an act—even though it's disputed'. In those circumstances, she explained, the alternative remedy is to sue for defamation to protect their reputation against the accusation being made.

As we explain in Chapter 6, the threat of defamation proceedings—and the cost risk of potential litigation—can work just as well as any contract to silence.

Rebekah argued that NDAs should remain an option for those who want to protect their identity, and for those who face the threat of having their intimate information shared in public. According to Rebekah, it allows women to have 'the opportunity to reach financial settlements early and without a protracted and expensive legal dispute' and prohibiting NDAs will mean that allegations 'will have to be determined in the court or in the media'. What is important, she told us, is that the process of putting the NDA in place ensures that the survivor is properly advised of the consequences of the contract and what it could mean for her in the future. As Rebekah explained, anyone seeking to put in place an NDA should—to ensure it will later be enforceable and safe from legal challenge—be certain that the complainant has independent legal advice and has been assessed by a medical professional to confirm that their trauma and any associated mental health issues do not affect their ability to enter the contract.

Can't buy my silence

While things have changed since Zelda first spoke out about Weinstein's NDAs, she doesn't think it's happening fast enough. In the four years since she first spoke out, there have been parliamentary inquiries and recommendations for law reform have been made—but no action has been taken to change the law on NDAs. Frustrated by the lack of action, Zelda has decided to join together with *Going Public* author Julie Macfarlane to start a campaign.

Professor Macfarlane had her own bad experience with NDAs. A fellow professor at the University of Windsor in Canada had left after allegations of bullying and sexual harassment were made by students. His employment settlement agreement with the university had included an NDA. When he applied for jobs at another university and she was contacted by his prospective employer, Professor Macfarlane was honest about the accusations that had been made against him in an email. She was concerned to ensure that the university considering hiring him was forewarned in order to safeguard students. He then sued her for defamation over her email, and not in Canada but in Trinidad and Tobago, where he is from and where he was living. He won at trial—because the university had refused, on the basis of the NDA, to release any information about the allegations against him to help her prove her case that what she said was true. She is appealing and had to sue the university for its failure to provide her with the information she needed to defend herself in the defamation claim.

As Professor Macfarlane said in a 2022 interview for *Elle* magazine, 'What NDAs are doing is taking away the natural instinct we have, especially as women, to warn one another.' Professor Macfarlane, herself a survivor of child sex abuse in the church, has campaigned to end the use of NDAs by the church in settlements—and, in her, Zelda found a kindred spirit with a common goal.

Launched late in 2021, Can't Buy My Silence is a global campaign to end the abuse of NDAs and the silencing of women who have suffered sexual abuse and harassment. As Zelda explained, the personal repercussions for people who are 'living under that shadow [of an NDA] are catastrophic'.

As part of Can't Buy My Silence's push to get NDAs back on the legislative agenda in the United Kingdom, the Conservative MP Maria Miller, who had chaired the committee inquiry into NDA misuse, launched a bill that intended to restrict the misuse of NDAs. Introducing the bill in September 2021, Miller said, 'NDAs have been weaponised to uphold a culture of abuse,' and added that the gagging orders continued to act as 'a safety net for employers to routinely cover up abuses without consequence'. The bill is up for consideration in 2022—so watch this space.

The campaign has already had a number of wins: in Ireland in 2021, a private member's bill to restrict the use of NDAs in relation to workplace sexual harassment and discrimination was introduced, and is currently at the committee stage in the Dáil, the Irish Parliament. This proposed legislation would restrict NDAs unless the woman prefers to enter into one and has been offered independent legal advice at the employer's expense, along with a host of other safeguards, including that the agreement must allow the employee to waive their own confidentiality in the future. In Canada, Prince Edward Island became the first province to ban the use of NDAs in sexual misconduct cases and other cases involving discrimination, for example, racism and pregnancy-related discrimination based on the Irish bill. The legislation, which came into force in June 2022, also preserves space for women to enter into these agreements where they choose to do so to move on with their lives and includes safeguards against coercion and the power imbalance between employers and employees. And in the Australian state of Victoria, a taskforce was recently established in July 2022 to develop a legislative response to restrict the use of NDAs in workplace sexual harassment cases, with the state government pledging to consult with stakeholders including victim-survivors.

In the meantime, fed up by the UK Parliament's failure to enact legislation, Zelda took another approach: she lobbied key organisations to sign a pledge to end the use of NDAs. In early 2022, the UK Department for Education committed to this pledge, which will make a huge difference in the thousands of cases of sexual harassment settled each year in universities and schools across the country.

And there are success stories elsewhere. In the wake of the MeToo controversies and the release of all Miramax and Weinstein Company employees from their contractual NDAs, pressure has mounted on other major organisations to do the same. Women have been campaigning to be released from their NDAs—and they've been winning. For example, in 2019, the US journalist Rachel Maddow announced that NBC was releasing all women who had settled sexual harassment claims against the network from their NDAs.

In 2021, California paved the way by passing the *Silenced No More Act*, which prohibits the use of NDAs and non-disparagement clauses in severance agreements and builds on enhanced employee protections introduced by the state in the wake of MeToo. The legislation was co-sponsored by Ifeoma Ozoma, a whistleblower who broke her NDA to speak out about the racial discrimination she and other Black women had suffered at Pinterest, and has campaigned for change since. The legislation was expected to increase pressure on Silicon Valley's tech sector, which has faced considerable pushback against its use of NDAs and mandatory arbitration clauses. It has since been adopted in Washington State and Microsoft announced in June 2022 it has dropped all NDAs. (Meta's board recently refused to do the same.) Ozoma said it was just the start.

It is clearly better to prevent than to fix after the fact, which is why women like Zelda are continuing their efforts to get more organisations to sign onto her pledge and continuing her efforts to change the law to ensure that contracts and NDAs cannot be used to silence survivors. But as Zelda told us, 'the law is a hard thing to move' and, in order to defend themselves and advocate for change, silence-breakers 'have to come to grips with alienating and technical legal language'.

Zelda also raised her concerns about how hard it was for her—and for other women she speaks to—to find lawyers who are able and willing to help, and that even the cost of seeking advice on NDAs is often beyond most women's means. 'Some lawyers simply don't understand speaking out to be a funda-mental human rights issue,' she told us—or they 'had too much skin in the game' and 'were more concerned not to alienate their high-net-worth clients who all use NDAs'. But there are human rights lawyers who take on these cases, and change is happening.

It is clear, thanks to MeToo and to Zelda and other silence-breakers who have spoken out about the abuse of NDAs, that the use of NDAs is becoming less acceptable from a PR point of view, whatever the law says. And we believe there is hope that, as more cases go before the courts, more arguments can be made about the need to recognise the reality of how the law is failing survivors, and how the public interest should privi-lege their free speech over contracts that seek to silence. As Zelda says—things need to change—and faster than the courts can move, so we hope to see more take-up of her pledge from institutions and corporates, and law reform.

Chapter 6

DEFAMATION ON TRIAL

By far the most common legal action we have seen used against women who have spoken out or reported gender-based violence is the libel suit. These defamation cases are about protecting his right to honour and reputation from the damage caused by her speech.

Defamation law allows a person to sue for damage caused to their reputation. The law is different in different countries; in some contexts, it is a criminal offence with those losing defamation claims facing penalties ranging from a fine to imprisonment. Civil defamation claims can involve monetary damages and legal costs into the millions.

In defamation cases involving allegations of gender-based violence, it is always a question of weighing his right to reputation against her right to free speech, weighed on Justitia's scales. But how and where is the balance struck? And are the courts getting the balance right?

Defamation, duels and defending the honour and reputation of men

Before there were defamation claims, there were duels. This was how men defended their honour against lies and libels. Two men, with pistols or rapiers, would meet at dawn—and had one shot each. It was a manifestation of an aristocratic honour culture in which nothing was more valuable than a man's reputation. Or a rich man's reputation, at least. And he was willing to pay for it with his life.

It was an act borne of extreme entitlement. Duels were known as 'judicial combat' for a while; it was said that God would oversee the encounter and decide the winner. Winning a duel was not a matter of luck or whoever had the best shot, but a matter of divine intervention—God was saying, 'This man is telling the truth.'

Over the centuries, various kings and governments tried to stamp out the practice of duelling but it continued well into the 20th century. In one of the most famous of all duels, popularised by the hit musical *Hamilton*, former Secretary of the Treasury Alexander Hamilton died in a duel with US Vice-President Aaron Burr in 1804. By then, reputation was meant to be decided in courtrooms, not on battlefields, through the action of defamation. So it is a great irony that, just months before he died, Hamilton had been in court defending the free speech of a client in a defamation case. In it, Hamilton made a crucially important contribution to early defamation law. In an appeal involving a criminal libel conviction against journalist Harry Croswell over statements he had published about then president Thomas Jefferson, Hamilton argued: 'The right of giving the truth in evidence, in cases of libels, is all-important to the liberties of the people. Truth is an ingredient in the eternal order of things, in judging of the quality of acts.'

The case was not ultimately determined, but the year after Hamilton's death by duel, the New York legislature adopted his argument and made it law that truth alone is a defence to libel, regardless of the subject matter. Whether you are speaking about the President of the United States or about gender-based violence, your right to free speech and your civil liberties means the truth must protect you against a defamation claim. As we explain, most countries around the world now recognise truth as a defence to any defamation claim—and international law requires it under your right to free speech.

In Hamilton's time, those who lost their duel were silenced by injury or death. The musical *Hamilton* ends with his death by duel and a song called 'Who Lives, Who Dies, Who Tells Your Story'—a reflection on narrative control and historical legacy. Duels may now be dead too, but the language lives on in defamation and the media's representation of it: a *New York Times* headline in 2020 read 'The Depp v Heard duel approaches its climax'. Today, those who lose their defamation claim are silenced not by death but by the law. Whoever wins gets to tell their story.

Invisible wounds

Today, defamation is the cause of action men most often use to vindicate their reputation after allegations of gender-based violence. Wealthy and powerful men sue, and women are often outgunned by men's teams of lawyers in this modern-day duel. Defending claims is expensive—and stressful. But it's so much more than that. Understanding the impact for women facing defamation claims requires us to look beyond the law as it appears in the statute books, and beyond the technical legal arguments we make in court, to look at the law's real-world impact.

Journalist Carole Cadwalladr was sued for defamation by Brexit-backer Arron Banks over allegations she made in her TED Talk about his alleged connections to the Russian government. Before winning the case in 2022, she wrote on Twitter about her personal experience of being sued for defamation:

> it's not just designed to silence you. Although it does. But also to destroy you. Which it does too. It's not a pissy business dispute. It's a full-frontal multi-million quid existential assault. On who you are . . . it is a rich man's sport . . . It's not just the trial or an act or an event, it's a process that goes on over years. It's a toxin that enters your central nervous system slowly & insidiously, until one day you can't move your limbs.

Cadwalladr wrote candidly about her experience of being 'trapped inside the airless machinery of the legal process', and how traumatic it was for her to be 'forced to hand your personal messages against your will in the certain knowledge that anything you've ever said can & will be used against you'. For Cadwalladr it was a traumatic, life-altering experience. She was being sued by a powerful, wealthy man she spoke about as a journalist, not someone she had alleged to have committed violence against her.

Many women are sued for defamation by their alleged abusers. A common manipulation tactic used by perpetrators to avoid being held accountable and discredit and silence victims is known as 'deny, attack and reverse victim and offender', or DARVO. As Professor Jennifer Freyd's book *Blind to Betrayal*

(2013) shows, one of the ways perpetrators assume the victim role is by claiming to be the victim of false accusations. Defamation claims provide the mechanism by which they become the victim in law, by making her the defendant—and him the complainant—in a claim that she lied and damaged his reputation.

Many of the women we have acted for and interviewed for this book have also described it as a means by which these men can continue their abuse and harassment. Court-mandated disclosure allows them access to women's personal messages and medical information, giving him access to the intimate details of her life long after she has left him. This also happens in criminal prosecutions, where women's rights groups have raised concerns about the extent to which women must give up their privacy to enable him to be prosecuted by the state. But here, he gets access to this information in a private claim against her, brought at his behest—not for the protection of the public, but to protect his reputation. Legal emails demand her constant attention. Court dates dictate where she can be—and ensure that he knows exactly where she will be. The costs can cripple her financially, affecting other aspects of her life.

Cases can take years to be resolved and, in the meantime, women are effectively silenced: as we have seen, women's lawyers will tell them not to repeat the allegation because it may increase the damages she might be forced to pay. And she will be told she can't speak to the media because she'll be cross-examined in court about whatever she says. But it also silences others: journalists and media will shy away from reporting on her allegation when they know the matter is before the courts because they could be sued too. But beyond the silencing, women facing defamation claims—as Cadwalladr explained—feel destroyed: emotionally, physically and financially.

One thing hasn't changed since the duelling days: these claims are mainly the prerogative of wealthy, powerful men. Men who are willing to spend a lot of money to defend their honour in court. In duelling days, equality of arms was dictated by each person having one shot. In litigation today, equality of arms is still an essential element of a fair trial, which is put at risk when one party doesn't have sufficient resources to properly defend themselves. Because of the astronomical costs, wealthy men can—in effect—take many more shots. They can get their way through pure attrition, bankrupting and bullying her and journalists into silence—and then calling it justice. What does your right to free speech mean if you can't afford to defend it?

Defamation, MeToo and movements for change

Each individual defamation case—even though it is a private dispute between two individuals—needs to be seen within its broader context. We want to highlight the impact these defamation claims have—and not just on each woman or survivor who is sued, but on society, and on our ability to end violence against women.

Since MeToo, there has been a global spike in defamation cases. In 2020, *The New York Times* reported the problem we were seeing in our work: the civil courts are becoming the 'alternative battlefield for accusations of sexual misconduct'. Take, for example, Jen's homeland, Australia. As women marched across the country to demand accountability for violence against women in 2021, Attorney-General Christian Porter sued the ABC over reporting a historic rape allegation and Minister for Defence Peter Dutton threatened Senator Larissa Waters with defamation—for alleging he was a rape apologist—and sued activist Shane Bazzi for making the same claim. Celebrated Australian soldier and alleged war criminal Ben Roberts-Smith is suing Fairfax for defamation for reporting on his alleged war crimes and domestic violence. Not long before, Oscar-winning actor Geoffrey Rush successfully sued *The Daily Telegraph* over publications making allegations of sexual assault and harassment, while former *Neighbours* and *Home and Away* star Craig McLachlan sued the ABC and *The Sydney Morning Herald* and Christie Whelan Browne for publishing similar allegations. All the men vehemently deny any wrongdoing—and have sought to demonstrate this by suing their accuser or the newspapers which reported the allegations. And it's not just in Australia.

In France, the founder of French MeToo was sued by her boss for defamation over her allegation of sexual harassment, which had started the French social media campaign #BalanceTonPorc or 'Out Your Pig'. In Canada, politician Patrick Brown sued a TV channel for broadcasting sexual harassment allegations. Meanwhile, also in Canada, academic and author Steven Galloway is suing twenty individuals for reporting or tweeting about accusations of rape made against him by a former student. In New Zealand, former Conservative Party politician Colin Craig sued his former press secretary over her allegations of sexual harassment. In the United States, actor Johnny Depp sued his ex-wife, actor Amber Heard, for US$50 million over a *Washington Post* opinion piece. Marilyn Manson is suing Evan Rachel Wood over her allegations, including in the HBO documentary *Phoenix Rising*, that he sexually assaulted her. Justin Bieber sued two fans for US$20 million over allegations of sexual assault they made on social media. The problem is so widespread in the United States that the American Civil Liberties Union (ACLU) put out a defamation guide because of the number of inquiries they had received from women being threatened with defamation in the wake of the MeToo movement. In the UK, women's frontline services and rape crisis centres have been seeking defamation advice from us, after seeing a spike in defamation threats against the women accessing their support services. The Women's Equality Party had to seek defamation advice from Jen for their election campaign plans to tackle sexual harassment in the British Parliament.

Women's rights groups are reporting numerous cases and concerns across the African continent too. For example, in Kenya, journalist Tony Mochama sued poet and activist Shailja Patel for accusing him of sexual abuse, together with her friend, academic Professor Wambui Mwangi, who tweeted about it to support Patel. Mochama won—and Patel is now reportedly living in exile in London as a result of the case. Similar cases are being reported in South Africa, Uganda and elsewhere.

In India, journalist Priya Ramani faced criminal defamation charges filed by Union minister and former editor M.J. Akbar after she tweeted that he had sexually harassed her in a job interview. Meanwhile, photographer and magazine editor Manik Katyal is suing 36 women who accused him of sexual harassment on a blog. Rajendra Pachauri, former head of the United Nations Intergovernmental Panel on Climate Change (IPCC), filed a civil lawsuit against well-known women's rights lawyer Vrinda Grover for assisting women to come forward with their allegations of sexual harassment against him. These cases are just some of the many of the 'retaliatory' defamation cases afoot against women who have spoken out in India—and those who have supported them—which the Indian Network of Women in Media warns will deter other women from coming forward. The list goes on and on—and on.

Our research shows this issue is not limited to Western liberal democracies, but spans the global North to the global South, from the Far East to the West. And it's not just rich and famous people—it's happening in every level of society. For example, Jen was recently approached at a women's leadership event by a woman in the mining industry who had been sexually assaulted by a colleague on a mine site and was then threatened with defamation for reporting it to her employer and talking to her colleagues about it. The pattern is striking, both in the kinds of allegations being sued upon and the biases and stereotypes deployed in courtrooms—and in the media—to undermine the women making the accusations. Defamation claims are not just silencing individual women but are collectively stifling the movement to end violence against women.

This is not the first time in history that we have seen defamation being used as a tool to stifle progressive movements for social change and maintain the discriminatory status quo. We need only look to how defamation claims were used during the US civil rights movement to stifle Black dissent. Aimee Edmondson explains this in her 2020 book *In Sullivan's Shadow: The use and abuse of libel law during the long civil rights struggle*: 'White government officials wielded libel law to protect white supremacy and waste the time and funds of those individuals and organizations that worked to dismantle segregation and end police brutality.' By silencing Black dissent, the white establishment was able to resist change. She has uncovered how the US courts were complicit in maintaining racial injustice with libel suits used 'to silence the media, civil rights leaders and activists'.

Out of the raft of litigation during the civil rights movement came one of the most important free speech judgments from the

US Supreme Court: *New York Times Co. v. Sullivan*. This was a libel case brought by a police commissioner in Alabama over an advertisement in *The New York Times* that aimed to raise money for civil rights leader Martin Luther King Jr. The advertisement referred to police brutality towards civil rights protestors in Montgomery, but it also contained some inaccuracies, including about how many times King had been arrested. The case was decided in favour of the police—because some of the information in the advertisement was shown not to be true—but the newspaper took the case all the way to the Supreme Court. Was defamation law stifling freedom of speech on civil rights? The court found that it was and laid down a test to better protect free speech. To win a defamation claim, public figures and officials now had to show not just that the defamatory statement about them was untrue, but that it was also made with malice and reckless disregard for the truth. It is a purposefully high bar, limiting the law's ability to stifle speech that is in the public interest.

This case shows both how defamation laws can be used to stifle efforts—and speech—designed to end discrimination, but also how the courts can play an important role in limiting the law's complicity in that effort and better protect free speech.

What does his right to reputation protect?

The right to protect one's reputation, like the right to free speech, is protected under human rights law. Everyone is entitled to protection against unlawful attacks on their honour and reputation. This is protected under Article 17 of the International Covenant on Civil and Political Rights (ICCPR) and in regional treaties such as Article 8 of the European Convention on Human Rights. International law makes clear that protecting the rights and reputations of others is a legitimate ground to limit the right to free speech. But her free speech is the starting point and any restriction on her right to free speech in order to protect his reputation—like defamation laws—must be limited to what is strictly necessary in a democratic society.

International courts and bodies have considered Justitia's balance between the right to free speech and the right to protect reputation and give guidance on how to get that balance right. To start with, criminal defamation laws should be repealed, and imprisonment is never an appropriate remedy. Whether defamation law is civil or criminal, defamation laws must always include Hamilton's rule: the defence of truth. His right to reputation cannot protect her from speaking the truth about his action.

The problem is that many countries don't respect this requirement and write their laws to protect men and to prohibit women from speaking out. For example, in South Korea, when a person's social reputation is tarnished, truth is no defence. Women accusing men of sexual assault face civil and criminal defamation claims in response, even after they have reported the offending to the police. As Seo Hye-jin of the Korean Women Lawyers Association has explained, 'Many abusers openly use the threats of lawsuits as an intimidation tactic, saying, "I'll drop the false accusation and defamation suits against you if you drop the sex abuse complaint against me".' In Colombia, truth is generally a defence to any defamation claim—unless you are speaking about sexual relationships. Article 224.2 of the Colombian Criminal Code provides that, while truth is generally a justification for speaking out, this is not the case when matters relate to allegations made in intimate, marital and conjugal relationships—even if they are about abuse. This law is being challenged before the Constitutional Court in Colombia and, with our assistance, the UN and Organization of American States (OAS) Special Rapporteurs on Free Speech have submitted a brief arguing that this law results in indirect censorship and affects survivors' free speech rights to report and contribute to public discussion on gender-based violence.

In most common law jurisdictions, including the United Kingdom and Australia, truth is a defence. But having a truth defence in the law is not enough to comply with the right to free speech under international human rights law. It also requires that women will not be held to unrealistic or excessive standards of proof to prove her truth and be able to succeed in a truth defence. As we explain later in this chapter, even in countries where truth is a defence, her right to tell her truth isn't always properly protected. It doesn't stop him suing her—and evidential difficulties, old male-centric myths about abuse and cost often mean that, in practice, he can defeat her truth and sideline her right to free speech.

Defamation laws should also contain a defence for speaking about and reporting on matters of public interest. This is reflected in the laws of most democratic countries, including in the United Kingdom and in most states in Australia. This means that even untrue statements (or, more accurately, statements that cannot be proven in court to be true) or statements made in error should not be penalised in defamation if they were made in the public interest and without malice. As we argue, her right to speak about gender-based violence is a matter of public interest and should be protected. UN experts have repeatedly emphasised that allowing women and girls to speak about gender-based violence is a matter of public interest.

In each legal system there are various other defences such as qualified privilege and honest opinion, which—like truth and public interest—are supposed to reflect the appropriate balance between the rights to reputation and free speech. Defamation law is highly technical, and each case requires specialist legal advice. It is impossible for us to cover each defence in detail in this book. In this chapter, we focus on truth and public interest.

In the end, free speech protection isn't just about the law as it appears on the books but also how it operates in practice: UN bodies have repeatedly warned that states must ensure that defamation laws 'do not serve, in practice, to stifle freedom of expression' and 'are not misused . . . to illegitimately or arbitrarily censor journalists and interfere with their mission of informing the public'. UN experts have warned states to ensure that defamation laws do not prevent survivors of gender-based violence from speaking out about the abuse they have suffered or have a chilling effect on the ability of the media to report on it. Are our laws and our courts helping or hindering women's ability to speak?

What can you be sued for?

It's important first to be clear about what you cannot be sued for. You cannot be sued for defamation for reporting your abuse or anyone else's to the relevant police or state authorities (at least in most jurisdictions). You also cannot be sued for what you say in court when giving evidence about it. But you can be sued for what you say and publish outside of court.

You can be sued for any accusation of gender-based violence you make on social media, in the print media or on TV or radio—and even for what you write in an email. Slander is spoken defamation, but anything spoken that is recorded or broadcast becomes libel. Libel is defamation in lasting form, and so includes any statement that is written, broadcast, posted online, tweeted or otherwise published. As we saw at the beginning of this book, Nicola Stocker had to fight all the way to the UK Supreme Court over a Facebook comment.

For him to be able to bring a defamation claim, he must show that she damaged his reputation. Unlike other kinds of allegations, any allegation of gender-based violence—rape, sexual assault or harassment, or domestic abuse—will generally be presumed to cause damage to a man's reputation. Even in the United Kingdom, and Australia (except in Western Australia and the Northern Territory), where a new 'serious harm' to reputation test was put in place to make it harder to sue for libel and better protect free speech, accusations of gender-based violence—particularly if published in the national media— will meet that threshold. But this is a fact-specific test, and a recent case in the United Kingdom suggests the test may not be met where a woman is simply talking to her friends and social circles about his alleged abuse. For example, in *Lee v. Brown* a man sued his ex-partner for claiming he had been abusive towards her during their relationship. He claimed she had been running 'an abusive smear campaign' against him. The publications he complained of included private emails and correspondence to eleven identified people and a Facebook post. Her Facebook post did not name him, though the judge found that didn't matter because he could still be identified from the post. The post was seen by between a hundred and thousands of Facebook users. This would have been enough to be defamatory under the old common law and allow him to sue her, but the judge dismissed his case because he had not proved that her statements had caused 'serious harm' to his reputation under the new test. Relevant to his conclusion was the fact that the allegations were made and published to people who were already 'partisan recipients' on either side of 'an acrimonious relation-ship break down'. As a result, the judge concluded that people would be unlikely to change their mind or allegiance and—in the absence of evidence to show otherwise—the publications of the allegations could not be said to have caused serious harm to his reputation. In short, it is all about context: where it was published, who it was published to, the extent and effect of publication on his reputation. In Nicola Stocker's case, her Facebook post was seen by a relatively small number of people but was enough to meet the serious harm test. And media publi-cations about gender-based violence will almost always enable him to sue.

Of course, he can only bring a claim if he has a reputation to defend: you can't harm, let alone do serious harm to a reputa-tion that has already been irreparably harmed. By the time tens of women had made credible sexual assault allegations against Harvey Weinstein, many lawyers argued that it was safe to report further since there was a good argument to say that he no longer had a good reputation to defend. But that's a hard argument to run and win, even when more than one woman speaks out.

You don't need to name your alleged perpetrator: it is enough that he is identifiable and someone who reads the story can connect it to him. We have noticed a trend towards women not naming the person in order to protect themselves against defamation proceedings. For example, in Australia, former member of parliament and lawyer Julia Banks recently published her book *Power Play: Breaking through bias, barriers & boys' clubs* (2021), about the sexism she faced in politics. In the book, and in the media, she has described an incident when she was inappropriately touched by a cabinet minister in the Prime Minister's Office. Banks has told that story out of her stated concern that, if he was willing to do it there, and to her—a fellow MP—imagine what he would do to women with less power, and elsewhere. In response to questions as to why she would not name the minister, she said, 'I'm not fearless,' and cited the risk of defamation proceedings.

While you're safer not to name him, not naming him won't necessarily protect you: what matters is whether or not he is identifiable—and what you've published causes his reputation harm. If you claim an ex-boyfriend raped you at a particular age, then he will be identifiable to those who know you both, and so he could still sue you. Banks perhaps felt some security in not naming that cabinet minister because there were sixteen men in Prime Minister Turnbull's cabinet in 2016 and only six women. Ironically, the historical discrimination against women that has caused the under-representation of women in politics, and in cabinet appointments, affords her some protection. That and the fact he probably doesn't want to name himself in order to be able to sue her.

He decides what she meant by her words

The first part of any defamation proceeding is to look at the alleged defamatory statement itself and determine exactly what it means. In the United Kingdom, the court will do this—with her lawyers, his lawyers and the judge poring over the words used to determine what an 'ordinary reader' would understand from them and what they imply or convey. It is often (but shouldn't be) a very technical exercise. The meaning determined by the judge will shape the rest of the trial. Even when it is a personal account of her own experience of violence, what she really meant by her words does not determine what her words mean in law for the purposes of a defamation claim.

Historically, defamation claims have been determined by juries of men and (more recently) women. They must decide, first, the meaning of the defamatory statement and, second, whether there is enough evidence to prove that the statement is true. Juries are still used in some places (for example, in the United States and in some jurisdictions in Australia). But in the United Kingdom, all this will be determined by a single judge—who typically will be a white, privileged man. And this matters.

The test is this: how would the ordinary reader understand the meaning of her statement? The test used to be how 'the reasonable man' would interpret her words, but we now use gender-neutral language. But does that change really matter if the people determining this test are still, in fact, predominantly white, privileged men? Her words could be given a spectrum of different interpretations. But when only a narrow subset of people sit on the bench, the 'ordinary and reasonable reader' may in effect come to mean 'a privileged white man'.

The impact of a male-centric approach to the meaning of her words is illustrated by what happened in Nicola Stocker's case. Did her words 'he tried to strangle me' mean that he forcefully grabbed her around the throat, or did it mean that he did so with an intent to kill her? What Nicola had meant was that he had grabbed her by her throat, and indeed she had police evidence to prove that he had. But Mr Justice Mitting imposed a different meaning on her words: using a technical definition from the dictionary, her words 'tried to strangle' meant that her husband had intended to kill her. (The new offence of non-fatal strangulation introduced by the *Domestic Abuse Act 2021*, thanks to feminist campaigning, remedies the problem that Nicola Stocker faced in her case: the new offence does not require an intent to kill.) On the judge's meaning, Nicola's evidence and the police evidence was not enough: the judge found that it was evidence that he had intended to silence her, but it was not sufficient to show that he had intended to kill her. And so she lost the case and was found to have defamed the man who had committed an act of domestic violence against her.

This is not to say the different interpretations were necessarily the result of gender difference—a majority male Supreme Court later overturned this decision on appeal, taking a more reasonable and realistic approach to the meaning of Nicola's words. But it does show how important perspective can be when it comes to determining the meaning of her words when she speaks.

Debates about MeToo—and the defamation cases that have followed—have also shown the important of nuance in language around gender-based violence. In English, the phrase 'sexual assault' can refer to a spectrum of conduct from unwanted sexual touching to that involving more forceful physical violence. In defamation, too, words matter and meaning matters: as Nicola Stocker's case shows, the meaning of your words could be construed in a way that makes it difficult or even impossible for you to prove your case. This is why you often read stories in the newspapers about 'sexual misconduct' or 'sexual assault' instead of more specific phrases in law like 'attempted rape', which is notoriously hard to prove because of the need to prove his intention. However, courts have begun to take a more expansive approach to the meaning of domestic abuse in defamation cases to reflect developments in law and understandings of abuse: it need not necessarily mean physical violence and can include non-physical abuse, such as 'controlling behaviour' and verbal abuse.

It is because of the courts' approach to meaning that journalists and their in-house lawyers will often choose language that a survivor might see as downplaying her experience. But they do this in order to make it easier to prove the truth of the allegation in court—if it comes to that—and to be sure they have sufficient evidence to prove it. This is also why you will always see 'it is alleged' or 'she said', rather than reporting her allegation as a fact: it is easier to prove later in court that there were grounds to suspect he raped her, than it is to prove he is guilty of raping her.

It also means that women speaking out, and the commentators who support them, have to be careful about the language they use. For example, a Canadian professor is suing a group of women for calling him a rapist or using the hashtag #rapist in tweets referring to him in support of a student who accused him of rape, sexual assault and harassment. He says it was defamatory because the university had, in an investigation which he said was flawed, only found that he had sexually harassed her, not raped her.

All of this means that when speaking about your abuse or anyone else's, you must be very careful in the language you use. This is particularly so when your words have a specific definition in law.

He decides who to sue and where

In our practice and more broadly, we have seen how someone can use defamation law to prevent an allegation against them from being reported on and repeated. This is because he can sue not just the woman speaking out, but also the journalist and the media outlet that published the allegations, and anyone else who repeats her allegation in order to support her. Friends and family, activists or frontline services organisations can be sued or threatened with a suit. Depending on the jurisdiction, these cases can be civil or involve the man pursuing criminal prosecution, with or without the support of prosecutors. It is possible to take these actions simultaneously—and in different jurisdictions. He can sue the woman, while also suing the journalist and the media organisation, together or separately. Defamation claims have the effect of silencing the women and journalists who are sued by deterring them and anyone else from repeating the allegation. As we saw in the Charlie Elphicke case in Chapter 4, a defamation claim can stop a story: *The Times* story about him was not reported on by any other media organisation.

But in some places, such as in India, men have been able to get orders and injunctions before trial to force the removal and repetition of her allegations. We interviewed Karuna Nundy, one of India's leading lawyers. She explained how artist Subodh Gupta sued an anonymous Instagram account, @herdsceneand, which had published allegations of sexual harassment against him, seeking 50 million rupees in damages and for the posts to be taken down. Controversially, Gupta was able to get a court order requiring Google and Instagram to remove the URLs and posts relating to the allegations before trial. Karuna explained that these orders can be obtained in India before trial because the legal system is so slow; in order to preserve his rights and protect him until the matter can be determined at trial, the material is taken down. The Indian Journalists Union argued that the orders violated the right to freedom of speech, and we agree. It privileges mitigating potential damage to his reputation over and above her right to free speech. In Australia and the United Kingdom, you can't get an injunction to prevent publication or remove material that you allege is defamatory publication until after trial—and the truth or otherwise of her allegations is proven in court. This rule is considered to protect freedom of speech and represent the correct balance between speech and reputation. Gupta later agreed a settlement with Herdsceneand, which resulted in the posts being removed permanently. Irrespective of the outcome in his case, a dangerous precedent was set in India. Orders which allow the removal of potentially defamatory material pre-trial in India will mean that men can legally silence women's allegations for years on end just by filing a claim, regardless of the truth of her allegations.

He can also choose where to sue: in most places, he will just have to show he has a reputation in that jurisdiction to protect, and that the publication has caused him damage there (i.e. it was published and distributed there or—in the case of online publications—it was downloaded there). For example, in India, Manik Katyal sued 36 women, and Facebook and WordPress, over an online blog in which women had accused him of sexual harassment. He chose to sue in the city of Dehradun, where he was from. But this was far away from all of the women he sued and added to the expense and difficulty they faced to defend themselves. Karuna Nundy, who represents the women, had to petition the Supreme Court of India to have the cases moved to Delhi in a process that took three years.

There is also nothing to stop a man from suing, on the same allegations, in multiple jurisdictions. Johnny Depp is just one high-profile example of this: he sued *The Sun* newspaper in the United Kingdom, and Amber Heard personally in the US state of Virginia—where neither of them live. Those suing for defamation can also 'forum shop'—that is, he can sue in the place where the law is most favourable to him. It also means he can sue in another jurisdiction if he doesn't like the outcome the first time around.

Around the world, we are seeing men use various kinds of action—against the woman, against the journalist and against the publication. And depending on which of these targets he decides to sue, the lawsuit affects her in different ways.

Where a woman is personally sued

In the first scenario, where the woman is sued personally, she faces the stress and cost of the proceedings, but she is in control: it is defended by her lawyers and it is for her to decide how the case is defended. If she cannot afford to defend her truth, she may be forced to settle for financial reasons, and perhaps forced to agree to never repeat her accusation: she is silenced. How many women have been silenced because they cannot afford to defend their right to speak?

Louise Reay, an award-winning British comedian, could not afford to defend herself when she was sued for defamation by her former husband for using material about him in her stand-up show. He claimed £30,000 in damages plus legal costs and an injunction to prevent her from repeating her allegation that he was abusive in their relationship. The case worried not just women speaking out about abuse, but all comedians who use material about their loved ones (or former loved ones) in shows. A crowd-funding campaign commenced to support her defence was not enough. But Louise settled the case and the agreed statement said simply that they had both 'agreed to make no further comment'. Louise cannot now speak about her own case, in her comedy show or anywhere else, but she has been vocal about others who found themselves being sued by their ex-partner. During the UK trial, *Depp v. News Group Newspapers*, she posted on Twitter in support of Heard: 'This is what real silencing looks like. Where you risk losing everything for speaking out.'

If the woman being sued for defamation can afford the fight, she will have her credibility questioned and undermined in a public courtroom, and be subjected to cross-examination by her alleged abuser's counsel. In some places, she might even be questioned by the alleged abuser himself. This is because, in many jurisdictions, the protective rules developed for criminal trials involving gender-based violence to protect complainants don't apply in civil defamation trials. For example, in New Zealand, Rachel MacGregor was sued by her former employer, former Conservative leader Colin Craig, for defamation over her claims he sexually harassed her. She countersued him for defamation and was later awarded NZ$400,000 in damages— but only after years of being dragged through the courts by him. During the case, MacGregor was cross-examined over two days in the High Court in Auckland, and not by a lawyer, but by Craig himself. She was reportedly brought to tears by his questioning. In the United Kingdom, in criminal cases judges can make an order to prevent a self-represented defendant from cross-examining the complainant and appoint a lawyer to do it for them. As Harriet Johnson explains in *Enough*, 'the rule is designed to stop the trial process from forming part of any abuse'. It was only after the *Domestic Abuse Act 2021* that 'the same rules were introduced to prevent abusers being able to cross-examine their victims in the family court and in civil proceedings'. Women should have this same protection in defamation cases where they are being sued in relation to allegations about gender-based violence.

If she gets through the process and wins—vindication. If she loses—she will have to pay him damages and costs, and could be subjected to an injunction making it a contempt of court if she makes the allegation again. She is silenced.

Suing a media outlet or publisher

In the second scenario, a media outlet that seeks to publish the allegation being made by the woman is threatened with legal action. The threat might be enough to stop publication if the media organisation can't afford, or doesn't want, the fight. She has no say—and her story is silenced.

If the media outlet does report her allegations, and the man sues it and the matter goes to trial, she is not a party to the proceedings and so will have no say over how it will be defended—or indeed whether it will be defended at all. The only agency she can exercise is whether to voluntarily assist the media outlet to defend her truth by providing them with evidence and appearing as a witness. Even if she doesn't want to be involved, she may still be subpoenaed. But in either case the woman has no say in how the matter will be handled. The media organisation could, at any time, choose to settle for commercial reasons, which can then forever be used by the alleged perpetrator to say she lied or at least to undermine her account and credibility, deterring other media from ever publishing her allegation. If the case goes to trial and the media organisation can't meet the burden of proof because she is not believed, it will be liable for damages and costs. An injunction might prevent the media organisation from repeating the allegation, which will deter other journalists from reporting on it too. She is silenced, and the media is silenced. This might be the case even where she had never wanted the allegations to surface in the media.

Eryn Jean Norvill's career was thriving. Cast in a series of Sydney Theatre Company (STC) productions, she was a darling of the Australian theatre scene, and had played high-profile roles, including Cordelia in *King Lear*, and won Melbourne Fringe Festival awards. But then, in late 2017, as the MeToo movement gained traction around the world, a news story was printed that would change her life forever.

The Daily Telegraph published a sensational front-page story, with the headline 'KING LEER' accompanying a portrait of Geoffrey Rush. The story the article was telling was Norvill's: it revealed allegations about inappropriate conduct she had made against the Oscar-winning actor. Rush was one of the most widely respected and revered actors in the world, one of the few to have won 'the Triple Crown' (an Oscar, an Emmy and a Tony) and a powerful industry figure in Australia. There was just one thing: she had never intended those allegations to be made public. Yet there it was: her story splashed across the papers. Several further sensational stories were published over the next week, making global headlines.

Back in 2015, Norvill had starred opposite Rush in *King Lear*. She reported certain behaviour, including 'inappropriate touching' by Rush during the production to the STC, her employer, in the hopes that the STC would deal with it and it would stop. She did not sue Rush or the STC for sexual harassment, nor did she ever seek out any media coverage. Indeed, as Tom Blackburn SC, the barrister for the media would later make clear at trial, she had 'desperately sought to stay out of the limelight'. But the allegations against Rush were leaked—without Norvill's consent—and published by *The Daily Telegraph*, Sydney's most popular tabloid newspaper, in November 2017, as MeToo was kicking off around the world.

The Daily Telegraph had not sought Norvill's consent before doing so, nor had it even sought comment from her.

As Norvill has since said, 'My experience was not #MeToo, it was #HerToo.' This was an example of the media failing to protect survivors—publishing her experience without her consent. 'My choice to participate was taken away from me by the media,' Norvill has said. 'I really don't like when decisions are made without you or for you, no one likes that, but particularly when it reshapes your entire sense of self and reality.'

When the story was published, Rush denied the allegations vehemently, and sued *The Daily Telegraph* for portraying him as 'a pervert' and 'a sexual predator' who 'had engaged in inappropriate sexual conduct' and 'sexual assault' during the *King Lear* production. The newspaper argued only one defence: that the allegations were substantially true. And so Norvill's account of the incidents was put on trial—years after she alleged they had taken place, and without her ever intending for them to be made public.

To defend itself, the newspaper needed Norvill to appear as a witness and give evidence. She was in an invidious position: if she chose not to participate, her truth would be put on trial in her absence and the newspaper would likely lose— and her allegations would be said to be untrue. But if she chose to participate to defend her truth, she would be cross-examined and subjected to a media circus that was not of her making. Either way, her credibility and her truth would be under attack. Norvill chose to give evidence. But in the battle of credibility between her and Rush, the judge preferred Rush—and he won the case. As we will explain later in this chapter, the decision has been criticised. It was devastating for Norvill.

Happily, however, it has not kept Norvill down. The STC has continued to support her, casting her in Oscar Wilde's *The Picture of Dorian Gray*, for which she received rave reviews. Some called it her comeback. But she should never have been in the position of having to make a 'comeback'. The defamation trial was traumatic for her. She told *The Guardian* about having to endure 'the most isolated period of my life' and has said that she needed to completely reshape her worldview as a result. Her words will resonate with the many women we have interviewed around the world who have said the same of their own experience of defamation cases.

The settlement of defamation claims against the media can be unsettling—for the women who make the allegations, and for their friends and family. Claims are settled or withdrawn for all kinds of reasons and can be used to undermine the credibility of her allegations.

As we explained in Chapter 3, Australia's then attorney-general Christian Porter sued the ABC in 2021 over the publication of a report about Kate's historical rape allegations. In the claim, his lawyers alleged the media reports had accused him of 'the brutal and anal rape of a 16-year-old', which 'contributed to her taking her own life', 'warranting criminal charges being brought against him'. The ABC defence did not allege that Porter had committed the rape but rather that he was reasonably suspected of doing so—which, as we explained earlier, is an important distinction. The ABC also argued there were reasonable grounds 'to warrant the Prime Minister urgently instigating an independent investigation' into Porter's conduct and sought to rely on other defences given the importance of free speech about political accountability and the conduct of a minister. Porter strenuously denied the allegations and proclaimed he would prove his innocence in court. Prime Minister Morrison refused to conduct an inquiry into Kate's allegations because it would be determined by a court of law—not in a criminal court, but in Porter's defamation claim.

But the matter never made it to trial. Porter agreed to a settlement with the ABC just before its defence was due to be made public. Porter had applied to strike out parts of the ABC's defence, arguing it was 'embarrassing and vexatious'. Before the court determined his application, a settlement was reached: Porter would discontinue his claim and the ABC would publish an agreed statement. The ABC published the following statement:

> On 26 February 2021, the ABC published an article by Louise Milligan. That article was about a letter to the Prime Minister containing allegations against a senior cabinet minister. Although he was not named, the article was about the Attorney-General Christian Porter. The ABC did not intend to suggest that Mr Porter had committed the criminal offences alleged. The ABC did not contend that the serious accusations could be substantiated to the applicable legal standard—criminal or civil. However, both parties accept that some readers misinterpreted the article as an accusation of guilt against Mr Porter. That reading, which was not intended by the ABC, is regretted.

The agreed statement was considered by many to be a statement of the obvious: the ABC had not said Porter was guilty of rape, even if some readers of the article had (wrongly) interpreted it that way. The ABC also agreed that the disputed parts of their defence would be removed from the court file, and was therefore never made public.

Porter claimed victory. He continues to vehemently deny the allegations and can now point to the ABC's statement that they had never contended that Kate's claims could be proven in court. Others claim it was no coincidence that his settlement came just before the strike out application, which would have determined how much of the ABC's defence would be made public: Porter didn't want his day in court after all, if it meant a public airing of the ABC's defence and the facts they would allege to defend the case. But his lawyer, Rebekah Giles, disputed that and told us Porter got what he wanted from the ABC without having to go to the expense of a trial.

For many, the settlement meant that no one was any closer to the truth. A court had not determined the matter, and the government still refused to set up a judicial inquiry. It is a tragic case. Rebekah Giles pointed out that some close to Kate had questioned the ABC's decision to publish the allegations after her death and cited the attempts made by her parents to stop the ABC from airing the allegations. The ABC did not and sadly could not have obtained Kate's permission to publish her allegations but continues to defend the public interest in reporting them. The most tragic part of this case is the fact that Kate is no longer alive to decide or to defend her truth. But even if she had been and was willing to give evidence, it would have been the ABC's decision whether or not to settle, not hers.

For Kate's friends, the outcome was anything but satisfactory. Dhanya Mani has lamented that because there has been no judicial inquiry into Kate's serious claims, and much of Australia has moved on, Kate's story 'will stop being told'. She has written that the 'most excruciating pain' in grieving

Kate's death was 'witnessing the public and press defile her', citing the many attacks on Kate's credibility after her allegation was made public. The settlement of Porter's defamation claim and the failure of the government to investigate, Dhanya wrote, meant that '[t]he priority thrown at the feet of Kate's loved ones—by the media and by politicians—is the task of restoring her'.

Sometimes claims are withdrawn before or even during a trial by the claimant. This can happen for a range of reasons: they run out of money or lose the will to sue. It could also be because evidence comes to light that they don't want aired in court or will mean they might lose. Withdrawing the claim before judgment is better than ending up with a judgment stating that what was said was true and mitigates his legal cost exposure. For the journalists and the women sued who could afford to get this far, it is cold comfort: you've been through years of stress, cost and silencing to be forced to prove the truth, only to have the ability to do so taken from you at the eleventh hour.

In a recent case in Australia, former *Neighbours* star and award-winning actor Craig McLachlan had sued media organisations and Christie Whelan Browne, one of three women who spoke out in the media with allegations of sexual assault and harassment during a theatre production of *The Rocky Horror Show*.

The defamation claim, filed in 2018, was stayed after Victorian police charged McLachlan with assault and indecent assault involving four women in the production. In 2020, McLachlan was acquitted of the charges. In the magistrate's opinion, the outcome could have been different if his conduct in 2014 was judged under Victoria's new consent laws. In other words, he may have believed the women consented, but his belief was not reasonable.

McLachlan then pursued his defamation claims against the media and Whelan, and the trial commenced in May 2022 before a four-person jury. In their defence, the media made clear that, since their initial publications about McLachlan, they had collected more evidence to prove the truth of the allegations against him. In a good example of how media reporting can 'shake the tree' and encourage more women to stand up and come forward, the media said that eleven women were now prepared to say in court that they were harassed by McLachlan. The witnesses included women who had worked with McLachlan not just on *The Rocky Horror Show*, but on the set of *Neighbours* and two other productions, and crew members who would support their accounts. Their allegations were going to include sexual assault, harassment, indecent exposure and bullying.

McLachlan gave his evidence in court, claiming that he was merely 'friendly and affectionate' on set. But on the day the defence was due to call their first witness, he abruptly withdrew his claim, citing mental health concerns and the stress placed on his family. He had his day giving evidence in court— and the media had reported his evidence—but the women would not have theirs. He claimed that discontinuing the case would 'finally bring to an end the four years we have endured since the publications were first made' and highlighted the fact he had been acquitted in the criminal case. For withdrawing, McLachlan will have to pay the legal costs of the defendants, which were reportedly $1.5 to $2 million.

But what about the distress his defamation claim had put the women through? Christie Whelan Browne, who was the only woman he sued alongside the media organisations, published a statement. In it, she explained that she and a group of women had initially tried to raise their concerns about McLachlan's conduct with the production company of *The Rocky Horror Show* because they wanted to protect the women due to perform in the next production. The production company refused to investigate and, she says, threatened to sue them for defamation. She emphasised that she and the other women only spoke out to the media to protect other women. The fact that they did resulted in the authorities deciding there was sufficient evidence to prosecute him. But then she was 'singled out and sued for defamation', by McLachlan. She describes how her 'name was dragged through the mud', and her character and behaviour, 'called into question'. Whelan said, 'I had thought this kind of shaming was a thing of the past, but I was wrong':

> The past four and a half years have significantly traumatised me and the other brave women who spoke up at that time and afterwards. I have received multiple threats and constant abuse and it continues to this day . . . I have lost my feeling of safety in the world, knowing someone wanted so badly to damage me for speaking the truth.

Whelan says she hopes that the fact that she fought and McLachlan ultimately withdrew his case will be 'a reminder that women will stand up for themselves and each other, even when threatened by those more powerful'. But how many women can afford to fight a defamation case for four years and through to trial? And how many women have to come forward before a powerful and wealthy man will withdraw his case? Or choose not to sue in the first place?

Suing friends, family, activists and other third parties

In the third scenario, if a third party speaks on behalf of the woman or in support of her, he might bring an action against them in defamation too. If they can't fight it for financial or other reasons and have to settle, he will claim that her friends and supporters don't support her or can't prove the allegations. Again, she has no agency over the action. She will not be able to decide whether to fight or to settle. We have seen women's friends, supporters, commentators, activists and those working to prevent gender-based violence sued and ultimately silenced from speaking about the matter and supporting her. Sometimes action has been taken or threatened against people who were simply expressing their opinion online about allegations on the public record. For example, David de Freitas, the father of a young woman who tragically took her own life after a private prosecution for making a false rape claim was brought against her, was sued for defamation in England by the man she had reported to the police. In Canada, a group of women are being sued for speaking in support of their friend, who made claims of sexual assault and rape against her professor. These types of legal threats and actions chill discussion and reduce the public space in which people can talk about gender-based violence and call for accountability or changes in the laws or processes.

Her truth on trial

It is a fundamental aspect of her right to free speech that she is protected for speaking the truth. But what happens when her truth goes on trial?

Many women have asked us: 'But he can't sue me for defamation if it's true, can he?' The short answer is yes: he can still bring an action, and it will be a matter of proving it at trial. There are many famous examples of wealthy and powerful men—from Oscar Wilde to Lord Jeffrey Archer—who have sued for defamation, at great expense, despite the allegation being true. In Archer's case, he sued and won his defamation case against a newspaper in 1987 by lying about his relationship with a sex worker, Monica Coghlan. Coghlan gave evidence at trial and told the jury the truth: Archer was lying. But the jury preferred the testimony of the peer and his wife over Coghlan's evidence (which is perhaps not surprising given that, in his directions to the jury, the judge famously described Lady Archer's 'elegance', 'radiance' and 'fragrance', giving credence to her claim about their 'full married life' and its implication that her husband would have no need to turn to Coghlan). He was awarded £500,000 in damages. But the truth would later out, and Archer went to prison for perjury in 2001, and had to repay the newspaper. Sadly, Coghlan struggled to work after the verdict and didn't live to see her vindication: she died in a car accident before Archer was convicted. The English Collective of Prostitutes wrote to *The Guardian* at the time, complaining about the discrimination and victimisation she and her family faced in the earlier defamation trial, the associated media coverage and the years since, asking, 'how will Ms Coghlan's son be compensated for the unjust slander of his mother?'

The point is that women, journalists and media organisations need to be prepared to prove her truth at trial. This means proving in court—to the civil standard of proof, on the balance of probabilities—that their allegation is true. This is different to the criminal standard of proof. For example, if she accused him of rape, a prosecutor would have to prove 'beyond a reasonable doubt' that he had raped her. For this reason, it should be easier in a defamation claim to prove that what she said was true. It is a risk that men take when they sue in civil courts—and may explain why men like McLachlan choose not to pursue defamation cases on this lower standard of proof, especially after being acquitted by the criminal courts.

Different jurisdictions have different rules about how the truth is to be judged. In the United Kingdom and Australia, the burden falls on the defendant. An allegation about gender-based violence will be presumed to be defamatory, and the person who made that allegation—or the journalist who reported it—must prove that it is what happened. If her allegation is one of serious criminality (such as rape, sexual assault or domestic violence), then she is required to have even stronger evidence if she is to succeed with a truth defence.

In the United States, however, the burden is reversed: the burden of proof falls on the person bringing the defamation claim. This reversal of the burden of proof is considered an essential element of the stronger free speech protections that are said to exist in the United States under the First Amendment to the Constitution. As a result, scholars and lawyers agree that US law better protects free speech—and her speech.

As in criminal cases, it is often challenging to prove allegations of sexual assault or domestic violence. More often than not, the offending has occurred in private, and so it comes down to the credibility of the witnesses: will a judge or jury believe her or believe him? Much has been written about the gendered bias in criminal prosecutions of sexual crimes, and how it undermines justice for women. For this reason, many countries have adopted rape shield laws, jury directions, and judicial guides and bench books to guard against gendered bias and to warn juries to ignore myths about gender-based violence and how victims 'should' behave. As our colleague Harriet Johnson writes in *Enough*, 'This has a significant impact in shifting the emphasis of the defence in such cases: if a barrister knows that, after her closing speech, the judge will tell the jury to disregard stereotypes about rape, she is unlikely to rely on stereotypes about rape in her speech.' But in defamation jury trials about sexual and domestic violence, there are no such protections: there is no requirement to give jury directions about harmful myths and no rule to prohibit cross-examining women about their sexual history. Evidence about sexual history should, of course, be considered irrelevant and inadmissible—but that doesn't stop lawyers trying to raise it (see discussion of the Depp case in Chapter 7).

When a woman's truth goes on trial, she also comes up against the problem of what is known as 'testimonial injustice'. When she speaks about gendered violence or sexual assault, her word is often not enough. A lot of the time, without corroborating evidence, she will not be believed (and sometimes even with it). In criminal cases, this may mean there is 'not enough evidence' for the state to prosecute. In defamation proceedings, it can mean a woman's testimony is not sufficient to establish the truth of her allegations.

One of the earliest feminist interventions in law was to try to remove the requirement for corroborating evidence for sexual assault and rape allegations. As we explained in Chapter 1, many common law countries had rules requiring corroboration evidence in sexual violence cases and judges would warn the jurors that it was dangerous to believe uncorroborated evidence (that is, it was dangerous to believe the woman's testimony alone). This was rooted in the idea that the testimonies of women and children were inherently unreliable. Yet in cases of gender-based violence, there may be nothing other than a woman's testimony—because it so often happens behind closed doors, enveloped in shame and secrecy. Many countries have since abolished the requirement for corroboration evidence, as we explained earlier, having appreciated that presuming all women to be unreliable witnesses is discriminatory. But some countries still require corroboration evidence.

The International Commission of Jurists has emphasised that this requirement is underpinned 'by the gender stereotype that women fabricate allegations of rape and sexual assault' and that they make allegations of rapes when they want to cause harm or seek revenge. The ICJ has produced evidence and data that the percentage of women who fabricate complaints is in fact very low and that 'it is increasingly accepted and understood that in fact allegations of sexual assault are not easy to make'.

The ICJ notes too that there is no legitimate reason for the application of a different approach to the testimony of survivors of sexual violence to those of other crimes.

Even where the corroboration requirement has been removed, women and girls often find that they are considered unreliable witnesses. According to feminist philosopher Kate Manne, judges treat women and non-white men less favourably, due to unconscious bias, and find 'their testimony suspect or their arguments unpersuasive'. This explains why men are often granted testimonial priority in 'he said, she said' situations. Judges or juries uphold his point of view and thus uphold the patriarchal order; women's testimony is found to be suspect, or they are told there is no 'evidence' when they make allegations.

As Rebecca Solnit has put it in her book *Men Explain Things to Me*, women are not considered to be reliable witnesses in relation to their own lives.

The testimonial injustice identified by Manne is a particular concern in defamation cases where women—or the newspapers and journalists reporting their stories—rely on a truth or justification defence. This has been starkly exemplified in Johnny Depp's defamation trial against Amber Heard in the US, as we shall discuss in more detail in the next chapter, and in many other defamation cases around the world. How much corroborating evidence do women need before they will be believed? How many women must make allegations for a truth defence to succeed?

These are questions that were asked after the decision in the *Rush* case in Australia. The trial was conducted under intense public and media scrutiny. Thanks to their own sensational reporting, *The Daily Telegraph* had a tall task: to prove the meaning of their articles—that Rush had committed sexual assault, had been a sexual predator and pervert, and that his conduct was such that he would never work at the STC again. The judge, Justice Wigney, came to the (correct) conclusion that the newspaper's reporting was 'reckless'—which was no fault of Norvill. But given the newspaper had pleaded truth as its defence, it was Norvill who was on trial. Norvill was the key witness and took to the stand to defend her initial reports made to STC.

But after Norvill's allegations were made public, she was supported by fellow crew members, who told *The Daily Telegraph* they believed her. And there was soon another twist: actor Yael Stone came forward with her own allegations about Rush involving sexually inappropriate behaviour during a different production at Belvoir St Theatre. Stone's decision to go public was widely praised.

Neither Stone nor Norvill had wanted to be caught up in a defamation trial. But both ended up offering their evidence. Stone decided to take to the stand in support of Norvill, but only came forward late in the trial. For this reason, the judge refused to let her evidence in, saying it would prejudice Rush despite the newspaper's arguments about the fact her evidence would help prove their case. So it would only be Norvill's allegations heard at trial: it was her word against Rush. Who would the judge prefer in the battle of credibility—and why?

In reaching his judgment, Justice Wigney acknowledged the difficulties women face giving evidence about sexual harassment because of stress and trauma they have faced. He also recognised that 'the absence of corroboration' is 'a common feature of cases involving sexual harassment'. But he nevertheless came to a decision about Norvill's credibility that has caused concern: he found that Norvill's account was 'exaggerated and unreliable'. The judge raised concern about Norvill's delayed report of some details, because she had 'remembered things that [she] hadn't before', as she thought more and more about the allegations. He thought it significant that Norvill had—after alleged incidents—caught an Uber with Rush and gone to dinner and a show with him, his daughter and another man. Surely, if he had done what she said he had (and she was a 'real victim'), she wouldn't socialise with him afterwards in groups or at industry events? Or so it goes—if you don't understand power dynamics in the workplace and in her industry. The judge also cited the fact that she had made positive statements about Rush during publicity interviews to promote the *King Lear* production. Surely, if it was true (and she was a 'real victim'), she wouldn't say anything positive about him in the press? The newspaper rightly pointed out it was 'fanciful' to expect her 'to sit silently or give a neutral or guarded answer' about Rush in promotional media interviews, especially given the fact it was her job to promote the show and be positive about her co-star to bring people to the show. Had the judge assessed her evidence by unrealistic or mythical standards of victimhood? The judge found in favour of Rush, awarding him $2.9 million in damages and an injunction.

The judgment received widespread criticism and the hashtag #IbelieveEJ flooded social media. Journalist Judith Ireland noted 'gendered discomfort about the way Norvill was treated as a witness'. *The Daily Telegraph* appealed, arguing the judge had demonstrated apprehended bias, including his treatment of Norvill as a witness and in his refusal to hear Stone's evidence. The judge had privileged Rush's desire for quick 'vindication' of his reputation over allowing the newspaper the opportunity to defend free speech with evidence that could have proved the truth of their case. But the appeal was unsuccessful.

The damage was already done. The judgment was said to change the game for Australian defamation law—and for all the women who watched how Norvill was treated in the case and in the media. What might have been a validating moment for survivors of abuse across Australia became just the opposite. The message was clear: we will not believe you. And your word alone is not enough.

After the decision, journalist Jenna Price raised concern about the worrying trend in defamation cases in Australia where it appeared one woman's evidence was not enough. She wrote, 'as one defamation lawyer joked today, you need three witnesses and a person of impeccable gender,' adding wryly, '[e]xcept that wasn't a joke'. Would the judge's conclusion have been different had he heard Stone's evidence too?

In Japan, Shiori Ito (see Chapter 2) went to great lengths to get corroborating evidence of her rape claim. She went to the hotel and got video footage of Mr Yamaguchi carrying her into the hotel before her alleged rape, because she was unable to walk. And she got testimony from a taxi driver to confirm her claims. And even when Shiori had this evidence, as she told us, the police investigation into what was happened to her was still closed. But her extraordinary determination and, in some ways, luck in being able to find this evidence—which later helped her win her defamation case—does not reflect what most survivors are able to do. Most women are unable to secure this kind of evidence, if it exists.

Without contemporaneous third-party accounts—and some-times even with them—judges and juries are deciding that women shouldn't be trusted, and are preferring his account. How many women does it take to come forward about a per-petrator before they are believed? How many witnesses does a survivor need to have before she is believed? What evidence does she need to back up her own words?

The failure to treat her testimony alone as enough, and the associated problem of testimonial injustice, denies women their truth and their right to free speech. This is—and should be treated as—a free speech issue: the failure to fairly consider the evidence denies her right to speak.

Her speech and the public interest

International human rights law—and her right to speak—requires that speaking out on a matter of public interest is a defence to any defamation claim.

Public interest is a defence in the law in England and Wales and now in Australia. In our experience, most women want to run truth defences in defamation cases because they want to defend their truth—and understandably so. But the public interest test is an important alternative defence. What it means is that journalists don't have to prove the truth of her allegations, but instead show that her allegations were credible, that adequate inquiries were made about the facts, that they reasonably believed that the publication of her allegations was in the public interest—and that they sought comment from him about her allegations before publication. Women's ability to speak out about gender-based violence should always be treated as a matter of public interest: it is an essential part of violence prevention and deterrence and is key to ending violence against women.

International human rights courts have recognised this. Let's look at the case of Neva Tölle in Croatia, the director of a domestic abuse shelter who faced a defamation and insult claim in the Zagreb courts. After a woman and her daughter fled their home and sought housing in her shelter, stating that they had faced domestic violence, the man then accused Ms Tölle of kidnapping his daughter. Tölle went on the radio to defend herself and the shelter, stating that she had not kidnapped the daughter—the mother and daughter had escaped and sought protection from an abuser. He then brought a private criminal prosecution against Tölle on charges of defamation and insult in relation to the allegation that he had abused his wife. The Croatian courts found Tölle guilty on the basis that she had tarnished his honour and reputation by alleging that he had abused his wife—privileging his right to good reputation over her right to free speech.

It took seventeen years for Tölle to fight her case, and ultimately the European Court of Human Rights found that the Croatian courts had got the balance wrong. It decided that it was wrong for the Croatian courts to have found that Tölle had defamed him simply because the father 'had never been convicted of domestic violence', making clear that speech about domestic violence is not dependent on him being convicted by a court.

The European court, which includes judges from all Council of Europe countries, also emphasised that there is little scope to limit free speech rights 'on questions of public interest'—which includes violence against women—even where his right to reputation is involved. The court concluded that 'the discussion in the present case—about violence against women and domestic violence—was clearly one of important public interest and the subject of a social debate, both at the material time and today'. Giving Tölle a criminal conviction for speaking on the radio and defending herself 'amounted to a sort of censorship' that might have discouraged the shelter from promoting its statutory aims in the future. His right to reputation had been improperly valued over her right to speak out about violence. The human rights court made clear that requiring a conviction for domestic violence to defend her speech was simply unrealistic and too much to ask.

The Tölle case is a landmark decision because it confirms that speaking out about gender-based violence and domestic violence is a matter of public interest.

The availability of the public interest test in relation to speech about sexual violence was first confirmed in the United Kingdom in *Economou v. De Freitas*. This was a libel case brought against the father of Eleanor De Freitas, a young woman who had

reported Economou to the police for rape and was later prosecuted for making a false report but committed suicide before
her trial. In the context of the inquest into her death, her father
spoke out in the media about the state's decision to prosecute
her. The father had sought to have the scope of the inquest into
the cause of her death expanded to examine the role of the state
prosecutors in taking over the private prosecution that had been
initiated by Economou. Mr De Freitas said:

> Eleanor was a vulnerable young woman, diagnosed with
> bipolar, who made a complaint of rape as a result of which
> she herself became the subject of legal proceedings. This was
> despite the fact the police did not believe there to be a case
> against her ... I feel that the system of fairness in this country
> has let me down terribly, and something needs to be done so
> that this can never happen again.

De Freitas did not name Economou as the alleged rapist, but
Economou was still able to bring the libel claim. He sued
De Freitas, claiming his comments were defamatory because
they implied that there was evidence that Economou was
guilty of rape. But the court ruled that De Freitas's speech
was protected by the public interest defence.

In considering the public interest, the court emphasised
the risk that women will be too afraid to come forward if they
risk facing prosecution for making false claims. In balancing
Economou's right to reputation against the public interest in
De Freitas's speech, and the need to ensure that women can
come forward to report their abuse, the court decided that the
balance was in favour of De Freitas being able to speak. The
judge reasoned:

Rape is a very serious crime, and deplored by society. Hence, as Mr Economou has emphasised, the making of a false allegation of rape can have very serious implications for the person accused. There is a public interest in deterring and punishing those who make accusations of crime against others which they know to be false. But to prosecute an accuser who has made a true report of crime would be a serious mistake. Especially so if the crime reported is as grave as rape, a crime usually carried out in private, without witnesses. There is a strong public interest in ensuring that the victims of rape come forward. There has, notoriously, been concern for many years that levels of reporting are low. There are no doubt many reasons for that. But there is a real and obvious risk that rape victims may be deterred from coming forward for fear that, by reporting, they will expose themselves to a risk of prosecution for perverting the course of justice.

This tragic case established that the public interest defence did protect Eleanor's father, with the court agreeing that it is in the public interest to speak about prosecutorial decisions in false reporting cases because of the impact it might have on other women coming forward to the police.

In another case in the United Kingdom, the courts have recognised that reporting about domestic violence and discrimination against women are matters of public interest to which the public interest defence will apply. This was in the case we first mentioned in Chapter 1, where Afsana Lachaux's ex-husband, Bruno, sued *The Independent* and *The Evening Standard* for publishing stories about Afsana's allegations of domestic abuse. The newspapers had reported how Afsana sought refuge with her son in a women's shelter in the UAE after she said she had suffered domestic abuse and was then prosecuted for kidnapping her son for taking him with her to the shelter. She lost custody of her son after divorce proceedings brought by Mr Lachaux in the UAE, under laws which discriminate against women. Afsana returned home to the UK to campaign to get custody back and sought the help of Southall Black Sisters. She told us that she and her family had also been threatened with defamation, but that her ex-husband had only sued the media. Lawyers for the newspapers reached out to Afsana who was—like Eryn Jean Norvill—willing to help the newspaper defend her truth and provided them with evidence to support her claims. The media defended the case arguing truth and public interest.

But while the defamation case wound its way through the courts, the decision of the family court was handed down. In 2017, a British judge rejected Afsana's allegations of abuse—in a decision which has been criticised as being based on misconceptions about domestic abuse (see Chapter 1). For Afsana, the family court decision was incredibly traumatic and a huge blow to her efforts to regain custody of her son. But the ruling also meant the media decided to withdraw their defence of truth. For Afsana, this too was difficult. But the decision was not hers to make. However, she spoke in glowing terms of the sensitivity and respect she was shown by David Price KC, who defended the media in the case, who had to break this news to her and who helped her understand why the battleground was shifting to the public interest in reporting her story.

The judge agreed that publishing information that a woman had been subjected to domestic violence by her husband, was mistreated by the UAE authorities and faced an unfair trial over the alleged kidnap of her son, were all matters of public interest. But the media still lost the case. The problem wasn't with the subject matter, but with the journalism. The journalists themselves could not say they considered the public interest in reporting Afsana's story before publication (one couldn't even remember why he wrote the article) and they had not taken steps to contact Afsana and verify her allegations, nor had they sought comment from Mr Lachaux before publication. Mr Lachaux was awarded £160,000 in compensation and an injunction to prevent repetition of the allegations.

The *Lachaux* case shows that reporting on gender-based violence is a matter of public interest. But it is also a warning to journalists about complying with responsible journalistic practices if they want to benefit from the defence. In Afsana's case in the United Kingdom, as with Eryn Jean Norvill in Australia, the journalists failed to do so, leaving lasting consequences for both women. Even if *The Daily Telegraph* had been able to defend the *Rush* case using the new public interest defence introduced in 2021 in parts of Australia (which was designed to reflect the same public interest test applied in *Lachaux*), they would likely not have succeeded. *The Daily Telegraph* would not have benefited from the defence because it had failed to properly verify the allegations with Norvill and because its reporting was sensational. Both cases have been cited as chilling the media from reporting on stories on violence against women, but they are, in fact, both lessons about how *not* to report these stories. Journalists can and should still report stories about gender-based violence, and the public interest test provides important protection for this reporting. But journalists must always have in mind that when you run a truth defence, the victim goes on trial; when you run a public interest defence, your journalism goes on trial.

What does your right mean if you can't afford to defend it?

Defamation law is complex: our brief explanation of the potential defences here is oversimplified and incomplete. To bring or defend a claim effectively, you need specialist defamation counsel, and they do not come cheap. Geoffrey Rush's case is reported to have cost around $6 million in legal fees, which News Corp was liable to pay after losing the case. How many media organisations, let alone individual women, can afford those kinds of costs? Nicola Stocker explained that she was fortunate to have defence counsel acting on a 'no win, no fee' agreement, but even the disbursements to run the case put her under financial strain and stress. If she hadn't won in the Supreme Court, she would have been liable to pay her ex-husband £300,000 in costs. What does the right to free speech mean if you cannot afford to defend it?

There is no legal aid for defamation cases. Many have run crowd-funded campaigns to raise funds from concerned members of the public to help with the cost of defending their free speech. For example, we explained earlier in this chapter that this was how British comedian Louise Reay raised funds to defend the defamation case brought by her ex-husband. In Australia, journalist Nina Funnell, founder of the #LetHerSpeak campaign with Grace Tame, created a GoFundMe campaign called 'Enough' to support Australian academic Professor Gemma Carey, and any other women who received defamation threat letters from powerful men in politics and the media: Christian Porter, Andrew Laming and Peter van Onselen. The defamation threat letters came from the same firm—Rebekah Giles' firm—but related to different tweets and comments that Professor Carey had made about each of the men. In response to the defamation threats, Professor Carey apologised to each of them. But the campaign wasn't just about Professor Carey: it followed a raft of defamation threats that had been made against journalists, commentators and activists tweeting or commenting about allegations of gender-based violence. The campaign, which was also supported by Australian of the Year Grace Tame, raised $250,000—far more than the original target of $10,000. Funnell told *The Daily Mail*:

> It just snowballed. It became very clear very quickly that this issue had hit a nerve. We want it to go to help as many people as possible but also we want to highlight the public's frustration with defamation laws and the clear impetus for reform . . . Clearly Australians feel passionately about this issue.

These campaigns must be carefully articulated to avoid his lawyers being able to claim you are aggravating the damage to his reputation by spreading the defamation further through the dissemination of your fundraising campaign. For example, Funnell's campaign page did not repeat the allegations that the men had threatened to sue over.

Some crowd-funding campaigns have been anonymised. For example, in 2017, a group of women in the United Kingdom started a crowd-funding campaign called 'Solidarity Not Silence' after they were sued for defamation by 'a well-known musician' over their 'statements concerning his mistreatment of women'. They said they were his former partners and feminist musicians—and raised almost £60,000 for their defence. In 2021 the fundraising website reported:

We're happy to announce that legal proceedings against members of Solidarity Not Silence have settled on mutually acceptable terms **without any admissions of liability**. We are enormously grateful for all of your support over the last four and a half years—<u>without it, we would never have been able to reach this outcome</u>. All of the money raised has been spent on our legal representation up to this point. [Emphasis in original]

For journalists wanting to report these stories, it's not just the cost risk if you are later sued. As Pia Sarma explained, getting a story wrong and apologising can still cost £250,000 without going to trial. But to investigate the stories to a standard that will pass muster—to ensure you can win on a truth or public interest case in court—takes time and resources that many media organisations no longer have. With more and more cuts to investigative journalism and their legal budgets, who can afford to pursue these stories?

Both plaintiff and defendant counsel have complained about the cost of bringing and defending defamation proceedings. For example, in the United Kingdom, two publishers have filed a complaint to the European Court of Human Rights after having to spend £578,000 to defend their decision to publish on truth and public interest defences. In their complaint, they assert:

The costs regime connected to the UK's system of defamation laws, rules and procedures, does not enable journalists and other media actors to contribute to public debate effectively and without fear, and discriminates against all but the wealthiest . . . The regime discourages the participation of the press in debates about matters of legitimate public concern . . . The sums involved are life-changing for any individual save for the wealthiest . . . Small publishers (and many other defendants) who are unjustly threatened with legal proceedings face the stark choice between offering an undeserved settlement and financial ruin.

The complaint, filed in 2021, is pending. As we pointed out earlier in this chapter, international human rights law requires states to decriminalise defamation because criminal penalties are considered a disproportionate interference with the right to free speech. But, as a media law expert colleague of ours has said, the costs involved in civil defamation claims are so huge that 'many would prefer to be prosecuted and cop a nominal criminal fine than lose their home'. Governments concerned with protecting free speech and the ability of women to speak out about their abuse must review costs regimes and their impact on her ability to speak.

Defamation today

The law of defamation has been weaponised by rich and powerful men to silence women who might speak out against them. Women speaking out and journalists reporting their stories cannot afford to defend the cases—and their freedom of speech. This must be acknowledged and made right. Defamation trials about domestic and sexual abuse also suffer from the same problems that have plagued criminal trials: difficulty proving allegations in court, compounded by persistent myths and prejudice that mean women are not believed and are denied justice.

In the next chapter, we explore how these issues played out in two of the most high-profile defamation trials in recent history: Johnny Depp's defamation claims in the United Kingdom and the United States about Amber Heard's allegations of domestic abuse. Jen will give her perspective on the two trials, which involved the same facts, but different defendants, in different jurisdictions, offering an unprecedented comparative perspective of what happens when a woman's truth goes on trial.

Chapter 7

HER TRUTH ON TRIAL, TWICE

'LIAR!'

This word was shouted, over and over, as our car pulled into the side entrance of the Royal Courts of Justice in London. The crowd of paparazzi and Depp fans pushed up against the car, jostling for a glimpse of Amber through the car window. It was the opening morning of the trial in *John Christopher Depp II v. News Group Newspapers Ltd*, billed by the tabloids as 'the libel trial of the century'. Johnny Depp was suing *The Sun* for defamation for calling him a wife-beater: he claimed his ex-wife Amber Heard had lied about the domestic violence she said she had suffered during their relationship.

We could hear them before we could see them. Bellowing, yelling, booing. Among the angry crowd were grown men dressed up as Johnny Depp—or at least as Jack Sparrow and Edward Scissorhands—pushing up against the car and milling about in the crowd.

'Amber, you lie!' a man screamed. His face pressed up against the window. Angry fists were banging on our car window. I flinched. 'You lie, you lie!'

These men weren't Johnny Depp. Some had dressed like him, but all of them had taken up his cause as if it were their own. They held up hand-drawn placards:

'Men too'

'Gold-digger'

'Amber LIES'

'Amber the Abuser'

I had worked on cases that had drawn a crowd before, but I had never seen anything like this. Celebrity fandom and misogyny converged. I reached out to squeeze Amber's hand. In some ways, she had seen it before. She was heckled outside court in 2016, when she first got a domestic violence restraining order against Depp, and had been attacked ever since: in the media, in Depp's PR statements and in the avalanche of social media trolling that followed. But it was shocking—for her and for me—to see it play out in person.

I was grateful to the newspaper and the court for making arrangements to allow us to enter through the judge's security entrance. We needed it. Amber had to have a personal security guard for the duration of the trial. On some days, police escorted us in and out of the court gates. Depp walked through the court's front door trailed by his usual security team, with women pressed against the security barriers handing him flowers, hoping for an autograph. His fans would shout their support and wave their 'Justice for Johnny' signs.

By the first day of the trial in London, it had been four years since Amber got the restraining order from a Californian judge. In 2018, when Depp had sued *The Sun* in the United Kingdom over an article that had called him a 'wife-beater', she reached out to me to advise her. In 2019 he sued Amber personally in the United States over an opinion piece she had written about the treatment of survivors. In the UK case he was claiming over £300,000 in damages and an injunction to prevent *The Sun* from ever reporting he was a 'wife-beater' again, which would also stop other media reporting it too. In the United States, he was claiming US$50 million in damages, more than enough to bankrupt Amber. Her legal costs were crippling, even for a Hollywood actor.

But our immediate concern on this day was getting her safely into court, where she was about to see Depp for the first time since their divorce. She was also about to be cross-examined about what she describes as the most traumatic experiences of her life, and they would then be splashed across front pages and TV screens around the world. As the intimidatory banging, shouting and abuse at our car windows continued, Amber squeezed my hand back to let me know she was okay. Our security detail looked alert, while gently telling us to remain calm: they would get us into the court as quickly as possible.

As we got out of the car and entered through the court's security gates, the angry crowd of mostly men and middle-aged women gathered at the fence, continuing to scream abuse at Amber. Their aggression was intense. Why did they feel the need to come out and show their support for Depp by shouting horrific abuse at Amber? Why did they feel so strongly about a case involving celebrities they had never met? How had Depp— and this case—somehow become, for them, an emblem?

In Johnny Depp, it was as if they saw the victim of a cancel culture supposedly obsessed with bringing white masculinity down. He was not just someone suing in costly defamation proceedings with a huge legal team and a PR campaign of the kind very few people can afford. He had somehow become an everyman, unfairly accused and subject to the same 'witch-hunt' that had seen the demise of every guy who had made an off-colour office joke since MeToo. Every man who had been sacked for coming onto the junior women at work or making 'now inappropriate' comments. They saw the jobs they had not been offered because of quotas. They saw their own ex-wives and custody battles, and the child support they had been forced to pay. Maybe they sympathised with Depp when they learned he had sent a message to Elton John calling his ex-wife and mother of his children, Vanessa Paradis, 'an extortionist French c***'. Maybe they agreed with his texts calling women sluts and whores and wishing ruin and death on Amber, his ex. They saw all of this in Johnny Depp—to them he was not an out-of-touch celebrity, but an anti-establishment hero, the kind he so convincingly played in movies.

Depp supporters found each other online, in Reddit forums and comment threads on YouTube, the same kind of algorithmic echo chambers in which alt-right culture thrives. Hashtags like #MenToo, #JusticeforJohnny and #AmberHeardIsaLiar flooded the internet, and were directed at Amber, at me as her lawyer, and at any film, any brand, any organisation or any individual associated with her. They were represented in the angry, disaffected men protesting outside court. Their sentiment was shared by 'Fathers for Justice', who drove by the court and around London with a giant mobile billboard bearing an image of Amber and Depp and the words 'Ditch the Witch'.

These online attacks and in-person protests weren't spontaneous: they were often reflecting and repeating the misogynistic language from Depp's own words; they echoed his text messages, made public as evidence in court, and the harmful myth-filled public messaging that had been coming from Depp's lawyer, Adam Waldman. Depp had sent texts calling Amber 'a scumbag, gold-digging cunt', a whore and a witch; he joked about wanting to drown and burn her—and 'fuck her burnt corpse to make sure she's dead'. Waldman ran a relentless PR campaign: he claimed it was Amber who was 'a violent abuser' and who had 'repeatedly violently attacked and severely injured' Depp. He claimed she had 'faked abuse allegations' against Depp, motivated by money, that she was a gold-digger who had even 'painted on [her own] 'bruises' to be able to 'masquerade as victim'. Waldman's constant refrain was that Amber was not a 'real victim'. According to him, she had 'abused the trust and experiences of real survivors for her own reputational gain' and 'defraud[ed] her abused hoax victim Mr. Depp, the #metoo movement . . . and other real abuse victims worldwide'. 'Does the #metoo movement care about male victims too?' Waldman asked. His narrative dominated online spaces and was amplified by parts of the media.

Amber had not spoken in public about the violence she said she suffered during her relationship with Depp, nor did she ever want to. Before Depp's defamation claim, Amber had only told a judge in California enough detail about the violence to obtain a restraining order back in 2016. Once she got the restraining order, she had no interest in talking about it again, and she had signed an NDA as part of their divorce that prevented her from doing so. When Depp sued *The Sun*, Amber had not given a single media interview about the violence she said she had suffered during their relationship. Depp sued over an opinion piece by journalist Dan Wootton, which *The Sun* had published without speaking to her and without seeking her comment. But the newspaper was going to defend the case on truth, so her truth was going on trial. Depp's defamation claim meant she would give evidence before a British judge to defend her truth, not because she wanted to but because he decided to sue and claim that she had lied.

The stage was set: he was the powerful, much-loved movie star calling her a liar. She was the younger woman, who left him, got a restraining order and was trying to get on with her career. She said he was violent, he vehemently denied it—so it would be left to the judge. Who was to be believed? The judge had to decide: had *The Sun* published things about Depp that were true? And, by extension, had Amber told the truth about his domestic violence?

Amber and I had spent two years gathering evidence to corroborate her allegations: photos, text messages, medical records, witness evidence. She had, in my view, far more evidence than most victims of domestic abuse. We worked together with the lawyers for the newspaper he sued to help build their defence. I sat with Amber and her sister through sixteen days of evidence in London. I watched on as she and Depp were cross-examined over fourteen separate incidents of violence, including sexual violence, which was heard in closed court to protect what was left of her privacy. As I sat in court, I watched as Depp's defence used all the old, gendered tropes: she lied, she nagged him, she picked fights, she stood up to him, she was not a 'real victim'. If it was true, why didn't you leave him? If it was true, why didn't you go to the police? Her answers were constant: I loved him. I wanted him to get sober. I thought if I could just help him get sober, the 'monster' would go away and the violence would stop. I was trying to help him to get better. I didn't want the media or anyone else to know what he'd done.

Everything about the UK trial—from the crowd outside court to the way it was covered in parts of the media and how it was argued in the courtroom—left me feeling depressed about how far we still have to go as a society when it comes to the treatment of women who have made allegations of gender-based violence.

As the trial progressed, friends and colleagues called me to check in. They were observing from afar, trying to understand the trial through media reports and discussion online. 'It doesn't seem to be going well for her,' was their almost uniform comment. It was striking to me because, with the benefit of being in the courtroom and having a close understanding of the evidence, the opposite was true: it was obvious to me that it was going well for Amber and for the newspaper. Where was the disjunct coming from? How was it that what I was seeing inside court was not being reflected in public understanding?

At the conclusion of the trial, Amber gave her one and only public statement about the case on the steps of the Royal Courts of Justice, amid boos and taunts from the Depp fans jostling behind the media's cameras. She said this:

> I travelled to the UK to testify in these proceedings as a witness to assist the Court. After obtaining a restraining order in 2016 and finalising our divorce, I wanted to move on with my life. I did not file this lawsuit and, despite its significance, I would prefer not to have been in court. It has been incredibly painful to relive the break-up of my relationship, have my motives and my truth questioned, and the most traumatic details of my life with Johnny shared in court and broadcast around the world. I stand by my testimony in court and I now place my faith in British justice.

Four months later, the judgment arrived in my inbox. I had been sitting at home, anxiously waiting for it to arrive. Because

Amber was a witness, and not a party, we had not had advance notice of the outcome (Depp and the newspaper had, but they were not allowed to tell us). When it popped up, I quickly scrolled through the 129-page judgment to understand the judge's findings on incident after incident of alleged violence. Amber's faith in British justice had not been misplaced: Mr Justice Nicol found that what *The Sun* had published was substantially true. With his decision, the judge gave Amber the message she had long deserved: I believe you. But it was much more than that: the judgment set out, in meticulous detail the witness evidence, issues of witness credibility and corroborating evidence to explain why the judge could reach the conclusion that twelve of the fourteen incidents of violence in dispute, including an incident of sexual violence, were proven to the civil standard of proof. I immediately called Amber to give her the good news: she had been vindicated. Messages of congratulations flooded in from friends, colleagues and journalists who had been covering the case.

Depp had lost his case. *The Sun* ran a triumphant headline and front page: 'On behalf of all domestic abuse survivors we can now confirm that HE IS A WIFE-BEATER.' His lawyers protested what they called 'a perverse and bewildering' decision, but his appeal was rejected.

The outcome was hailed by domestic violence charities, after 'a trial which exemplified tactics used to silence and discredit victims'. Lisa King of Refuge, the United Kingdom's largest specialist domestic violence service, said the ruling was 'a very powerful message . . . power, fame and resources cannot be used to silence women'. Harriet Wistrich from the Centre for Women's Justice said the decision 'will serve as a warning to men who think they can silence those who speak out about their abuse'. All of the charities highlighted the problem that had prompted us to want to write this book long before the Depp case came across my desk: defamation laws are being used to silence women.

It was a big win—for Amber, for the newspaper, and for all women—setting a precedent that would deter the powerful from suing to silence.

The judgment had restored my faith about the progress that had been made in how women are treated in the courts, if not in the media and online. 'Surely, no one could doubt her now?' I thought to myself. But how wrong I was. Whatever had horrified me about the media coverage, online trolling and angry mob of Depp supporters during the UK trial was nothing compared to what was to come in the United States.

Two years later, on the same set of facts, the same outdated arguments were run again before a jury in Virginia. Only this time it worked. The jury found against Amber.

Two cases, two very different outcomes—which shows what can happen when her truth goes on trial. But how did it all come about?

The backdrop

In 2016, a story circulated. It was widely reported, but it didn't set the world alight—or spark a movement in Hollywood or anywhere else. Amber Heard had taken out a restraining order against her husband, and soon to be ex-husband, Johnny Depp.

'During the entirety of our relationship, Johnny Depp has been verbally and physically abusive to me,' said her witness statement to the court, a public document. But their divorce settlement contained an NDA, and a non-disparagement clause, and for a while neither of them spoke about the matter—or each other—again. All that could be said publicly after the divorce was contained in this joint statement: 'Our relationship was intensely passionate and at times volatile but always bound by love. Neither party has made false accusations for financial gain. There was never any intent of physical or emotional harm.'

I remember reading this carefully worded statement in the media, years before I met Amber. I was struck by its wording: it did not say there was no physical violence; it merely said that none was intended. And it included language that addressed any suggestion she had lied in order to extract a bigger divorce settlement. Amber's actions spoke even louder than those words: the amount of her divorce settlement was low by Californian standards—given Depp's wealth and earnings—and she pledged all of it to charity. These didn't seem to me to be the actions of someone out to ruin a man's reputation or get rich by making unfounded domestic violence claims. (The judge in the UK case would later agree, concluding that Amber's actions were not those 'one would expect of a gold-digger'.)

But the world moved on and the restraining order became a footnote in the glossy magazine timelines of their relationship and in their public profiles. Depp continued his career as a star leading man, including in J.K. Rowling's billion-dollar franchise films. The following year, when MeToo exposed Harvey Weinstein and the PR and legal machine that had protected him, Amber's allegations against Depp were not part of the conversation, nor did she seek to make them so. Having signed an NDA, she did not talk to the media. Again, these did not seem like the actions of a woman who made allegations for money or fame.

But tides had turned enough after MeToo that people started to question why Rowling had cast Depp in the role, and a discussion about the restraining order resurfaced (even though Amber was not able to and had not spoken about her allegations outside of court). In response to growing public criticism, Rowling put out a public statement defending her decision, saying she was 'genuinely happy' to cast Depp. That's how it came to be that Johnny Depp sued *The Sun*—for an article it published titled 'GONE POTTY: How can JK Rowling be "genuinely happy" casting Johnny Depp in the new Fantastic Beasts film after assault claim?'

In it, journalist Dan Wootton quoted actor Caitlin Dulany:

> 'We would like to see things change in this industry and not see people who have allegedly victimised women. It is not much of a change if you are seeing people rewarded with roles. Amber has been through a difficult time with him. But it seems like what happened hasn't really affected Johnny.'

What was striking about Depp's decision to sue *The Sun* was that the article wasn't the first to report on the claims of assault made against him, nor was it the first article to raise concerns about J.K. Rowling's decision to cast him.

Four months before the *Sun* article, a very similar opinion piece by Hadley Freeman had appeared in *The Guardian*, in December 2017, referring to Depp as a 'wife batterer'. Both articles referred to the restraining order and criticised Rowling's casting decision, pointing out that it did not sit easily with her public advocacy for women. But Depp chose to sue *The Sun*, not *The Guardian* or any of the other publications in the United States or elsewhere that had published stories about the abuse allegations.

For lawyers who understood media law, it came as no surprise that Depp chose to sue in London. Defamation law in the United Kingdom is notoriously pro-claimant—and, for this reason, has been described as 'the libel capital of the world'. As we explained in Chapter 6, by suing in the United Kingdom, the burden of proof fell on the newspaper to prove its claim about Depp's abuse. The actor and his lawyers chose *The Sun* as the defendant, a tabloid that would be unlikely to arouse the sympathy of much of the public, or of fellow celebrities or Hollywood executives. For those in the film industry, it was no coincidence that he chose to bring suit over this article, which focused on J.K. Rowling and her upcoming film franchise. And with concern for gender-based violence on the rise around the world after MeToo, an investment worth hundreds of millions of dollars was at stake.

In the lead-up to the trial in London, I asked a talent agent in Los Angeles why Amber was not receiving more support in a post-MeToo Hollywood. He replied, 'To be frank, no one wants to be on the wrong side of Depp's comeback.' It became clear to me that Amber was up against every film industry executive and agent who stood to make, or wanted to make, money from Depp.

Depp had chosen to sue *The Sun*. Amber had not been interviewed for the article or asked for comment. Wootton had based his opinion piece on the publicly available evidence that had been before the Californian judge who had granted the restraining order. Amber was not a party to these defamation proceedings, and had no control over how they were conducted. She was merely a witness, asked by *The Sun* to give evidence to help them prove she had not lied about the abuse she suffered in their relationship.

When Amber first called me about the case, I explained how she—like Eryn Jean Norvill in the Geoffrey Rush defamation case in Australia, and so many other women in cases like these—was in an invidious position. *The Sun* had published its piece without speaking to her since it was an opinion piece, but was pleading truth as its defence and relying on Amber's statement to the Californian court as proof. The burden of proof was on the newspaper, not on Depp, and he would turn up to court and say that she had lied to the Californian court. Amber did not want to have to get involved, but she wanted to defend her truth and was concerned about what would happen if she didn't. I explained to her that *The Sun* could at any time choose to settle for commercial reasons—and if it did, Depp would use the settlement to say she had lied, and that Rupert Murdoch's paper agreed with him or weren't prepared to defend it in court. If it went to trial, whatever he said about her in court would be reported around the world, without her side of the story being told. And if Depp won, she would be called a liar, and he would get an injunction preventing *The Sun* from repeating the claim that he was violent towards her, which would also deter others from repeating it.

In considering Amber's position, I always had in mind how Norvill was treated in the *Rush* trial in Australia. Norvill had been, like Amber, understandably reluctant to give evidence for a tabloid. She had only agreed to participate just weeks before trial, which meant the newspaper had not had the benefit of her assistance in preparing the case, and her initial witness statement had been prepared without consulting with the newspaper's lawyers, so it was not as comprehensive as it needed to be. As they would complain in their appeal, the judge made adverse findings about Norvill's credibility because of the deficiency in her witness statement. I did not want Amber to be put in that same position. If she wanted to give evidence, we needed to be prepared and we needed to work closely with the newspaper so they could win.

Faced with this prospect, Amber chose to give evidence. News Group Newspapers, their editor and their brilliant legal team were committed to fighting the matter—and free speech—all the way, and treated her with respect and sensitivity throughout.

After Depp filed the defamation claim, his PR campaign kicked into gear. It did not start well.

In July 2018, Depp gave an interview to *Rolling Stone* that resulted in a profile piece entitled 'The Trouble with Johnny Depp'. The article was later described as 'damning' and a 'PR disaster', outlining—among many problems—Depp's issues with drugs and alcohol, his financial woes, his failure to perform on set, and Amber's 'persuasive allegations of physical abuse'. It described Depp as 'an aging man-child', 'oblivious to any personal complicity in his current predicament'.

Crisis-management firm Hawthorn was brought in. Later, *GQ* would explain that Hawthorn acts for 'exceptionally wealthy clients [who] call if there's no one else to call'; its staff were 'the Harvey Keitels of this world: wolf men, fixers, public-image adjustment specialists'. The result was a new—fawning—profile in *GQ*, titled 'Johnny Depp Will Not Be Buried'. In it, Depp asserted that 'there's no truth' to Amber's allegations of domestic violence, and that 'the truth will come out in all of this and I will be standing on the right side of the roaring rapids'.

The *GQ* cover story epitomised the stereotypes, biases and assumptions we see in the media when reporting on gender-based violence. A *New Statesman* article issued a reminder to the men's magazine: '*GQ*: being accused of domestic abuse does not make you cool.' In her critique of the *GQ* profile,

Anna Leszkiewicz highlighted how 'Depp is glorified as a modern-day Odysseus or Perseus', noting *GQ*'s references to Odysseus's triumph over the Sirens, and how Depp had metaphorically 'looked into the Gorgon Medusa's eyes to see for himself life's savage reality'. Leszkiewicz sardonically pointed out the obvious reason why these particular myths were deemed to be relevant to Depp's story: each involve 'legendary tales of heroic men overcoming tempting, manipulative, or vengeful women'.

This was just a snapshot of the media messaging in the lead up to trial to paint Amber as a liar and abuser and Depp as the 'nice guy' victim. Celebrity friend after celebrity friend gave statements in support of Depp. He was a 'sweet', 'kind' friend and father, and a 'gentleman'. Javier Bardem, in a declaration for the US proceedings, even claimed that Amber's allegations were 'false facts' and 'lies', though it is unclear how he was in a position to attest to the truth or otherwise of what happened behind closed doors. His ex-wife Vanessa Paradis said it was not the 'true Johnny' she knew, repeating the exact same phrase as Bardem: the allegations were 'false facts'. Winona Ryder said in her statement that the allegations were 'impossible to believe', though neither she nor Paradis would appear in the London court to allow us to cross-examine them about what they had said in their statements about their relationship with Depp. (Depp's lawyers would later say in court that they were not needed, but it was later reported that Ryder had hired a former US prosecutor to block the use of her testimony in the UK trial.) But their statements were still used in the PR campaign to undermine Amber's credibility with the public: if he didn't do it to them, then he didn't do it to Amber—or so it goes.

Whatever was said about his character, there was nothing sweet or kind about Depp's PR campaign. His US attorney,

Waldman, speaking on Depp's behalf and at his behest, was aggressive. His regular missives repeated all the old tropes. To build his desired public narrative that Amber was the abuser, and to place pressure on *The Sun* to settle before trial, Waldman selectively leaked evidence to the media, in violation of a US court order, which would later result in the US judge kicking Waldman off the court record. Waldman later admitted to having leaked a heavily edited version of a recording of an argument Depp and Amber had about domestic violence in their relationship in which Amber admits to having hit him. (Her evidence was that she had acted in self-defence.)

This fed a public narrative that their relationship was one of 'mutual abuse', a harmful myth that has been rejected by domestic violence experts. They point out there is always a primary aggressor in an abusive relationship; the fact that a woman acts in self-defence should not be seized upon as evidence that she is the abusive partner. This didn't stop the term from being thrown around in the media before the UK trial (and later in the US proceedings). For example, Piers Morgan claimed that their relationship was 'a mutually abusive situation' and that the case 'diminishes people that go through real abuse' (again: Amber was not a 'real victim'). Morgan wasn't alone: Sharon Osbourne also opined that 'she gave him as good as she got'.

Meanwhile, a sea of online trolls targeted Amber, us as her lawyers, and the journalists reporting on the case. An online petition calling for her to be dropped from the *Aquaman* sequel attracted 400,000 signatures. After Amber appeared at an International Women's Day event for my chambers, my Doughty Street colleagues and I were flooded with what appeared to be bot-generated emails and tweets saying that we had been associating with a 'criminal' and an 'abuser'. It was sophisticated: it targeted everyone who had been pictured with Amber, tweeted about Amber or tweeted about being at the event—not just with tweets, but with emails addressed to their workplace. Colleague after colleague forwarded me the identical tweets and emails they had received. UN Women, who Amber had worked with, was also targeted, along with the brands Amber worked with. The message was clear: don't believe Amber, don't associate with her, don't defend her—and don't hire her.

Despite Amber's position as a witness, the UK defamation case was repeatedly mischaracterised in the media as a spat between Depp and Amber in which she had equal agency, even though she had been dragged into it as a third-party witness. For example, *The Times* ran a headline describing Depp's case against the newspaper as the 'Depp v Heard court duel'. Meanwhile, Piers Morgan raged on *Good Morning Britain* that Depp and Heard were 'spoiled brats' for subjecting Britain to a 'circus' during a pandemic. At the same time, Depp's team complained that because Amber was not a party, she didn't have the same disclosure obligations as he did. As was pointed out during the various pre-trial hearings about disclosure, and by the judge in his final judgment, Depp was well advised when he chose to sue the newspaper—and should have been aware of all the consequences that would flow from that decision.

The UK case was mired by Depp's repeated failures to disclose relevant evidence—in fact, Depp's entire case was nearly struck out because of it. His firm, Brown Rudnick, disclosed by accident 70,000 of Depp's personal text messages (every lawyer everywhere will shudder at the thought of being responsible for clicking send on that email). But within the material accidentally disclosed were text messages that were relevant to the case and should have already been disclosed, including the now infamous texts between Depp and actor Paul Bettany joking about wanting to drown and burn Amber and rape her corpse. And Waldman, the US attorney, had been leaking evidence to the *Daily Mail* that had not been disclosed to the newspaper in the UK case. Just before trial it emerged that Depp had failed to disclose even more relevant text messages—this time, texts showing Depp had lied about his drug use in Australia at the time of one incident of alleged violence—and thereby violated court orders for disclosure. The existence of these texts was only brought to the British court's attention because Amber had received them in disclosure for the US proceedings, and we were able to identify the gap and alert the newspaper's lawyers. Depp then sought sanctions against Amber in the US proceedings for having pointed this out. The newspaper sought to have the proceedings struck out and argued that Depp's conduct amounted to 'threats' and 'intimidation' of Amber, as a witness seeking to assist the court. The judge allowed the UK trial to go ahead—despite Depp's violation of court orders for disclosure—but on one condition: Depp had to provide an undertaking to the court that he would not seek sanctions against Amber in the United States.

Depp also sought to exclude Amber from attending the trial until after she had given evidence. The newspaper opposed his application on the basis that it would have meant Amber would not have been allowed in court while he and his witnesses gave evidence and so would not be able to assist the newspaper in responding to the allegations made about her and what happened. His lawyers argued that she was a witness, not a party, and that she should not be allowed to observe the rest of the evidence before giving her own. The judge refused Depp's application, stating that while the newspaper was defending the case, it was relying 'heavily' on what Amber said and excluding her 'would inhibit the defendants in the conduct of their defense'. So the trial was going ahead—and Amber and I would both be in the courtroom to assess Depp's evidence and help the newspaper rebut it.

The UK trial

It was one thing for Depp and his supporters to make all kinds of claims in the media and online, but it was another to make them in court where a judge would decide. *The Sun*'s opening statement to the court made this distinction clear:

> The assaults upon Ms Heard have continued, no longer through the physical assaults by her ex-husband but by the campaign of vilification which has been orchestrated by others on his behalf. Documents that have been provided during court proceedings have been leaked, often selectively, providing a distorted picture of the reality. This case will not be decided on media leaks and public relations campaigns but on evidence.

In court, I observed how Depp's evidence and arguments continued with the gendered tropes we had seen in his lawyer's public statements—the kind you find warnings about in judicial bench books for family and criminal proceedings. Depp's lawyers claimed that Amber's allegations of domestic and sexual violence were 'fiction' because they were delayed, raised 'very late' and only in the context of the defamation case (even though this was the first time she was ever asked to set them out in detail). Her allegations couldn't be true because her friends hadn't witnessed them, because she had not sought medical treatment for her injuries after each and every incident, because she had not reported him to the police, and because she had only documented her injuries in respect of some incidents, but not all of them.

On this last point, Amber was damned if she did and damned if she didn't: Depp argued that the fact she had photos of her injuries was evidence that her claims were a hoax, but the fact she didn't have photos of injuries from some other incidents also meant those incidents did not happen. His counsel, David Sherborne, even went so far as to say:

> [I]n all the years of violence she alleges, when she has her phone at the ready, where is the secret recording of Mr Depp knocking seven bells out of her, grabbing her by the throat, pulling her hair, screaming at her, threatening to kill her, or any of the other acts of brutality which he is said to have perpetrated against her on a regular basis throughout these years? Nowhere, is the answer.

What was Amber expected to have done while Depp dragged her by the hair, punched her and threatened to kill her—take a selfie? As the one video of Depp in a violent rage (widely available on YouTube) shows, after Depp smashes his wine glass and violently kicks a cupboard, his discovery that Amber is filming him only infuriates him further.

The tropes continued. If he really hit her, why didn't she just leave? It couldn't be true because she hadn't left him. He couldn't have controlled her because (he alleged) she had extramarital affairs (for which he had no proof). Mr Sherborne even quipped in court, 'She was not controlled. She was barely controllable as a witness.' Depp's counsel asserted in court that Amber was not a 'vulnerable victim' or a real victim because she didn't go to the police or a hospital, because she was capable of 'standing up to' Depp and hitting him, because she was 'a financially independent woman and an actress' and 'a woman with all the choices', and because she was capable of documenting her injuries.

At times, it even seemed as though Depp was running a provocation defence from the 1960s, with his lawyers arguing that Amber 'deliberately provokes arguments': she had nagged him, 'berated him', verbally fought him, 'lied about extra-marital affairs', denied him certain drugs he was supposed to be detoxing from, and driven him to drink. As Sasha Wass KC pointed out in closing for *The Sun*, 'It is as though Mr Depp is seeking to justify his physical assaults on Ms Heard on the basis that she may have deserved it.' She contended, too, that he had 'sought to deploy the more old-fashioned methods to discredit women, that she is a gold-digger, a shrew, an adulterer'—none of which, of course, was relevant to the central question: had he ever hit her?

Depp's lawyers repeated in court the offensive lines run in Depp's PR campaign: Amber had 'concocted' her allegations, the restraining order was 'a publicity stunt', she was doing 'a huge disservice' to 'genuine victims' and 'the MeToo movement', and she was 'exploiting the rising popular movements for speaking out against violence against women for her own ends'. Never mind that she had sought the restraining order in 2016, long before MeToo went viral.

Depp's own text messages, which were evidence in court, were worse. On the day after his divorce was finalised and their respectful joint statement—which his lawyers had agreed—was published, it emerged that Depp had written this text to his agent about Amber:

> She's begging for global humiliation. She's gonna get it . . . But she sucked Mollusk's [a reference to Elon Musk] crooked dick and he gave her some shitty lawyers. I have no mercy, no fear and not an ounce of emotion or what I thought was love for this gold digging, low level, dime a dozen, mushy, pointless dangling overused flappy fish market . . . I cannot wait to have this waste of a cum guzzler out of my life. She will hit the wall hard. I met a fucking sublime little Russian here . . . which made me realise that time I blew on the 50cent stripper . . . I would not touch her with a goddam glove. I can only hope that karma kicks in and takes the gift of breath from her. Sorry man but now I will stop at nothing!

In Depp's texts, his desire to ruin Amber's career was clear: 'I want her replaced on that [Warner Bros] film'—an aim that, as we saw earlier in this chapter, was later pursued by his fans via an online petition. Despite describing himself as 'a Southern gentleman' who had respect for women, Depp's text messages showed a different picture. Depp describes women as sluts and fat whores, boasting in one exchange that he would 'smack the ugly cunt around'—he was speaking of his ex-wife Vanessa Paradis, whom he also described as a 'worthless hooker'.

It was in a text message exchange with Paul Bettany that Depp joked about murdering Amber to see whether she was a witch, with Depp saying, 'I will fuck her burnt corpse afterwards to make sure she's dead.' 'My thoughts exactly,' Bettany replied.

When Bettany was asked in a later media interview about the texts, he complained that it was 'embarrassing' and 'unpleasant' to have his texts read in court. 'I'm not sure there's anybody who has one of these devices that would feel comfortable having a team of lawyers scour their private text messages,' he said. Let it be a warning to anyone bringing a defamation claim, as Depp did: you must be prepared for the disclosure obligations you are subjecting yourself to in order to bring your claim. Notably absent from Bettany's response was any apology or regret for the language he had used about women (or, if he did make such a statement, the media did not publish it). His sole regret appeared to be that the texts were made public.

In her closing address, Sasha Wass KC was forensic. Bringing her perspective as a criminal barrister who had acted in sex offence cases, she debunked myth after myth about domestic abuse that had been raised by Depp's lawyers in what she described as their 'outdated and facile' arguments. She began with the question of corroboration, pointing out that Amber's evidence alone was enough to prove *The Sun's* case, and noted that we are 'long past the days when the courts in this country required corroboration before accepting the unsupported testimony of a female complainant'. Not only was Amber a reliable and consistent witness, she was supported by 'a wealth of supporting evidence', including emails, text messages and the accounts of those she had told at the time, including her mother, her sister, her friends and medical professionals.

Wass then pointed out that many of Depp's witnesses had made the 'unmeritorious' point that no one had seen him hit her: it was unmeritorious since domestic violence is usually behind closed doors. It was 'misconceived' to suggest that

Amber could have left when she wanted to, and to say that, just because she chose to stay with him, she was not 'a genuine victim'. Wass explained Amber's family history: her father had been violent to her mother, and her mother had stayed with him until her death; it was 'trite to suggest that a person who chooses to stay with a violent partner cannot be a victim'. As the LA police officers called to give evidence explained when cross-examined about their training for responding to domestic violence incidents, 'a victim may love a perpetrator and still be in fear of them', and victims may try to protect the perpetrator, refuse to give a statement and be so ashamed of the abuse that they are reluctant to disclose it. And this was no ordinary case: Amber knew that the moment she made a police report about Depp, it would cause a media storm and global controversy; the details of their lives would be out there for all to see. He could also face prosecution and prison. She didn't want that. As Wass told the court, '[T]he last thing [Amber] wanted was to expose herself or Mr Depp to ridicule.'

Wass was cutting about Depp's 'risible' theory that Amber's documentation of her injuries was some kind of 'hoax' or an 'insurance policy', especially since 'what exactly Ms Heard was insuring against in the course of this hoax remains unexplained'. She dismissed any suggestion Amber was a 'gold-digger', pointing to the joint statement that Depp had agreed to sign upon their divorce, which made clear she had not 'made false accusations for financial gain', and to the fact that she had pledged her divorce settlement to charity. As Amber had said in her evidence, she knew it would not assist her career to make allegations of domestic violence; in fact, it was quite the opposite. After all, how many women have ever benefited from making abuse allegations?

Depp had denied everything and accused her of being the abuser, which Wass explained was 'to reverse his role with hers'—the well-known DARVO tactic to 'deny, attack and reverse the role of the victim and offender', which we explained in Chapter 6. Wass raised concern that the way Depp had put his case assumed that if Amber had hit him once this 'absolved Mr Depp from any responsibility for the many occasions when he assaulted her' and that 'she may have deserved it'. As Wass made clear, the court was not concerned with whether Amber had fought back or lost her temper. In other words, as the experts say, mutual abuse is not a thing. There is always a primary aggressor and, on the *Sun*'s case, it was Depp.

Wass also pointed out that much of Depp's case was irrelevant to the central question: had he hit her? It was irrelevant whether or not she had affairs, with Elon Musk or anyone else. Depp had applied to try to get third-party disclosure from Amber of all her personal text messages with Musk, which he believed would prove his theory about Amber's supposed affair. The judge, rightly, refused: the issue of adultery was irrelevant to whether or not Depp had hit her. As Wass argued, Amber had denied having affairs, and Depp's evidence was 'thin' at best, dismissing Depp's 'old-fashioned methods to discredit women'.

Turning to Depp's evidence, Wass showed that Depp had lied about his drug use—indeed, many forget that Depp's failure to disclose the text messages that proved that lie had almost seen the entire case thrown out. But Depp also showed himself to be an unreliable witness on the stand. Amber's evidence was that, in one incident, he had headbutted her, leaving her with bruising and a suspected broken nose. In Depp's witness statement about the same incident, he had claimed he had not touched her and that she was left uninjured. Long after Depp's witness statement was served, a recording came to light. As part of their couples therapy, Amber and Depp had been recording their discussions and fights. In a recording that we discovered, and submitted as evidence just before trial, Depp said this: 'I headbutted you in the fucking forehead, that doesn't break a nose.'

When confronted with this evidence in court, Depp conceded he headbutted her but claimed it was 'accidental'. When pressed about why—if this were true—he had not included this in his written statement, he admitted that he had not read his own witness statement. It was all 'too much information' for him and he blamed his lawyers for the factual error.

The reaction among the lawyers in the courtroom was palpable. A lawyer for the newspaper turned sharply to catch my eye and we shared a knowing look: this was a huge blow to Depp's credibility.

There was a problem with Depp's answer, as the judge would abruptly remind him: he had been asked at the outset of his evidence to confirm for the court that he had read his witness statement and that it was true, and he had done so.

Depp had also tailored his evidence when confronted with unfavourable evidence. For example, when confronted with evidence from his former girlfriend and co-star Ellen Barkin that he had been jealous and had thrown a bottle at her, he said he didn't remember it; then he said it had never happened; and then he claimed that she bore a twenty-year grudge against him—yes, that old chestnut: the scorned woman. Other parts of his evidence were contradicted, rather than supported, by the evidence. For example, he claimed that he had not controlled, or tried to control, Amber, despite evidence of the texts he had written to her forbidding her from taking work ('NO GODDAM MEETINGS???? NO MOVIES'), and a text to his sister complaining about her working, 'I don't need actress bullshit and her fucking ambition.' Depp also had direct communication with their personal nurse, ordering her to medicate Amber to control her ('CALM HER DOWN KEEP HER UNDER CONTROL').

Amber's evidence was that drugs and alcohol would often bring out 'the monster' and result in outbursts of violence towards her. Depp denied he ever hit her, but it was also clear his recollection of events was seriously affected by his substance abuse. For example, he admitted that during an incident on a private plane where he had disputed Amber's evidence that he kicked her, he had in fact 'blacked out' and couldn't remember parts of the flight. Amber's account of being kicked was also corroborated by a text message from Depp's assistant Stephen Deuters after the flight, saying 'When I told him he kicked you, he cried.'

There was also evidence that Depp was prone to violence, especially when using drugs and alcohol, and he himself admitted to 'losing control'. The newspaper presented evidence of his history of violent outbursts, which included trashing a hotel room and causing US$10,000 worth of damage, assaulting a photographer with a piece of wood, and throwing a bottle at Barkin, his former partner. At the time the UK case was heard, Depp was also facing legal action in the United States for assaulting a crew member on a film set in 2018. (Depp claimed his actions were in self-defence. The case against him has since been settled—the terms of settlement have not been made public.)

In her closing submission, Wass said it was clear from the evidence that Depp had 'no accountability for his actions'. He was surrounded by people who never told him no. When giving evidence, Amber expressed concern that he never faced up to the consequences of his actions and was being enabled, rather than helped by, the people around him: his security and staff would clean him and the mess up after his benders, make excuses for his absences from set, and—rather than help him get clean—prop him up just enough to try to keep him in work.

Wass also pointed out how Amber had tried to help Depp kick the drugs, but he had grown to resent her for it. This was demonstrated by his text messages to her, including one in which he accuses her of being 'a lesbian camp counsellor' for questioning his substance abuse. 'Mr Depp has spent his entire adult life doing exactly what he wanted and he was not about to answer to a woman at this stage of his life,' Wass concluded.

The full 129-page judgment is worth reading in detail. There is a separate, closed judgment, in which the judge made findings about Amber's allegations of sexual violence. He found the evidence supported Amber's account in twelve of the fourteen incidents of violence pleaded by the newspaper.

Depp's team called the decision 'perverse'. His supporters and online trolls went into meltdown. Wild claims were made about the judge—and about me. A flowchart appeared on social media that depicted all the ways in which I was supposedly connected to the judge—through my chambers and professional relationships—in an attempt to make the false and absurd claim that I had improperly influenced the judge's decision, and that he somehow had conflicts of interest. Thousands signed online petitions calling for the judge to be sacked. It was just another online misinformation campaign that bore no relationship to reality—or what had happened in court: when Depp appealed, no such complaint was raised.

Depp's appeal was rejected by the Court of Appeal: the hearing had been 'full and fair', with an 'extremely detailed review of the evidence', and the judge's conclusions had 'not been shown even arguably to be vitiated by any error of approach or mistake of law'. As *The Sun* said, the 'decision vindicates the courageous evidence that Amber Heard gave to the court about domestic abuse, despite repeated attempts to undermine and silence her'.

But what troubled me was that it didn't seem to matter. It didn't seem to matter that Depp had lost the case. It didn't seem to matter, to many at least, that the British courts had found him to be a wife-beater. The vile, misogynistic and violent language that Depp had used about the women in his life—which was on display in court and reported in the media for all to see—didn't seem to matter either. It was Amber who continued to face suspicion and online attacks and abuse. The online noise attacking her drowned out the fact that a judge had ruled she was a survivor—and that Depp had been violent towards her. What consequences were there for Depp?

While it was announced that he had been asked to resign from his role in Rowling's films, he was reportedly paid his full US$13.5 million salary because of his contract. Depp continued to win awards for his acting—over and above the protests of women in film—and kept his ad campaigns for luxury brand Dior.

For years I had been turning up at Heathrow to see huge Dior advertisements with Depp's image promoting a men's perfume named 'Sauvage'. Long before I had met Amber, the ads had troubled me ever since I had read about the domestic violence restraining order against him; 'sauvage' is the French word for savage. But these advertisements remained up around London during and after the defamation trial in 2020—for Amber and all to see—despite the evidence in court of his violence, and even evidence that Depp had called himself a 'fucking savage'. In 2015, Dior had immediately dropped a previous advertisement with Depp after complaints and controversy about the appropriation of Native American culture. But after the US court granted a restraining order against him in 2016, and even after the UK court found Amber's domestic violence allegations to be true in 2020, his Dior ads remained up—a decision that was slammed by domestic violence campaigners. In 2021, after the UK trial and before the US trial, Dior promoted a new fragrance with Depp called 'Sauvage Elixir', describing him as 'uncompromising, profound, authentic', and proclaiming, 'Never has he been so mesmerising, so rock'n'roll.' As one global cosmetics website noted, 'That's certainly an interesting take on domestic violence, Dior.'

The US trial

So how was it that the case ended up being run again in the United States?

Almost six months after Depp sued *The Sun*, and the year before the UK trial, Amber was asked to write an op-ed in her capacity as Women's Rights Ambassador for the American Civil Liberties Union (ACLU). Her piece, which was originally drafted by the ACLU team for her, was published in *The Washington Post* in December 2018. In it, Amber wrote from personal experience about how women who speak out need to be supported, and about necessary law reform to better support survivors. She wrote these words: '[T]wo years ago, I became a public figure representing domestic abuse, and I felt the full force of our culture's wrath for women who speak out.' She also described her experience:

> I write this as a woman who had to change my phone number
> weekly because I was getting death threats. For months,
> I rarely left my apartment, and when I did, I was pursued

by camera drones and photographers on foot, on motorcycles and in cars. Tabloid outlets that posted pictures of me spun them in a negative light. I felt as though I was on trial in the court of public opinion—and my life and livelihood depended on myriad judgments far beyond my control. I want to ensure that women who come forward to talk about violence receive more support. We are electing representatives who know how deeply we care about these issues. We can work together to demand changes to laws and rules and social norms—and to right the imbalances that have shaped our lives.

Amber didn't mention Depp or any of the underlying factual allegations of violence. She was advocating for change for all women—and for more support for those who choose to speak out. But in January 2019, Depp sued her personally for US$50 million for writing this op-ed. In response, Amber later filed a defamation countersuit for the 'malicious' public campaign he had run against her to ruin her reputation and her career, 'because she was the victim of domestic abuse . . . and had the audacity and temerity to finally come forward to end the abuse'.

Depp put her on trial again in Virginia. We explained in Chapter 6 how people forum shop and choose the most advantageous place to bring their claim. So why did Depp choose Virginia, a state where Amber said she had never been before? Depp could sue there because it is where *The Washington Post* is printed. As Depp's lawyers admitted in court, they chose to sue Amber in Virginia, rather than in California where they both live, because there were no anti-SLAPP laws in Virginia that could have enabled her to strike out his claim and stop him from suing her. We discuss the possibility of anti-SLAPP laws further in the next chapter.

It should have been more difficult for Depp to win in the United States: the burden of proof fell on him. By rights, she should have won—on the evidence, and based on the United States' supposedly more stringent free speech protection under the First Amendment to the Constitution and the rule in *New York Times Co. v. Sullivan* that we discussed in Chapter 6. She tried to have the case thrown out on this basis: the UK court had already found her allegations to be true, so why do it all over again when he couldn't prove it the first time?

The judge refused, and Depp got another day in court—or another month, in fact. And this time it was before a jury.

The trial was, at Depp's request, broadcast live online. Depp had wanted the trial televised, Amber had opposed it. There are rules in Virginia prohibiting the broadcast of evidence about sexual violence in criminal trials. But in civil trials, the judge has the discretion to allow it—and she did. When I spoke to Amber before the trial, she was devastated by this decision: it was hard enough giving evidence in court in front of the media and public in London. But in Virginia she was going to have to do it again—and this time broadcast live for the world's entertainment. In granting Depp's request, the judge said there would be restrictions on what could be photographed and filmed. 'It will be a tight leash,' the judge is reported to have said, though in practice it didn't seem to work out that way.

Depp had vowed to take revenge upon Amber after she left him back in 2016. As he had written in a text message to his agent, 'She is begging for global humiliation. She is going to get it.' In 2022, the court let him have his way: Amber was required to give evidence about domestic violence and sexual assault streamed live on television and on YouTube.

I did not act for her in the US trial and was merely observing from afar. Watching the YouTube stream was thoroughly depressing: the live comments function was enabled, showing second-by-second comments from people from all over the world, which were filled with misogyny and harmful myths about gender-based violence. Thousands of pro-Depp social media videos and internet memes mocked her and her evidence, promoting the same harmful myths. Friends called me during the trial, concerned that their children were beginning to repeat the old sexist tropes they were absorbing via Instagram and TikTok videos. One day Chanel Contos a survivor advocate, contacted me, distressed, after she saw videos of young women mocking Amber's testimony of sexual violence—about being raped with a bottle—and saying they wished Johnny had done it to them. It made us both feel sick.

It also painted a skewed picture of the facts and the evidence—in a case where the jury was not sequestered.

Depp's team ran the same 'outdated and facile' arguments that did not sway the British judge, pandering to the male-centric myths about violence that studies have shown successfully sway juries and deny women justice.

And, sadly, it worked.

His lawyers—again—claimed that she was the abuser, that she lied, and that she had doctored the images of her injuries. The fact she had so much evidence was suspicious—but the evidence she had also wasn't enough. In closing, Depp's lawyer Camille Vasquez told the jury to consider all the evidence and 'You either believe all of it, or none of it.' She said that Amber didn't cry enough on the stand (so she couldn't be a real victim), and yet, at the same time, Vasquez claimed Amber had given 'the performance of her life'. Much was made of Amber being an actor, to

undermine her credibility, even though Depp is also an actor—
and one of the highest-paid in Hollywood. Amber's was 'a case
of me too without a "me too"', claimed Depp's lawyer Ben Chew,
since no woman had accused Depp before Amber, and no one had
accused him since. The submission may have sounded catchy, but
it revealed a fundamental misunderstanding of what MeToo was
actually about: it was not about more than one woman speaking
about the same man (though that happened); it was about women
speaking out to acknowledge they had also suffered abuse. But
the clear message to the jury was that Amber's word was not
enough. And that the word of one woman is not enough.

Depp's lawyers called expert evidence, with one claiming
Amber suffered from 'borderline personality disorder' along
with 'histrionic personality disorder', a controversial, outdated
term that has been heavily criticised for perpetuating sexist
stereotypes about women. As author and survivor advocate
Dr Jessica Taylor explains, it is 'outrageous' that the diagnosis
would be used in 2022, 'considering the wealth of evidence that
it is nothing more than a made up, misogynistic label to beat
women with'. She pointed out that making these kinds of allegations is 'the go-to tactic of a legal team intent on discrediting a
woman', and that she sees it every day in her work: 'Thousands
of women are going through the same thing as Amber as
we speak.'

And it worked.

It didn't matter that a British judge had already found that
Depp had repeatedly and violently assaulted Amber. It didn't
matter she had more corroborating evidence than most domestic
violence victims. It didn't matter that Amber's expert evidence
confirmed that she suffered post-traumatic stress disorder,
and had symptoms consistent with being a victim of abuse, and

that Depp exhibited behaviours consistent with perpetrators of intimate violence.

It wasn't enough.

There was no jury direction warning about all the myths and stereotypes that had been paraded before them. If it had been a criminal case based on the same facts, they would have been so warned (at least, in the United Kingdom and other jurisdictions).

The jury found in Depp's favour. They decided Amber had defamed him, that she had lied, and that she had done so with malice, and they awarded him US$10 million in damages and $5 million in punitive damages.

But the jury also found that Depp had defamed Amber, through the statements of his lawyer, Waldman, claiming that her allegations were a hoax. She was awarded US$2 million. As Amber's appeal motion states, these two findings are 'inconsistent and irreconcilable'. How can it be that Amber was defamed when Depp's lawyer said that her allegations were a hoax, and yet Depp was also defamed when she said she became a public figure representing domestic abuse?'

The outcome was absurd. It wasn't just that the jury had ignored evidence that had convinced an expert and experienced British judge that Depp had been repeatedly violent. It wasn't just that the jury ignored Depp's documented history of violence and the expert evidence showing that he exhibited the traits of an abusive partner. The burden of proof was on Depp to show he had never been abusive towards her. There was evidence, which he and his security team had accepted, that Depp had trashed Amber's belongings, and—as her US counsel pointed out—that instance of property damage alone was domestic abuse according to Virginia law. It also seems that the jury didn't understand the law: one juror would later tell the media that they believed that Amber and Depp 'were both abusive to each other', which meant that Amber's defence of truth was made out and she should not have lost the case.

The jury had found that Amber had acted with malice, when it was Depp's texts that were filled with spite and ideations of violence, having expressed his hope 'that karma kicks in and takes the gift of breath from her' and that her 'rotting corpse is decomposing in the fucking trunk of a Honda Civic'. In evidence before the jury, Depp had sworn to subject her to global humiliation, and wanted to have her removed from films. He had even had the tattoo on his hand changed from her nickname, 'Slim', to read 'Scum'. Her evidence was that she hadn't wanted to speak out about the violence because she was trying to protect him but, in the end, she had to. And yet it was Amber the jury found to have acted with malice. This is the important test from the *New York Times Co. v. Sullivan* case we discussed in Chapter 6: the jury may not have believed her (or the evidence supporting her account), but they did not have evidence she made the allegations *with malice*. There was no evidence she did not believe she was abused, and said it anyway. Quite the opposite: she said she was abused, she believed it and she had evidence to support it.

The jury awarded Depp US$5 million in punitive damages, despite the $350,000 statutory cap, which the judge had to correct (reducing the amount from $15 million to $10.35 million). As Amber's appeal explained, the $10 million damages award was made without any evidence that Depp's reputation had actually been damaged by her opinion piece: the jury was not permitted to see the UK judgment, which clearly showed that, if anything, his reputation was harmed by the British judge's decision, which found that he is a wife-beater, and the large amount of evidence before the jury that showed he had already been losing roles because of his own conduct, including his substance abuse problems.

One of the key points used to attack Amber's credibility was the question about the donation to charity that she had pledged after their divorce. Depp claimed she lied: she said she had donated her divorce settlement when she hadn't actually given all the money to charity yet. Amber's answer was the same as it was in the UK trial: she had pledged the donations ($7 million, split equally between the ACLU and the LA Children's Hospital) and had started making payments, but could not continue to pay the instalments after Depp sued her— she needed the funds to defend herself from the defamation action Depp brought against her. Indeed, the ACLU confirmed for the jury that Amber had made $1.3 million in payments until 2019 (the same year Depp sued her in the United States), when they 'learned she was having financial difficulties'. On the stand in the US trial, she said she used the words 'pledge' and 'donate' as synonyms and made clear that she had started making charity payments and intended to complete the payments when she could afford to: 'I would love him to stop suing me so I can.' Depp had raised this point on appeal in the United Kingdom, claiming her statements about her donations were misleading. The Court of Appeal refused his argument, noting that Amber had pledged to pay the charities US$3.5 million over ten years from 2016, that she intended to meet that pledge, and that 'her charitable donation was in itself nothing to do with the case the Judge had to decide'. Indeed, the court stated explicitly that the issue of donations came up 'fairly peripherally' in the context of Depp's 'insurance/hoax thesis' and that Depp's own counsel in the United Kingdom had (rightly) accepted that 'the question of whether Ms Heard was a gold-digger was irrelevant'. Accordingly, the Court of Appeal found there was no reason to believe that the judge's decision was influenced by what Amber had said about the donations. But for the US jury it was a 'fiasco', according to one anonymous juror who gave media interviews after the verdict; it had contributed to their decision that her story about abuse 'didn't add up'. It is quite something when her charity commitment, which she now can't meet because he sued her, is being held against her, not him.

Depp's lawyers' submissions about what a 'real victim' would look like clearly resonated with the jury. A juror told the media that the jury had considered Amber's crying to be 'crocodile tears', which made her account of abuse unbelievable. In other words, she didn't cry the right way when recounting her abuse.

Amber's US counsel, Elaine Bredehoft and Ben Rottenborn, confirmed that she will be appealing the verdict because it was not 'just and fair'.

Among the complaints raised was the exclusion of evidence—by Depp's team—that had been before the British judge, including medical notes that confirmed Amber had been telling her therapist about Depp's abuse going back to 2012, and that she had sought medical treatment for concussion after one of the disputed incidents of violence. Depp did not call his assistant, Stephen Deuters, which also meant that his text messages—used by the British judge to corroborate Amber's version of events—were excluded, including the one in which he told Amber that Depp was sorry to have kicked her. There is some irony in Depp's lawyers trying to exclude so much evidence that was before the British court, especially after his lawyers' statement: '[W]e hope that in contrast to [the UK] case, the ongoing libel proceedings in America are equitable, with both parties providing full disclosure rather than one side strategically cherry picking what evidence can and cannot be relied upon.'

Amber's legal team have also raised concerns about the fact the jury members were not sequestered and had access to social media, where thousands of pro-Depp posts were circulating, presenting a distorted and unfair picture of what was happening in court.

Amber's op-ed had spoken of the wrath she faced for speaking out about abuse—and, ironically, the trial and the backlash she has faced has only proven her original point. The hashtag #JusticeforJohnnyDepp had 10 billion hits on TikTok. The trial captured global attention, with 3.5 million people watching the verdict.

As Jessica Winter observed in *The New Yorker*, a quick glance at YouTube, Facebook and Instagram reveals Amber as 'the Medusa of Sunset Boulevard'. Right-wing media spent thousands promoting anti-Amber content on Facebook, while YouTube channels pivoted to anti-Amber videos, recognising their money-making potential. Merchandise was sold online, including T-shirts saying 'Don't Be An Amber', 'Justice For Johnny' and 'Flappy Fish Market'—a reference to Depp's vile, misogynistic texts. The worst I have seen was a dildo created by a sex toy company in the shape of a bottle, so women could 'pleasure' themselves to new 'Depp-ths'.

Social media analysis that has since been released by the organisation, Bot Sentinel, showed how the trending of anti-Amber hashtags on Twitter was not organic, but manipulated. In their July 2022 report, 'Targeted Trolling and Trend Manipulation:

How Organized Attacks on Amber Heard and Other Women Thrive on Twitter', concluded that this had been 'one of the worst cases of platform abuse'. There was 'widespread targeted harassment' of Amber and women who spoke out in support of her, with 627 accounts that focused on negative tweets about Amber and her female supporters, who were doxed and faced death threats. At least 24 per cent of the accounts were created in the past seven months. It also showed how the same accounts, since the US trial, have started tweeting negative content about Evan Rachel Wood, who is being sued by Marilyn Manson (a close friend of Depp's) over her abuse accusations about him.

The findings of the report resonated for me: it is precisely what I had seen and experienced during the UK trial. Twitter trolls would copy and paste the tweets posted by Depp's lawyer, Waldman (who had been warned by the judge in the UK trial about making intimidating threats about witnesses), and by other trolls. The discussion I saw on social media often bore no resemblance to what was happening inside court: it was overwhelmingly pro-Depp. I have worked on high-profile and controversial cases in the past, but I had never faced anything like it before; the trolling was relentless. Everything from my ethics and professionalism to my appearance and my personal relationship history were attacked. Trolls vowed to 'ruin' me and make sure I never worked again because I had represented Amber in the United Kingdom, and had proven Depp was a wife-beater.

And it wasn't just directed at me: those who spoke about the trial in ways that were perceived to be critical of Depp or supportive of Amber—whether journalists or commentators— were trolled. Jess Phillips MP was attacked for pointing out that women need not be perfect, or even of good character, to be a victim of abuse. Mark Stephens, who was a disinterested commentator on the trial, told *The Guardian*, 'I've seen some high-profile cases, but I have never seen a response like this . . . the campaigning online has felt one-sided.' He also expressed suspicion about the pro-Depp bots during the trial and how 'comments supporting Depp are popping up in real time, just as evidence is being produced in court'.

But whatever I had seen and experienced during the UK trial, it was even worse during the US trial. Amber received death and rape threats—and threats towards her baby daughter. I observed how women who spoke in support of her or simply called out the misogyny on display were shouted down, attacked and threatened online. I did not act for her in the US trial, I was not there, and I made no public comment. But I still faced constant online trolling and threats, with men and women sending me messages filled with violent threats, misogyny and hate, including telling me that I had 'a punchable face too' and making comments on my appearance, my intellect and my professional ability. It was striking how many of the comments and threats appeared to celebrate and justify the violence Amber had alleged and the vile language used about her. The clear message—to Amber, to me, to any woman—was to shut up and stay silent. And don't dare support Amber.

So, for me, the Bot Sentinel report confirmed what I had seen and experienced in both the UK and US trials. And separate from how this could have affected the jury, is how it affected every other survivor and woman who watched all of this and might now be deterred from speaking out because of it.

The televised trial has been described as a modern-day witch trial. I had been concerned about the judge's decision to allow it: it would never be allowed in Australia or the United

Kingdom, and it would not be allowed in the United States in criminal cases involving evidence of sexual violence. It would later emerge, through the unsealing of court documents, that Depp had—in a televised trial—tried to introduce evidence including nude pictures of Amber, evidence about the sexual histories of Amber and her sister Whitney, and about Amber's brief stint as an exotic dancer to 'maliciously' suggest or imply that Amber had worked as a sex worker. It was irrelevant and was not permitted in evidence before the jury, but Amber faced questions about it in her deposition and it is part of the now unsealed court record (and is now being used by trolls on social media). This line of questioning and type of evidence is also prohibited in criminal cases about sexual violence.

The consequences were even worse than I could have imagined—for Amber and for women everywhere. As Jessica Winter wrote for *The New Yorker*:

> [I]f you spend enough time inhaling the sulfurous fumes of the Depp–Heard live stream, what it starts to resemble most is a high-budget, general-admission form of revenge porn, an act in which the person with the upper hand in a relationship forces the other to be complicit in the sharing and dissemination of raw, vulnerable, literally sensational moments for the delectation of an unseen audience . . . This is who she is now—the victim of an unprecedented Internet pile-on, a bruised face on an iPhone, a woman who makes people laugh when she cries.

The trial had 'turned into a public orgy of misogyny', wrote Moira Donegan in *The Guardian*—and she was right. Arwa Mahdawi also wrote for *The Guardian*, 'If the trial showed us anything, it's that misogyny is more alluring to many people than facts'—and she was right too. For Donegan, the case marked a 'tipping point' in the backlash against MeToo. That backlash was not just against Amber, but against every woman who dares to speak out.

And the fallout has been global.

Lawyer colleagues around the world have told me their clients are worried about taking action against their abusers after seeing what happened to Amber. Some decided not to go ahead. Others reported that abusive partners were threatening them, saying they were 'an Amber' and no one would believe them.

What message does all of this send to women who might want to speak out about their abuse? How many women will speak out if this is how they will be treated? How many more women will have watched this case and thought, 'I can't go through that'? How many women now feel unable to confide in family members about their experiences after hearing them ridicule Amber? How many women are now silenced and afraid to come forward? How many more women will be sued and silenced? And how many women have to go through this before the cultural narrative shifts away from the oldest tricks in the book—calling women liars, gold-diggers and whores?

As journalist Constance Grady wrote back in 2016, Amber did everything that victims are 'supposed' to do. She called the police when it happened (though she decided not to report and press charges out of concern for the consequences for him and them both). She then went to a court with evidence, photos and text messages to get a restraining order. She showed she was not after the money by pledging to give it all away (though even that was held against her later for not giving it away quickly enough). 'She was, in every way, exactly the kind of victim we say women should be if they want us to believe them. It didn't matter. We still said she was lying.' After that, Amber didn't give media interviews about it. But Depp sued a newspaper and her personally. She gave evidence in court and a British judge believed her. But the public—and a jury—still didn't believe her.

Depp's ability to litigate the case in two different jurisdictions means that people can and will continue to believe what they want, and take diametrically opposed positions on the case, on Depp and on Amber. But it raises serious questions about what happens when allegations of gender-based violence go before civil juries without the protections we have for complainants in criminal cases. So concerning is the US verdict that it has been described as 'the biggest blow to the #MeToo movement since its inception'. Amber's own statement outside court says it all:

> The disappointment I feel today is beyond words. I'm heartbroken that the mountain of evidence still was not enough to stand up to the disproportionate power, influence and sway of my ex-husband.
>
> I'm even more disappointed about what this verdict means for other women. It is a setback. It sets the clock back to a time when a woman who spoke up and spoke out could be publicly shamed and humiliated. It sets back the idea that violence against women is to be taken seriously.
>
> I believe Johnny's attorneys succeeded in getting the jury to overlook the key issue of freedom of speech and ignore evidence that was so conclusive that we won in the UK. I am sad I lost this case. But I am sadder still that I seem to have lost a right I thought I had as an American—to speak freely and openly.

Chapter 8

WHAT ABOUT HER RIGHTS?

A woman tweets on social media that she is a survivor of abuse, using the hashtag #MeToo. She doesn't name the alleged abuser but he sues her anyway.

A woman speaks in a private safe space of survivors about being raped. She tells the group that her ex-boyfriend raped her. Information is leaked. He takes his ex-girlfriend to court and gets a gag order that means she can never tell anyone about the rape again. The judge finds her guilty of 'emotional abuse' and harassment against him.

The members of a feminist academic collective publish a report condemning their universities for failing to tackle sexual harassment and abuse on campus. A male professor accused of sexually harassing a male student sues the report's author in criminal libel proceedings, saying she has damaged his right to honour and reputation.

The director of a domestic violence shelter is convicted for defaming a man who accused her of kidnapping his wife and child after they fled to her shelter.

Amber Heard writes in *The Washington Post* to advocate for better laws to protect survivors, and draws on her own experience as a survivor. A British judge finds she is a survivor in a decision based on detailed corroborating evidence, but she loses a defamation case on the same facts in the United States before a jury, which orders her to pay her ex-husband US$15 million.

In each of these cases from around the world, the law failed to properly protect women's right to speak.

As Justitia reminds us, the law is a constant balancing act, weighing interests and rights to achieve a just outcome. When it comes to freedom of speech about gender-based violence, she is weighing his right to privacy and reputation against her right to free speech and the general public interest in reporting that speech. Yet courts around the world are too often getting this balance wrong. The effect of this is to silence women and silence speech that is necessary to end violence against women. Victims and survivors of abuse are increasingly demanding that courts uphold her right to free speech and stop privileging his right to reputation and privacy.

Through our work, we have become convinced that we need to reclaim free speech from a feminist perspective. We want to make it clear that speaking out about gender-based violence, in the medium of your choice, is a human right, protected not just by the right to freedom of speech, but also the right to equality and the right to be free from violence. As human rights lawyers, we believe these rights must also be placed in Justitia's weighing scales to ensure her right to free speech is better protected in our courts, so that we can put an end to gender-based violence.

What about his rights?

Let's first begin with what his rights are—and the concerns we see raised in response to women choosing to speak out. What about his right to be presumed innocent? What about his right to a fair trial? As any of our barrister colleagues in criminal law will tell you, when a woman goes to the police to report that a burglar breaks into and enters a house and steals an iPhone, she is believed. But once she mentions a sexual assault, a cloud of suspicion descends. In the wake of MeToo, where women are choosing to speak to the media or post online rather than go to the police, even more questions arise. Why didn't she report it to the police? What if she is lying? What if she ruins his reputation and his career with a false allegation? Shouldn't he have the right to a fair trial, rather than trial by media?

In the opening essay in *The Right to Sex* (2021), 'A Conspiracy Against Men', Oxford philosophy professor and essayist Amia Srinivasan explains how in the United Kingdom only '0.23 per cent of rape reports led to a false arrest, and only 0.07 per cent of rape reports led to a man being falsely charged with rape'. Srinivasan concludes that 'a false rape accusation, like a plane crash, is an objectively unusual event that occupies an outsized place in the public imagination'. She also explains that the myth of the false rape accusation is 'a predominantly wealthy white male preoccupation'.

Nevertheless, this myth—that women often make false rape and abuse claims—is having a resurgence alongside other regressive forces that threaten to undermine decades of feminist activism and legal progress on women's human rights, gender equality and LGBTQI+ rights. Authoritarian right-wing figures have built platforms arguing that feminism and feminist activism have made gains at the expense of men and that MeToo has been an overcorrection. Some have described feminist reforms as a 'backlash against masculinity' and 'reverse discrimination'. Some argue that domestic violence perpetrated by women against men is under-reported and left out of media narratives. Some say that public allegations of gender-based violence undermine the presumption of innocence, a fundamental tenet of justice.

These views, which perpetuate old sexist myths and are not supported by empirical data, have filtered through digital spaces, with a growing online subculture of men who hate women. *The New Yorker* has reported on the violent political ideology of 'incels', who believe that women have unjustly refused certain men a 'right to sex' and often 'subscribe to notions of white supremacy'. Incel ideology has inspired murders, and aims for 'absolute male supremacy'. This is the extreme end of the misogyny spectrum, but offers important context to the idea that there is a conspiracy against men—or that there is inevitably discrimination against men in any development for equality for women. This is all part of the backlash against the MeToo movement, and has led to calls to strengthen the presumption of innocence and privacy protections.

In 2017, the same year as the MeToo social media movement took off, the UK Supreme Court handed down an important judgment about open justice and how it interacts with the presumption of innocence. The case known as *Khuja* concerned the arrest by the police of someone suspected of being involved in sexual offences against children. He was never charged and wasn't prosecuted, but his name came up in court. He sought to keep his identity secret but the newspapers challenged it. The Supreme Court explained that the constitutional principle of open justice meant that Mr Khuja could be named. 'The law must of course take the presumption of innocence as its starting point,' the court said. However, the court also said that, 'experience suggests that as a general rule the public understand that there is a difference between allegation and proof.'

This ruling affirmed the presumption of innocence as a fundamental legal principle guaranteeing and protecting the rights of the accused in a criminal trial. The presumption of innocence is protected by the laws of contempt, which make sure that the trial is fair and that a jury isn't prejudiced by media reporting (for example, by reporting that states a person is guilty before their guilt is determined at trial). But the court's ruling also affirmed that this principle must be balanced against other interests, including freedom of speech and the open justice principle. This means that when accusations are made in the courtroom, they can be reported by the press, subject to contempt of court laws.

The debates in the wake of MeToo have not been over whether alleged perpetrators can be named in court (clearly they can be), but rather about whether newspapers and survivors can name those alleged of abuse online or in newspaper articles *before* any court proceedings have commenced. Many have argued that doing so amounts to 'trial by media' and 'violates the presumption of innocence'.

Men's rights groups have argued that the naming of men online in relation to allegations of sexual assault, rape or abuse violates the presumption of innocence. They have even claimed that online movements such as #IBelieveHer (or #YoTeCreo in Spanish) violate this legal presumption. This is a basic misunderstanding of the principle. As Amia Srinivasan explains, this is a 'category error', since 'the presumption of innocence does not tell us what to believe. It tells us how guilt is to be established by the law: that is, by a process that deliberately stacks the deck in favour of the accused.' She explains that believing women operates therefore 'as a corrective norm, a gesture of support for those people—women—whom the law tends to treat as if they were lying'. As the UK Supreme Court said in *Khuja*, the public understands that there is a difference between an allegation and proof.

The right to be presumed innocent is already well protected—by both contempt of court and privacy laws. As we explained in Chapter 3, contempt of court laws protect his right to be presumed innocent once he is charged. But even widespread media reporting on allegations does not amount to 'trial by media' or necessarily violate his presumption of innocence.

███
███
███
███
█████████████████████████████████

As Justice McCallum said, '[e]xtensive media reporting of allegations of criminal conduct is not a mischief in itself' and recognised that 'the media play an important role in drawing attention to allegations of criminal or other misconduct and any shortcomings in the treatment of such allegations'. But the trial was later postponed after certain media reporting ██████████ ██████████ failed to respect the distinction between an untested allegation and guilt. In postponing the trial, the judge warned everyone about reporting, publishing books and even making comments ██████████████████████████ ███████████████████████████ in order to protect his right to fair trial. This is a good example of how his right to a fair trial is well protected and will, in certain circumstances, trump everyone else's right to free speech.

As we explained in Chapter 4, in the United Kingdom, there are increasing (and problematic) privacy protections that protect him from any media reporting while under police investigation and until charge. And, of course, there are also defamation laws. Our point is that his rights are well established and protected in law. The danger is that the creeping mythology that his rights are under threat is leading to ever greater restrictions on her right to speak.

The right to speak

Freedom of speech or expression is a fundamental human right and the cornerstone of a democratic society. International human rights law is clear that free speech can only be subject to restrictions that are necessary in a democratic society—and this includes 'for respect of the rights or reputations of others'. Human rights courts have explained that free speech also admits a degree of exaggeration or even provocation—and speech that may be offensive. In other words, free speech should be the starting point, and it should be limited by libel and privacy laws only where that is strictly necessary.

Free speech also protects the right of the press to impart information and ideas that are in the public interest; the public has a right to receive such information. The MeToo allegations and reporting on powerful and wealthy individuals such as Harvey Weinstein, R Kelly and Jeffrey Epstein have underlined the importance of such reporting and its role in 'shaking the tree', as more women come forward after seeing other women speak out. Public interest reporting like this has warned and protected other women, and led to criminal prosecutions and justice for survivors.

In the balance between his right to reputation and her right to free speech, there is one important question that we think courts too often overlook: whether the comment contributed to a debate of general interest. In other words, the wider context is crucial. There is immense public interest in women being able to speak out about violence. As we argued in Chapter 5 about NDAs and in Chapter 6 about defamation, we believe courts must place greater emphasis on the broader context of violence against women in society and the public interest in her speech about it.

Women's freedom of expression is under attack by state and non-state actors, as UN experts have repeatedly and recently warned. Women need to be able to speak out to realise their civil and political rights, and to participate in political life and public debate, but also to advocate for gender equality and to call out violence and abuse. Free speech rights ensure that we can speak about structural and systemic issues that discriminate against women, such as gender-based violence, to ensure they are addressed and eradicated. The same rights also ensure that people can express themselves—their sexuality, their gender identity, their art and their culture.

But there are other rights to consider too.

In recent years, the United Nations has reminded states and governments that women's human right to live a 'life free from gender-based violence is indivisible from and interdependent with other human rights, including . . . freedom of expression, movement, participation, assembly and association'. There is also mounting recognition that freedom of speech is an equality issue. The United Nations and regional human rights bodies have recognised that every woman is entitled to the free and full exercise of her civil, political, economic, social and cultural rights, including freedom of expression, and they recognise that violence against women prevents and nullifies the exercise of these rights. Yet too often we see courts fail to recognise a woman's right to speak, her right to equality and to be free from violence, and the broader context of the need to protect. So let's talk about her rights.

Her rights to equality and to live her life free from violence

In most defamation cases, discussion of the rights to equality and to live a life free from gender-based violence is conspicuous by its absence. These are human rights, just like free speech or the right to privacy and reputation. While some courts are beginning to recognise how these rights intersect with free speech, we still have a long way to go. This is the argument we wanted to raise in the UK Supreme Court as interveners in Nicola Stocker's case but were refused permission. Jen also tried to intervene in the case involving Afsana Lachaux's allegations of abuse on behalf of the Centre for Women's Justice with Caoilfhionn Gallagher KC to make similar arguments, and was again refused permission. Yet when courts around the world have considered the rights to equality and to live a life free from gender-based violence together with the right to free speech, they have handed down important judgments protecting women's right to allege abuse or misconduct.

Women and girls have fundamental human rights, which are protected by international law. The United Nations reaffirmed this in 1979 with the enactment of the Convention on the Elimination of All Forms of Discrimination Against

Women, a human rights treaty that guarantees gender equality, and it was repeated in 1993 at the Vienna World Conference on Human Rights. Before this, the Universal Declaration of Human Rights (UDHR) was meant to ensure that all persons had fundamental human rights but, as we explained in Chapter 1, Jessie Street's recommendation that it include an explicit right to be free from violence was not adopted. Despite all these efforts, it soon became clear that states and governments needed specific guidance and legal obligations to make sure they were protecting, respecting and promoting women's rights, including the right to be free from violence.

The aim of legal instruments such as the convention, and its monitoring body, CEDAW, is to achieve gender equality. Since its enactment, which we mentioned back in Chapter 2, international human rights law has developed: it now makes clear that violence against women is a gender equality and human rights issue. This is because violence against women is a form of gender discrimination. Every woman and girl on this planet has a right to live her life free from violence—free from the fear of walking down the street and being raped or killed.

Today there is an understanding that gender-based violence encompasses various manifestations: sexual violence such as rape; other forms of unwanted sexual touching and harassment; forced nudity; sexual assault; trafficking and forced prostitution; reproductive and obstetric crimes including forced pregnancy, forced abortion and sterilisation; other forms of violence including domestic and intimate partner violence; and violence against women committed over the internet. International treaty committees and regional courts have handed down landmark judgments recognising violence against women as a human rights violation and a form of discrimination against women, while regional human rights conventions have been drafted that set out state obligations. The courts have recognised that domestic violence, sexual violence and violence against women violates a number of human rights, including the right to life, the prohibition on torture, cruel, inhumane and degrading treatment, the right to private and family life, and equality and non-discrimination. International and regional courts have recognised the particular vulnerability of victims of domestic and sexual violence, 'who often fail to report incidents'. They have also recognised that women are often frightened to speak out about the violence they suffer.

The former Special Rapporteur on Violence Against Women, Dubravka Šimonović, the United Nations' expert on the issue, has called attention to the fact that we live in a world in which systemic and structural gender-based violence forms a part of women's everyday lives and daily routines. She has explained that '[g]ender-based violence against women is a global plague that affects one in three women worldwide in their lifetime and, as such, it creates a culture of normalization and tolerance of such violence in society'.

International law has imposed obligations on states and governments to ensure that violence against women is prevented, investigated and prosecuted, and that women are protected from such violence. This is called the due diligence principle. The right to free speech and the right to live a life free from violence are both protected under the law. If women can't talk about violence, if they are facing libel and privacy claims and injunctions for talking about their experience of abuse, how can society tackle the issue?

A number of very worrying legal cases show how women face retaliation for reporting an abuser to the authorities, including civil suits in defamation. CEDAW considered a case involving this issue against Kazakhstan. Anna Belousova tried to report her employer, the director of a school where she worked, for pressuring her to have sex with him in order to keep her job. He sued her for defamation and she lost her job—and the defamation case. The fact that she lost the defamation case was then used against her by the police, who said there was insufficient evidence to investigate her allegations against him. This left Anna with no job and no remedy for reporting the harassment she had experienced in the workplace. Even worse, the defamation ruling meant she had to apologise to him. CEDAW found that Kazakhstan violated her human rights.

Irene Khan, the Special Rapporteur on Freedom of Opinion and Expression, has highlighted the issue: 'Weaponising the justice system to silence women feeds impunity while also undermining free speech,' she explains. Free speech is essential for accountability. A person who sues for defamation can effectively steal a woman's voice, and force her into litigation to get it back, which undermines our ability as a society to tackle violence against women.

But there are some important developments: courts are beginning to recognise that other rights belong in Justitia's balancing scales, along with the rights to speech and reputation, and this is tipping the scales towards her right to speak about the violence she has suffered.

In 2018, the Indian journalist Priya Ramani, who we mentioned in Chapter 6, found herself facing a charge of criminal defamation for an article she published in *Vogue India* and a series of tweets about M.J. Akbar, a member of the Indian Parliament and the Minister of State for External Affairs. His lawyers referred to him as a veteran Indian journalist. In 2017,

Ramani named Akbar as having sexually harassed her and other women in the media. In one tweet she alleged that he was 'the media's biggest sexual predator'. Akbar made a complaint of criminal defamation, claiming that her allegations were made 'with the sole ulterior motive of maligning his reputation and his political standing'. Ramani was arrested but released on bail pending the determination of the case.

Akbar complained that Ramani had not reported his conduct to any authority—neither her employer nor the police—and claimed that this proved it was a 'figment of her imagination'. Like many women, she was accused of being vengeful and malicious, and found herself facing the argument that she shouldn't be believed because she hadn't gone to the police when she said the offending occurred.

The court in New Delhi handed down its carefully considered judgment on 17 February 2021, acquitting Ramani of the charges. The court stated that women cannot be punished for criminal defamation for raising their voice against sexual abuse, as 'the right of reputation cannot be protected at the cost of the right of the life and dignity of woman [sic]', which is guaranteed in the Indian Constitution under the right to equality. The court explained that, most of the time, victims of sexual abuse and harassment only realise the extent of what happened to them years later, and that it is common for there to be a long delay before victims feel comfortable talking about what happened. The court emphasised: 'The woman has a right to put her grievance on any platform of her choice and even after decades.' M.J. Akbar has appealed the ruling and the Indian courts in 2022 have said that they will hear his appeal.

The rights for women—to speak about their abuse on a platform or medium of their choice, to come out as a survivor of abuse, even to name their perpetrator—have been confirmed in other courts around the world. Courts have dismissed libel claims on the basis that such legal action leads to censorship, silencing and the denial of a woman's free speech rights, including her right to self-fulfilment, and her rights to equality and to be free from violence.

The Colombian Constitutional Court has recently considered a series of cases in which women have taken to social media to tweet about their experiences and have named their alleged abusers. In one case, a woman wrote on social media that a man she knew did not understand the meaning of 'no', and accused him of harassing and abusing her. He sued her, arguing she had violated his right to reputation and honour. She defended the case on the basis of her right to free speech.

The court explained that while he had a right to reputation, this had to be weighed against her free speech rights, and that social media publications denouncing sexist conduct receive special free speech protection given that they aim to defend other fundamental human rights, namely women's human rights. The court affirmed that a state's due diligence obligations to prevent gender-based violence must also be placed on the judicial scales. In this case, her speech and broader societal goals to ensure women's right to live free from violence meant that his libel claim against her could not succeed.

Through this and other decisions, the Colombian Constitutional Court has explained that the suffering caused to his reputation is outweighed by the suffering that would be caused by censoring her right to speak out about being a victim of sexual violence. It has held that the victims of alleged crimes have a right to freely and publicly denounce what had happened to them.

These MeToo allegations published on social media in Latin America have a name—*escraches*—and legal decisions have held that they are a legitimate form of expression protected by the constitution. The Constitutional Court has confirmed that women, journalists and other social media users are not required to wait until there has been a judicial decision on the allegations, since that would be a disproportionate restriction of free speech, making these accusations invisible and contributing to gender discrimination. In other words, calling yourself a victim or calling out your perpetrator on social media in Colombia is a constitutionally protected right.

However, the Constitutional Court warned that making such accusations online should be done carefully and responsibly; it is important to ensure that the accused's presumption of innocence is protected. The court explained that this could be achieved by making an allegation rather than saying he is guilty of a criminal offence.

The court acknowledged that *escraches* are a response to the lack of justice for women, given that most reports of sexual violence are ignored. Women have been forced to seek an alternative way of bringing visibility to the violations of their fundamental human rights. The court held that digital *escraches* aren't protected only by free speech principles, but also by the right to protest. It is a public manifestation of protest against a justice system that has failed to protect women from violence. *Escraches* have constitutional protection especially where official reports have been made but nothing has been done about them; in the context of such inaction, the person turns to the online world as the location for a form of social protest about the authorities' failure to act.

Importantly, the Colombian courts have held that the right to live a life free from violence and the right to free speech are heightened in certain contexts. Around the world, there has been a raft of libel cases brought by university professors or faculty members against a university or against students who have named them in relation to accusations of 'creepy' behaviour or misconduct. Al Jazeera's podcast *Degrees of Abuse* and work by feminist academics such as Sara Ahmed have highlighted the problem of sexual harassment in universities and the issues students face within internal complaint procedures when they report such abuse by other students or by faculty members. Meanwhile, faculty members who have been named and accused of harassment or more serious offences, such as rape, have argued that there has been a witch-hunt, and that their lives have been ruined by spurious allegations.

In one case in Colombia, the court made it clear that accusations made in an academic setting required the special protection of the right to live a life free from violence, as an important part of the state's obligations to protect free speech and the right to education. In a groundbreaking decision, the Constitutional Court considered a case in which a male professor was named in a report circulated online that stated he had sexually harassed a male student. The named professor decided to bring a case against the faculty member who wrote and published the report, a feminist academic. The court had to decide whether the information was protected by her right to free speech or whether it was a violation of his right to honour and good reputation.

The court held that the document, which detailed the testimonies of students and the names of alleged harassers, was protected by free speech because it had the objective of denouncing human rights violations and tolerance of sexism in the university. The court recognised that 'victims of gender-based violence turn to *escrache* given the recognised weaknesses within institutional mechanisms (of the state, universities and companies) to tackle these facts, protect victims and respect their dignity, and to provide solutions'. The court held that it would be unfair to hold individuals speaking out on the internet to the same standard as newspapers, and that social media had an important role in 'making the private public'.

These cases understand that defamation proceedings operate as a means of censorship. Censorship violates an individual's rights to share and provide information, but also the right of members of society more generally to receive that information. It also fails to properly account for why women and others are speaking out: to end violence against women in our societies. Instead of starting with the question 'Is the statement defamatory and does it damage his reputation?', the court asks itself a different question: 'What was the woman's objective when she spoke out?' In examining this crucial question, the court time and time again has found that her statements are protected free speech, because talking about gender-based violence is protected by her fundamental human rights.

Her right to tell her story

As we have seen, the starting point of international law in cases about her right to speak is freedom of expression. The European Court of Human Rights explains that this right 'constitutes one of the essential foundations of a democratic society and one of the basic conditions for its progress and for each individual's self fulfilment'.

Let's pause there, as it's an important point. Free speech isn't only about campaigning and media reporting—it is also about an individual's right to self-fulfilment. International and regional human rights courts have explained that the right to free speech contains within it a hierarchy, with greater protections for three kinds of speech: first, matters of politics and of public interest; second, information relating to those holding public office and candidates who are seeking to hold public office; and third, speech that relates to an essential aspect of a person's identity and their human dignity.

Free speech protects our expression of our own experiences—and our right to report our truth and to tell the world about it. As the UK Supreme Court explained in 2014 in holding that the pianist James Rhodes was entitled to publish his own account of the abuse he experienced:

> A person who has suffered in the way that the appellant has suffered and has struggled to cope with the consequences of his suffering in the way that he has struggled, has the right to tell the world about it. And there is a corresponding public interest in others being able to listen to his life story in all its searing detail.

As many of the women we interviewed for this book explained, winning a libel lawsuit meant getting her voice back and being able to speak about her own experiences. Otherwise, she is being silenced, prevented from speaking about a part of herself and about something that she has gone through in her life.

For many survivors of abuse, their experience of abuse becomes part of their identity, and their ability to overcome it is also part of who they are. Being able to talk about it can be an important part of their healing. Survivors shouldn't have to fear being sued and even bankrupted for speaking about their abuse, and the law should protect those who speak out and identity themselves as victims of gender-based violence.

Blaming women for the law's failures

'Women are being blamed for not using a system that has consistently failed them,' Sibongile Ndashe told us.

Sibongile is the director of the Initiative for Strategic Litigation in Africa (ISLA), a pan-African feminist organisation that works with the law to obtain justice for women there. Sibongile has identified a pattern in cases in Africa, which we are also seeing around the world: women are being asked, 'Why didn't you go to the police?' Too often, negative inferences are made against women who speak out about gender-based violence simply because they did not report their claim to the police when it occurred. Too often, her decision not to report him to the police is being used to deny her right to speak out about it. This is despite the fact that we know, as Sibongile points out, that 'the system is broken when it comes to violence against women'.

ISLA supports women facing gendered violence, but Sibongile told us that their work had to shift when they became aware of an avalanche of defamation and libel suits against women and survivor groups in Africa. It wasn't only defamation cases: women were being prosecuted for cyber-bullying and facing all kinds of legal actions to silence their allegations of rape or sexual violence. They created a targeted project, 'Women Who Speak', in response to the incredible surge in these claims across the African continent.

In one astounding judgment from South Africa, the judge used the facts that the woman hadn't reported the assault and no charges were laid to grant an order that would prevent the woman from ever repeating her claims of rape again. The District Court in Cape Town provided a man with a Protection from Harassment Order (PHA), which prevented his ex-girlfriend from 'disclosing to anyone in any manner that the Respondent had allegedly raped the Appellant' and that he had committed emotional abuse.

Before the court case, the judge explained, the couple had been in a relationship for three years. They both worked in the fashion industry. The woman victim described having suffered emotional and mental abuse; her ex-boyfriend's mother had even placed him in a clinic to deal with his anger problems. She said that she was raped and she was advised by a social worker not to report the rape to police. She decided to apply for a protection order, but she withdrew the application at a later date and instead they made a settlement agreement not to make contact with each other. Over time, she told the court, she began to tell people in confidence about the rape. She started talking about her experience in a private group of survivors of gender-based violence. She said she needed to speak out as a way to heal, and that she had never publicly named him as her rapist.

She was then alerted to the fact that private messages she sent to others in the survivors' group about the rape, including her ex-boyfriend's identity, had been made public—they were leaked and posted on Twitter—without her consent or her permission. She was devastated. But the court held that the case involved 'cyber-bullying', 'gender-based violence' and the MeToo movement. The judge stated that while he empathised with her belief that she was a victim of abuse, 'she cannot continue to tell others that the applicant had raped her', given it 'is a very serious allegation'. In the judge's opinion, even though the victim had only told members of a safe space group, her case confirmed that 'no one can be trusted with your secrets'. The order the judge granted meant that she was completely censored and unable to talk about her experiences at all, to anyone, anywhere and at any time.

She appealed and challenged the silencing order, arguing that it constituted a regression in the national fight against gender-based violence. She also explained that she did not want to press criminal charges because she didn't have faith in the criminal justice system. He argued in response that 'rape culture in South Africa is endemic, but that [she] cannot make him the poster child for rape', since he claimed never to have raped anyone. He told the court that her conduct illustrated malice.

In the appeal decision, the High Court of South Africa held that the magistrate was wrong to draw a negative inference from the fact that she had not gone through the criminal justice system. The court set out detailed evidence about her fears, the context of the relationship, the circumstances in which she said she was raped, and contemporaneous text messages in which she accused him of raping her and asked him for an apology. The court held her version of events to be more credible. It noted that he did not deny the allegations in reply to her texts, and that he had started harassing her directly and indirectly through family and friends and on social media. The court described 'damning evidence' against him.

According to the High Court, 'there was no need for her to lay a charge against him and to have him prosecuted and convicted to be labelled as a rapist, based on the evidence in this case'. As in the case of *Tölle v. Croatia* heard by the European Court of Human Rights we discussed in Chapter 6, the court explained that the absence of a conviction does not mean that a person who committed an offence like theft 'cannot be called a thief or, as in this case, a rapist'. That is, there doesn't need to be a criminal conviction for you to call someone a rapist if the facts show that he is a rapist.

The court went on to explain that this is particularly important when speaking about an accusation of rape, since 'it is a notorious fact, which has been judicially recognised, that most victims do not report rape to the police. It does not render the true facts, that a victim was raped, untrue or non-existent.' The court said that survivors are often threatened and shamed into silence, and that the characteristics of sexual violence often make it seem impossible for victims to report what happened to their friends and loved ones, never mind to state officials.

The court found that the woman in this case was a survivor of gender-based violence, and that 'she was trying to be heard, to find healing and to protect others from suffering the same fate'. She had 'the right to speak and to express herself about the experiences she had endured', and it was her right to talk about her rape with other victims.

This was not a defamation action, though, and the High Court made it clear that its finding was confined to the facts of this case. It was a case in which a man brought his ex-girlfriend to court, arguing that she was harassing him by calling him a rapist. She had never published or publicly named him as her rapist. Instead, he brought her to court for telling other victims of rape, in a private group, that he had raped her. This information had become public without her consent. The court found that the magistrate, in granting the protection order, 'perpetuated the notion that victims of gender-based violence should not speak out, should remain silent about their experiences, and should be careful who they speak to'. Unsurprisingly, the High Court set the protection order aside and found that she had not harassed him.

This is not a unique case. In another case from South Africa, the judge found against a woman who made allegations of sexual assault on Twitter and awarded damages of 65,000 rand. The court emphasised the damage caused to the accused man by allegations of this nature: 'at a time of increased awareness of gender-based violence and when the general public is increasingly vigilant against it (rightfully so), the mere accusation of being guilty of sexual assault and of being a sexual predator can ruin a person'. The court also placed emphasis on the fact that she had not gone to the police at the time:

> To be accused of sexual assault and to be identified as a sexual predator in such manner and circumstances can only be defamatory, especially since at the time of publishing this tweet the respondent had not pursued any criminal charges or any other steps against the applicant for a period of six years. The manner and circumstances in which the respondent elected to publish her tweets served to accuse and convict the applicant in the realm of social media without affording him an opportunity to defend himself or of challenging the allegations against him.

The problem with this legal reasoning, which requires a conviction before a woman can speak publicly, is that it fails to acknowledge the reality that the criminal justice system is deeply flawed. There is no regard for the context in which these laws operate: instead, it relies on an idealised version of how allegations like this should be investigated and prosecuted. In England, as we mentioned in the Introduction, only 1.6 per cent of rape allegations are prosecuted. The figure is even lower in many other places—and given how under-reported rape is, the actual figure is likely a fraction of this.

Given this reality, requiring criminal prosecution before a woman speaks out severely undermines the ability of survivors to speak. It completely ignores the fact that many survivors of abuse do not disclose their abuse immediately, it can take time before they feel able to approach police, and too often the police fail to act. Many choose not to go to the police at all—to protect him, to protect their children, to protect herself or for a range of other reasons, including because she has no trust in a broken criminal justice system. It does not mean that what she says is not true or that she is not permitted to speak about it. But in too many cases, the courts are blaming women for the law's failures: by finding she shouldn't speak out before he is convicted—or drawing negative inferences from her not going to law enforcement. It is vital that the courts recognise her right to speak even when she hasn't gone to police or other state officials. Her right to speak is her right.

The cases Sibongile has highlighted in her work are important because they are taking place in magistrates' courts. These are disputes at the lowest levels of courts, which often go unreported and unnoticed. Such cases demonstrate that this isn't a problem that only actresses and celebrities face. It has permeated the legal system, across cultures and social classes. Around the world, there are women today who have been gagged by court rulings, and we will never know about them because she cannot speak.

Fighting back through the courts

One of the most incredible things that we have found from speaking to women from around the world is not only that they are highlighting lawfare—the use of the law to silence them—but they are using the law to fight back.

We have seen more and more women around the world taking defamation claims against men who accuse them of lying about gender-based violence—and winning. It is defamatory to be called a liar, and we are seeing a growing trend of women countersuing men for defamation for accusing them of lying for speaking their truth about their experience of violence.

Often women have decided to take legal action in order to push back and defend themselves when libel proceedings have been brought against them. By countersuing, the women have made a strategic decision to take a stand, often to make it easier for themselves and for other women to speak out, by setting a precedent that might deter other people from suing women. These examples show that the age-old technique of suing someone for making an accusation can be countered.

In Chapter 2 we set out why Shiori Ito, the Japanese journalist, decided to go public with her experiences and frustrations with the Japanese police and the prosecutor over their decision not to charge the man she alleged had raped her, Noriyuki Yamaguchi. Here we pick up her story again to explain what happened after she decided to go public.

Shiori was deeply affected by the tragic suicide in 2020 of *Terrace House* reality TV star Hana Kimura after she experienced online trolling. Around the same time, Shiori was contacted by a young girl who said she was too scared to talk about her own abuse, given all the abuse she was seeing online against women who had spoken out, including against Shiori. This spurred Shiori to action: she decided she had to do something to tackle the online harassment and abuse she was receiving, not only for herself but because of the impact it was having on other young women who were witnessing it.

According to newspaper reports in Japan, Shiori filed a number of defamation cases against people who tweeted that she was lying about her sexual assault. She also sued an anonymous Twitter troll for defamation. Through her legal action, she discovered that the troll was Osawa Shohei, a former associate professor at the University of Tokyo, the most prestigious university in Japan. Shiori won in court, and Osawa was ordered to pay compensation and apologise.

This was an important symbolic and personal victory for Shiori, but it also sent a clear message to those who were trolling survivors, and to the survivors themselves: the people trolling them could and would be held to account.

Shiori also sued a cartoonist for insinuating that she had slept with Yamaguchi to help her career, which was also effectively calling her a liar. She won that case in November 2021, and the people who retweeted the cartoonist were also found to have libelled her.

She is now bringing a case against Mio Sugita, a Japanese politician and member of the governing party. The female MP has courted controversy previously for saying that 'women lie' about sexual assaults. *The Japan Times* has reported that she apologised in the following terms: 'I am sorry for offending people by giving the impression only women lie when lying is not restricted to a gender.' So—sorry not sorry, it seems.

The case might be one of the first of its kind anywhere in the world. In a suit filed before the Tokyo District Court, Shiori is seeking damages from Sugita for liking tweets by other people who had called her a liar, including tweets claiming that she is pretending to be a rape victim, which are defamatory. The idea behind the suit is that the liking of tweets criticising Shiori and attacking her credibility is itself defamatory and a form of 'group bullying'. For Shiori, it's important to hold prominent people who are in positions of power to account when they participate in and even encourage online attacks and campaigns against survivors.

Suing someone for liking tweets for defamation isn't a crazy idea. Back in 2018, *Law Technology Today*, an online platform, published an article called 'Think Before You Tweet'. It reported that, in Switzerland, a court fined a defendant for liking a defamatory comment on Facebook: the Zurich court had found that the 'defendant clearly endorsed the unseemly content and made it his own'.

The use of likes on social media platforms to intimidate and undermine women in public spaces has become part of a wider debate in the United Kingdom around the policing of sexual violence and protests against such violence, and how likes on social media can be used as a form of intimidation designed to silence women. In Chapter 2 we discussed the vigil for Sarah Everard. During the vigil, Patsy Stevenson, one of the protesters, was arrested. Images of Stevenson pinned down by a large number of male police officers went viral and led to criticism of the police's handling of the protest (even though the independent police complaints commission later exonerated them). Stevenson spoke out about her experience and the problems of policing of women's protests. After the controversy around her arrest, the 28-year-old said that she received 50 likes on her Tinder account from police officers and security guards. She told *The Guardian* that it 'is almost like an intimidation thing, saying, "Look we can see you," and that, to me is terrifying'.

Shiori's decision to countersue Yamaguchi for defamation is part of a global trend. ██████████████████████

But fighting back in defamation claims doesn't always work, and can have mixed results. For example, in Australia, Wendy Dent decided to sue TV personality Don Burke after he claimed that she lied when she said that he had asked her to audition naked for his TV program *Burke's Backyard*, and that she had made a false allegation as part of a 'witch-hunt' against him. He had made the comments on the national TV program *A Current Affair* in response to the many allegations of sexual misconduct that he faced in the wake of MeToo. Dent said of her experience of Burke, 'I went from feeling like this talent with a future to feeling like I was just a pair of boobs to him.' He defended the case, arguing the defences of truth and qualified privilege. But the case turned on the meaning (or imputations) of what he said in the context of the entire broadcast. Burke himself argued that what he said, considered in the context of the entire program, was not defamatory because the presenter, Tracy Grimshaw, had made clear that she was 'utterly rejecting' his assertion of a witch-hunt—and that, as a result, a reasonable observer of the program would not have come away thinking Dent was lying. The judge agreed, saying that the reasonable member of the public would have understood the allegations against him were credible, and his denials were not, but noted the 'irony of the defendant obtaining judgment in his favour on the basis that he has will be obvious'. When one considers how easy it is to sue for defamation in Australia, and how many men have successfully sued women and newspapers for defamation for making allegations of sexual misconduct, the irony that a woman suing would lose—and on this basis—is immense. Dent's lawyer claimed it was a 'pyrrhic victory' for Burke: he had won, but the judge agreed Dent was the one to be believed. Dent had been maligned by him as having lied and being part of a witch-hunt, and yet when she sued, he won and she was left with the costs of the case. Dent said she felt vindicated by the judge's comments about her credibility— she had defended her truth—which is what 'counts most'. But she added, 'I have been through hell 100 times because of Don Burke, and because of this ruling today, it was 101.'

Instead of suing for defamation for calling them a liar, some women have taken a different route and instead countersued for the assault itself. Consider, for example, the case Taylor Swift took against the man who sued her for defamation and then claimed she lied about him groping her. In 2015, a radio DJ, David Mueller, attended Swift's concert. Before the concert she hosted a meet-and-greet for fans, where she met Mueller. When they were taking a picture together, Swift said the DJ groped her by reaching under her skirt and grabbing her bottom. She had him ejected by security, and he received a lifetime ban from her shows; according to news reports, he was also fired from his job over the incident. Mueller then sued Swift for defamation, claiming she had lied and ruined his reputation, asking for US$3 million in damages.

Swift responded by countersuing him for assault, claiming only US$1 in damages. She sued him back not to win damages but to hold him to account: by defending and winning the defamation case, she would prove the truth of her allegations. In 2017, Mueller's defamation claim was thrown out of court, with the jury finding he had assaulted her.

Swift's victory was lauded at the time for drawing attention to the under-reporting of sexual assault and as a bigger symbolic victory to empower women to speak out. Swift herself has said that she countersued to take a stand and to help other women come forward. Many of the women we have spoken to told us that they were motivated to take action in the hope that the precedent they set might make it easier for the women coming after them. For others, countersuing was simply the only option to fight back against a suit and to obtain some form of justice.

Where the domestic courts fail, international and regional mechanisms—including the United Nations and its special procedures—can be important alternative sites where silence-breakers, campaigners and journalists can fight back against silencing. These mechanisms have been extremely important in upholding women's right to free speech and in setting out how gender-based violence affects free speech and women's rights more generally.

For example, in the case of Amal Fathy in Egypt, Jen and some Doughty Street Chambers colleagues, working with the free speech organisation Index on Censorship, obtained a ruling from the Working Group on Arbitrary Detention that her imprisonment and prosecution for speaking out on Facebook about sexual harassment was unlawful. While Amal has since been convicted and sentenced to prison in Egypt, the United Nations' ruling in her favour—showing that Egypt's silencing is unlawful because speaking out about sexual harassment is protected speech under international law—has assisted in demonstrating that Egypt's actions are wrong and continues to form part of her ongoing advocacy from Switzerland, where she now lives in exile.

In another example, the UN Human Rights Committee issued a landmark decision in 2018 about the case of Lydia Cacho, the Mexican journalist we mentioned in Chapter 2; it recognised that the inhuman and degrading treatment she suffered after being arrested for criminal defamation amounted to gender-based violence and violated her rights to free speech. Her UN case has been used by free speech organisations to advocate for better protections for women journalists in Mexico and elsewhere.

We have acted in cases before international and regional human rights courts to ensure that women can speak out and to challenge gendered online attacks against women journalists aimed at silencing them in online spaces. Human rights courts can provide important remedies, ensure state accountability and provide recognition for human rights violations suffered by women speaking out about their abuse and by the journalists trying to report on it.

While women are fighting back with the law, their ability to do so depends upon having the funds to do so—or finding lawyers willing to act for free. The cases take a huge amount of time and resources, and the fact is that women shouldn't be put in the position of having to countersue: the legal action they face shouldn't have been brought in the first place. Are there other solutions to shutting down abusive legal claims?

SLAPPing down women's speech: Is anti-SLAPP legislation the answer?

Defamation or privacy suits are not in themselves bad—but they can be wielded in ways that entrench already significant power differentials. When a powerful man is able to use the law as a weapon to silence criticism and discussion of his abusive behaviour, we think it is worth questioning why the law is permitted to operate in this way and to look critically at how that law operates in practice.

There is increasing global concern that SLAPP suits—standing for Strategic Litigation Against Public Participation—are stifling free speech.

The term 'SLAPP suits' was first coined in the 1980s by George Pring and Penelope Canan, who explained in their book that a SLAPP suit is a legal action taken against people or organisations who speak out on issues of public interest. The point of the suit isn't to win, but to silence, which is why they're known as litigation 'against public participation'. The ACLU has explained that defamation is one of the most common legal claims but other kinds of legal actions can be taken too. There is now growing understanding that these retaliatory lawsuits are a form of legal and judicial harassment. The European Parliament has warned that the problem is growing, and represents a substantial threat to free speech. A further worrying trend is that these suits appear to be organised—being funded by third parties to help pursue a common target. Newspapers are being coerced into deleting factual reports and individuals are being forced into silence.

The concern within the European Union arose after the assassination in 2017 of the Maltese journalist Daphne Caruana Galizia. Daphne was an investigative journalist in Malta reporting on corruption and human rights abuse. For her work reporting on matters of immense public interest, she was sued for defamation by Maltese government ministers, politicians and businessmen. The SLAPP suits didn't silence Daphne, but they did silence others in the media space in Malta, making her the sole voice in the media willing to hold power to account. The investigative journalist had 47 SLAPP suits pending against her at the time of her death, and her sons, Paul, Matthew and Andrew, have described how the family—Jen's clients—and her estate are still having to fight these lawsuits. After her death, her husband, Peter, had to appear in court twice a week to defend the cases against her estate, extending the harassment she faced to her bereaved family. The legal harassment she suffered, through the repeated use of defamation suits against her, together with the online attacks, has been seen as part of a broader strategy—a spectrum of attempts to silence Daphne and her important public interest reporting—that ultimately led to her assassination. But those who sought to silence her by killing her have failed: journalists have committed to continuing her work, and her family have built a foundation in her name to campaign for change. Thanks to this work, and to Daphne, politicians began a campaign to enact anti-SLAPP suit legislation in the European Union.

Organisations such as Greenpeace, Index on Censorship, the American Bar Association and the free speech organisation Article 19 have all been documenting the worrying rise in SLAPP suits against journalists and human rights defenders. Organisations are advocating for anti-SLAPP legislation, including early dismissal mechanisms, support for victims such as legal aid, advice and representation, and compensation for loss of income and stress. There also need to be deterrent measures. Laws like these have already been developed in the United States, some provinces and states in Canada, and Australia.

The European Parliament has recommended that there should be expedient, efficient and affordable legal procedures to dismiss SLAPP suits, that penalties should be introduced for people abusing the legal system via SLAPP suits, and that judges and lawyers should be trained to recognise and stop these types of suits. In our view, if the ultimate goal of SLAPP suits is to silence rather than to win, then they must be prevented for the sake of free speech and media freedom. Typically, the push for this legislation has come in the wake of David and Goliath litigation including a mining company or other major transnational company suing environmental activists. The idea of anti-SLAPP legislation is to ensure that wealth and influence cannot be harnessed to force people into silence through the law. But we also believe that anti-SLAPP legislation should specifically protect speech about violence against women—as it is speech in the public interest—and should stop men abusing their wealth and power to silence women and journalists.

And we aren't alone in that view.

Mandi Gray is a Canadian academic and survivor advocate who was the complainant in a high-profile rape trial and made a film about her experience to highlight how badly women are treated in the criminal justice system. That work led to an academic interest in how women are being sued for defamation for speaking out about their abuse. She worked on an academic paper exploring the problem of defamation suits in Canada and whether Canada's new anti-SLAPP legislation, which would allow courts to strike out certain types of legal claims, might be the answer to protect women from abusive suits that censor their speech about abuse. She didn't know at the time she was working on her academic research that her own case would become a test case on this very issue.

Mandi explained to us that she was being sued in British Columbia, along with nineteen other women, for tweets in support of a woman known as A.B. who made allegations of sexual harassment and rape against the author Steven Galloway. Galloway is suing A.B. as well as the people who tweeted in support of her. Galloway was at one time a tenured professor and chair of the creative writing program at the University of British Columbia. But he was fired after 'serious allegations' were made against him by A.B., a student, and were subsequently made public. Galloway says that he had a consensual relationship with A.B., while she described it as 'an ongoing abusive relationship'. The university hired a retired judge to investigate and she found on a balance of probabilities that he did not commit sexual assault. The case generated a media storm in Canada where authors such as Margaret Atwood weighed in, expressing their opinions on whether the university had treated Galloway fairly. But when we spoke to Mandi we were interested in her academic expertise and her experience of going through an anti-SLAPP motion and trial in British Columbia.

Twelve of the defendants in the case, including Mandi and A.B., brought an application before the court to get the case against them thrown out. In 2019, during their ongoing defamation proceedings, British Columbia had enacted a new piece of legislation, the *Protection of Public Participation Act*. This meant that they had a chance to test out the legislation. The test to be applied under the law—and the matters to be considered in Justitia's scales—is to weigh the public interest in allowing meritorious lawsuits to proceed against the public interest in protecting expression on matters of public interest. They argued that they had spoken out in the public interest and that there was a greater public interest in the lawsuits against them being dismissed.

The group being sued argued that 'the reporting of gender-based violence must be protected, and that victims must be able to come forward without fear that they will be sued for defamation'. If Galloway's defamation lawsuit proceeded, they argued it would have a chilling effect on victims or complainants of sexual violence in the future and that 'sexual assault survivors will be silenced even more'. On this basis, the group argued that the public interest weighed in favour of dismissing Galloway's claim against them.

A.B.'s lawyer argued that the lawsuit sought 'permanently to shutter A.B. making it difficult or impossible for her to identify as a "survivor" in any capacity, and to engage in advocacy and activism on issues of sexual violence'. If Galloway's reputational harm were permitted to trump A.B.'s public interest in reporting and healing from sexualised violence, then the question would arise: 'Why report?'

Galloway's lawyer argued that those submissions amounted 'to the absurd proposition that, in order to engage in important public discussions and to protect victims of sexual violence and encourage reporting of such violence, the Applicants must be free to publish defamatory statements—that he is a rapist and guilty of criminal conduct—about him, without consequence'.

After considering the anti-SLAPP motion, the judge concluded that 'it is beyond argument that there is a very significant public interest in encouraging reporting of sexual assault'. But she decided that allowing the proceedings to go ahead was the only way to ensure justice, since it would allow either A.B. or Galloway to have complete and public vindication. Most of the applicants had their applications dismissed but a few of the applicants, including Mandi, received a split decision: some aspects of their case were struck out, but portions of the claims against them could proceed. Those decisions are now under appeal—and the hearing has been listed for March 2023—meaning that the proceedings will hang over the women's heads for even longer. Has the new anti-SLAPP law really achieved its supposed goal?

This example shows that anti-SLAPP legislation may not be as simple a solution as some have hoped. As Mandi explained to us, the anti-SLAPP motion resulted in a three-week mini-trial before the defamation trial; the multiple cross-examinations will all have to be repeated during the defamation trial. This was not a quick fix solution, and has only prolonged the proceedings, their cost, and the associated stress for everyone involved.

The judge's decision, which runs into hundreds of pages, raises a separate and important issue: how do you distinguish a SLAPP claim from a meritorious claim? In other words, how do you tell the difference between an unmeritorious claim that aims to silence, and a claim in which someone is simply trying to protect their right to reputation? To dismiss a claim at a preliminary stage could deny a person their legal rights. The judge in this case held that if she dismissed the claims, 'There would be no legal consequences of any kind attached to publicly calling someone a rapist, completely outside of any formal reporting, and no obligation ever to prove the statement was true.' The judge's reasoning raises question marks, then, about how such anti-SLAPP legislation in Canada—or anywhere else—can be used by those who make accusations of sexual assault or rape on social media to defend themselves. Mandi's case is a test case to determine how the courts will treat allegations of gender-based violence in anti-SLAPP motions: and we will all be watching what happens in the appeal.

Online violence—the new frontier

We couldn't write this book without addressing the new frontier of violence against women: violence in the online space. This is another, increasingly problematic, form of violence that is silencing women's speech and undermining women's public participation, along with their ability to speak out and share information about gender-based violence.

As the former UN Special Rapporteur on Violence Against Women notes, 'gender discrimination and patriarchal patterns that result in gender-based violence offline are reproduced, and sometimes amplified and redefined' online and we are seeing 'new forms of violence emerge,' such as image-based sexual abuse. She has highlighted how women—in particular women journalists and women who have spoken out about their own abuse—are facing online violence that reproduces the harmful stereotypes we have discussed throughout this book and forces women to 'retreat from the internet', leading to 'self-censorship'. It's not just legal actions against women for speaking out about the abuse online: the online violence they are facing also silences them. Online abuse is 'a direct attack on women's visibility and full participation in public life', and its consequence is 'a society where women no longer feel safe either online or offline, given the widespread impunity for perpetrators of gender-based violence'.

In Japan, Shiori Ito had to hire a team to go through her social media and report the horrendous abuse that she received after she went public with her allegation of rape and her criticism of the police decision to stop investigating her case. ████████████

██
██
██
██
██████████████████████

The vitriol and abuse that Amber Heard faced online after making allegations of domestic abuse against Johnny Depp and during the two defamation trials that followed was unique and unprecedented. The trolling of Amber, her friends and lawyers, and the witnesses who gave evidence for her in court was relentless. But it has also sparked an important global conversation about misogyny, online harm, the responsibility of platforms like Twitter and TikTok, and the need to better protect women making accusations of domestic and sexual violence. We hope that conversation continues and that it is never allowed to happen again.

As commentator after commentator has explained, online abuse like this has the effect of silencing accusers and of deterring other victims from coming forward.

In our experience with our clients, it doesn't just silence women—it can also have serious mental health consequences, and these are slowly being recognised. For example, in 2021 the Australian media union recognised that women journalists are suffering post-traumatic stress disorder as a result of the online violence they face and is now describing it as an occupational health and safety issue.

The problem we see in our practices, representing survivors who have spoken out about their abuse and women journalists trying to do their job who face online violence, is that domestic law offers few useful remedies in a global information environment; online trolling happens across borders by often anonymous accounts. Shiori Ito and other women are pioneering interesting legal strategies against trolls, but it requires resources and the ability to identify the troll, and where they live, to be able to take legal action against them (whether in defamation, harassment or any other type of claim). As Jen has found representing women journalists working for BBC News Persian in London, how is a defamation claim or a police report going to deal with trolling coming from a country like Iran? And how many women have the resources to sue a troll on the other side of the world? The major social media platforms where the abuse takes place, like Twitter, Facebook, TikTok and Instagram, have their own internal complaint systems, which are notoriously slow. By failing to take action, they enable the abuse of women.

Various governments are looking to introduce law reform to address this problem. For example, in the United Kingdom the Online Safety Bill 2022 has been introduced with the aim of creating a safer online space, including, for example, creating a new offence of making a rape threat online. It has, however, been criticised by the End Violence Against Women Coalition for failing to explicitly reference online violence against women and failing to place greater accountability on online platforms for facilitating abuse.

In the absence of adequate responses from either the platforms or from governments tasked with law reform, feminists around the world have been thinking about how we can 'take back tech' and ensure that women's rights to free speech are protected and respected. Through our work with Article 19, we have spoken with and interviewed women from around the world who have set up incredible, practical initiatives to help other women protect their digital rights through holistic safety mechanisms. For example, American journalist and academic Dr Michelle Ferrier, founded TrollBusters, which provides first-responder assistance to women facing online abuse and other 'troll behaviour'. TrollBusters helps journalists with free lessons on digital hygiene, conducts training on digital security and publishes a monthly magazine online, *Toxic Avenger*. It tailors its approach specifically to freelancers and independent journalists, categories in which women often find themselves. The organisation VitaActiva similarly provides support and strategic solutions for women and LGBTQI+ journalists, activists and defenders of gender, land and labour rights, and freedom of expression. The organisation provides a number of resources online, which focus on self-care in resistance (*autocuidados en resistencia*) and cyber-security against digital violence.

These organisations respond to the urgent problem of online abuse, harassment and misogyny that women face for carrying out their work. For example, Vita Activa runs a helpline for those experiencing stress, trauma, crisis, burnout and gender-based violence: twelve trained responders who work around the clock, responding to messages they receive via Signal or Telegram. Feminist journalists and social communicators are creating solidarity networks. *The New York Times* has held solidarity parties, where journalists gather and teach each other how to protect themselves from 'doxxing', or the release of their private information online.

In countries from Chile to Paraguay, Bangladesh to Pakistan, online and offline movements were launched during the Covid-19 pandemic to support women who are speaking out about gender-based violence and women's human rights issues. Women who have spoken out on social media have told us how, in the face of coordinated online attacks, feminists have organised to create hashtags calling out abuse and providing emotional support to women who are being targeted. Free speech organisations, the United Nations and women's rights organisations are increasingly understanding how a feminist approach to women's free speech rights can help empower women to speak out and combat 'the chilling'.

Protecting all of her rights—to end violence against women

Women's right to speak about the experience of gender-based violence is about more than just her free speech. For too long, courts have been approaching the balance as one between her right to free speech and his right to reputation—and have too often got it wrong. Her right to speak about gender-based violence is also protected by the right to equality and the right to be free from violence, and when these rights are considered in Justitia's weighing scales, courts come to better decisions. As human rights lawyers, we want to see more lawyers make these arguments and more courts start listening and recognising the public interest in enabling her right to speak if we are ever going to end violence against women. And as women face new challenges with developing technologies, we must continue to innovate to find better solutions to protect her ability to speak, using whatever media she chooses.

Conclusion

FREE HER SPEECH

'Different legal systems, same story.'

Shiori Ito's simple words sum up what we have learned in writing this book. It has become clear to us, in our research, that the legal strategies and harmful stereotypes being deployed to discredit and silence women span continents and cultures. The interviews we have conducted with women across Africa, Asia, Europe and Latin America show that this is not just happening in Japan, or in Australia, or in the United Kingdom, or in the United States. It is happening everywhere.

To understand the law, we need to look beyond how it is written on paper and see how it works in the real world.

On paper, there is nothing wrong with being able to defend your reputation and your privacy. But in our opinion, which is drawn from what we have seen in our own legal practices and our work on this book, it is clear the law can be used to silence women. Women have told us how they have been silenced after being sued, sometimes for years, before winning their case, or been permanently silenced because they couldn't afford to defend their right to free speech.

The effect of this gendered censorship is all-pervasive: some women we have spoken to even felt unable to talk about their rapist in private conversations. 'My alleged rapist,' one woman said to us—before catching herself in a moment of self-reflection about her subconscious choice of language. After years of being sued for defamation and being forced to carefully choose her words, she realised she had become conditioned to referring to him in this way. 'See, I can't even speak my truth and call him what he is—my rapist—here with you.' She and many other women we have spoken to are afraid, and so conditioned by the threat of litigation or from the process of being sued, that they don't feel safe to speak their truth about rape or abuse, even behind closed doors. Many women report developing mental and physical health issues as a result of the stress they have experienced as a result of speaking out and the legal consequences that they have faced. But we also know that women who remain silent out of fear of facing those very consequences also suffer adverse physical and mental consequences because they must endure their pain in shame and isolation. We need to address this problem so it is easier for women to speak. We also know that if women remain in silos of silence, repeat perpetrators can get away with their crimes—and we, as a society, cannot understand the problem and how to fix it.

Many women who have suffered gender-based violence and been through the criminal justice system have told us they wish they had known more about it before it happened to them: what you need to know before a rape trial, you need to know before you are raped. But what we see in our work is different. Many women don't realise that after you've been raped or assaulted, there are all kinds of laws that regulate what you can say, to whom you can say it and when—and each decision you make has legal risks and ramifications. But knowledge is the key to empowerment: we want more women to understand this and to be aware of the issues they could face so they can make decisions that are right for them and find healing and justice. Understanding the problem is the first step towards fixing it: we hope this book sparks more conversations about what we can do to create change.

Privacy and defamation laws can operate to silence women for years through private claims in our legal systems. These arguments are framed as contests between his right to reputation and privacy, and her right to freedom of speech. But what about her rights to self-determination, self-fulfilment and a life free from violence? What about her right to equality? In many courts, these rights are simply not being considered—and the result seems to be a system that fails to respond to the reality of gender-based violence and fails to respect her right to speak. That denies her right to speak about her own experiences, her past, her history, her life. Are we really getting the balance right? And if not, how can women get their voices back?

Is it time for a different set of laws—or is there at least a way to ensure the laws we already have provide gender justice? We believe the courts can take a different approach to these kinds of cases—one that adequately weighs all these rights and prevents the law from being used as a weapon to silence women. An approach which recognises that when victims and survivors speak out about abuse they do so in the public interest, and that doing so is a powerful and important part of breaking the silence around different forms of gendered violence. An approach which recognises that there is immense public interest in ensuring that victims of rape and abuse are able to talk about their experiences, in private and in public. And an approach which recognises that speech provides a form of protection—a warning system—and a different form of justice for women in a world where our criminal justice systems too often fail. The public interest is in breaking the 'tyrannies of silence', as Audre Lorde has described them. 'My silences have not protected me. Your silence will not protect you,' she warned. We must turn the silence into language and action. Lawyers need to start making these arguments in our courts, and our judges need to listen. The law and the courts must work to promote equality. We believe that we, as lawyers, must ensure that our work promotes human rights and dignity, equality and free speech for all.

The threat of legal action and its use against those who make accusations of abuse and violence—or those who speak about their experiences—has to be called out, and stopped. Otherwise, the endemic and pervasive gender-based violence that terrorises women and girls, online and offline, will continue unabated. Every woman you know can tell you a story of rape, assault or harassment. Or of how they have been scared to walk home at night because we all know the statistics and are reminded of them with each new story we read about. Technology is facilitating digital forms of violence against women: image-based abuse, online attacks, digital kidnapping. All of this needs to be addressed and to change, and for it to change, we have to be able to speak about it. The law is being used against us instead of working for us. It is being used as a tool to maintain and re-assert the old status quo when it comes to gender-based violence: silence. If we don't call this out, and talk about how the law is being used to SLAPP down women's speech, then women around the world will continue to be silenced. The law cannot act as the handmaiden of the tyranny of silence, to aid and abet violence against women. And the law should not be weaponised by abusive men to allow them to continue their abuse. The law should ensure that women and girls can speak out so that we can end violence against women.

We also need to have conversations about how women who make accusations are treated in civil proceedings about sexual and domestic abuse. We believe that all courts, whether criminal or civil, should have the same protections for women, wherever courts are ruling on matters involving allegations of gender-based violence. Why is it that juries are given directions about gender-based violence in criminal but not civil claims? Why is it that we accept that a woman giving evidence about sexual assault should be protected from live broadcast in criminal trials, but not in civil trials?

In our view, costly defamation proceedings are not an appropriate venue to resolve allegations of gender-based violence. No one can afford to defend them. It is an action for the privileged and the rich. And even when you win, your vindication can often be costly: if the court awards you legal costs, it might not cover all the costs you incur in the case. And there is no compensation for the stress you have suffered, or for the years you have been silenced.

So how can we free her speech? How can we ensure that victims and survivors are able to come forward without the fear of being sued and silenced? How can we make sure that the law is balanced and fair, that it protects the presumption of innocence, privacy and reputation while upholding women's rights to live a life free from violence? How can we ensure women can afford to defend their free speech? What damages should a survivor obtain for being sued and silenced? Shouldn't women be compensated for the years of silencing and the stress of proceedings that they face?

These are just some of the questions that we believe we all need to start asking—and our lawmakers need to start debating.

In this book we have told inspiring stories of women who have broken the silence and faced a brutal backlash—a backlash which plays out on the internet, in the media and through the courts. But we have also seen how women are organising, campaigning, litigating and fighting back. We hope their strategies and stories inspire more women to see that they aren't alone and that they have options. Legal change is possible. And fight back we must.

Because if we don't, how many more women will be silenced?

ACKNOWLEDGEMENTS

Many people have made this book possible.

It was Baroness Helena Kennedy KC who first raised the idea of writing this book. Back in 2018, Jen did the libel review of Helena's latest book, *Eve Was Shamed*, about how the British criminal justice system was failing women. Jen sent Helena a long list of notes to consider for her book about another area where the justice system was failing women: defamation. 'Darling, that's your area—use it for *your* book,' Helena replied. We are so grateful to Helena for her support and encouragement—for us and for so many other women in the law—and for suggesting a book on this subject.

We decided to do this book together after our many rich discussions and debates on media law, women's rights and our respective clients and cases. We think the book is better for it. The decision was inspired, in part, by our respective academic mentors, Professor Hilary Charlesworth and Professor Christine Chinkin, who together wrote the first feminist analysis of international law, supervised our early academic work on opposite sides of the globe and have inspired us ever since. Hilary's recent appointment as a judge on the International Court of Justice, the first Australian woman and the fifth woman *ever* appointed is another sign that progress is being made, if slowly, and will inspire so many more women.

To our brave clients and the many courageous women, survivors, silence-breakers, journalists, lawyers and advocates who have generously given us their time and told us their stories—this book would not have been possible without you. Whether quoted, named or not—for legal reasons or otherwise—your perspectives shaped our thinking and our words, and enabled us to write this book to inform and empower so many others about your struggles, your strategies and your triumphs. This book is for you—and because of you. Thanks in particular to Zelda Perkins, Julie Macfarlane, Shiori Ito, Amber Heard, Mandi Gray, Catalina Ruiz-Navarro, Matilde de los Milagros Londoño, Pragna Patel, Nicola Stocker, Afsana Lachaux, Chanel Contos and Dhanya Mani.

We are grateful to the brilliant Doughty Street Women—our colleagues in chambers, led by the indefatigable Caoilfhionn Gallagher KC—who have created a feminist, collective and safe space for support, inspiration and discussion, which has enriched our lives, our careers and our thinking for this book. We are proud to be members of Doughty Street Chambers, together with so many colleagues so committed to justice and equality, and we thank Edward Fitzgerald KC and Geoffrey Robertson KC, as heads of chambers, for championing us and creating the space for us all to do the work we do as barristers.

Our agents, Jane Novak and Jane Finigan, have provided constant support, wisdom and encouragement. Our publishers, Kelly Fagan at Allen & Unwin in Australia, and Claudia Connal and Evie Dunne at Octopus in the United Kingdom, saw the potential in this book and backed it. Emily Meller, Julian Welch and Angela Handley helped us make it the book that it is.

Thanks to the brilliant women who conducted research and supported our work— Phoebe Cook and Georgie Trevelyan-Clark—and to those who so generously offered to read drafts and gave us useful feedback and further inspiration and ideas: Susie Alegre, Harriet Johnson, Seumas Milne, Connor Woodman, Gema Fernandez Rodriguez de Lievana.

We would also like to thank the lawyers who gave us their time and spoke to us: Galina Arapova, Gill Phillips, Pia Sarma, Matthew Lewis, Rebekah Giles, Jonathan Price, Karuna Nundy, Ana Bejarano Ricaurte, María Camila Correa Flórez, Mónica Roa, Sibongile Ndashe, Mark Stephens, Tom Blackburn SC and Professor David Rolph. Thank you to all of the women, journalists and women's rights activists who spoke to us, who are not mentioned here. And to Nicola Solomon at the Society of Authors for her guidance and support.

Finally, thank you to all the journalists upon whose work we have drawn for this book. Journalism is invaluable—on this subject and all others. We wrote this book, in part, because of our concern about the cost and difficulty of doing journalism on this particular subject. We hope this book makes a small contribution towards making your work easier in the future.

CHAPTER NOTES

The main sources cited in the chapters are listed below.

Prologue

The description of *Stocker v. Stocker* has been taken from the High Court, Court of Appeal and Supreme Court judgments. All these documents are available online through the UK Supreme Court's website or through other free court service websites such as BAILII. The term 'himpathy' comes from Kate Manne's book *Down Girl*.

Stocker v. Stocker [2016] EWHC 474 (QB)

Stocker v. Stocker [2019] UKSC 17

Manne, K., *Down Girl: The logic of misogyny*, New York: Oxford University Press, 2017

Introduction

The introduction draws on the work of the *New Yorker* journalists who have written about the MeToo movement and on the work of academics, including Cynthia Enloe, who have been discussing the broader implications of MeToo for women's security.

Chandra, G., Enloe, C. & Erlingsdóttir, I., 'No peace without security: Shoring the gains of the #MeToo movement', in S. Smith & K. Yoshida (eds), *Feminist Conversations on Peace*, Bristol: Bristol University Press, 2022, pp. 76–91

Johnson, H., *Enough: The violence against women and how to end it*, London: HarperCollins Publishers, 2022

Tolentino, J., 'One year of #MeToo: What women's speech is still not allowed to do', *The New Yorker*, 10 October 2018, <www.newyorker.com/news/our-columnists/one-year-of-metoo-what-womens-speech-is-still-not-allowed-to-do>

Chapter 1: Silencing Justitia

For a historical overview of the treatment of women by the law, and of the gendered nature of the legal system, we have drawn on the work of academics and practitioners who have been influential in the United Kingdom and in Australia. Susie Alegre, Harriet Johnson and Baroness Helena Kennedy KC, barristers and part of Doughty Street Chambers, have all written about human rights and the biases in the legal system in a practical and accessible way. Susie Alegre currently sits as a Deputy High Court Judge. Baroness Kennedy KC is a founding member of Doughty Street Chambers and a member of the House of Lords. Harriet Johnson is an author and practising criminal barrister. This chapter has also drawn on the seminal book by Brenda Hoggett (now Baroness Hale, a retired UK Supreme Court judge) and Sue Atkins, which has recently been reprinted in a digital format as part of the IALS open publishing series. For those who wish to study this topic more, we highly recommend reading the book. This chapter refers to a number of legal cases, UN reports and newspaper articles, all of which are also detailed on the website for further reference.

Lachaux v. Lachaux [2017] EWHC 385 (Fam)

Lachaux v. Independent Print Ltd and another [2019] UKSC 27

Alegre, S., *Freedom to Think: The long struggle to liberate our minds*, London: Atlantic Books, 2022

Atkins, S. & Hoggett, B., *Women and the Law*, 2nd edn, London: Institute of Advanced Legal Studies, 2018

Barr, C. & Topping, A., 'Fewer than one in 60 rape cases lead to charge in England and Wales', *The Guardian*, 23 May 2021, <www.theguardian.com/society/2021/may/23/fewer-than-one-in-60-cases-lead-to-charge-in-england-and-wales>

Johnson, H., *Enough: The violence against women and how to end it*, London: HarperCollins Publishers, 2022

Kennedy, H., *Eve Was Framed: Women and British justice*, London: Vintage Press, 1993

Kennedy, H., *Eve Was Shamed: How British justice is failing women*, London: Chatto & Windus, 2018

Macfarlane, J., *Going Public: A survivor's journey from grief to action*, Toronto: Between the Lines, 2020

Morgan, J. & Graycar, R., *The Hidden Gender of Law*, 2nd edn, Sydney: Federation Press, 2002

Noel, A. & Oppenheimer, D. (eds), *The Global #MeToo Movement: How social media propelled a historic movement and the law responded*, Washington: Full Court Press, 2020

Opeskin, B., 'Dismantling the diversity deficit: Towards a more inclusive Australian judiciary', in G. Appleby & A. Lynch (eds), *The Judge, the Judiciary and the Court: Individual, collegial and institutional judicial dynamics in Australia*, Cambridge: Cambridge University Press, 2020, pp. 83–115

Thornton, M., *Dissonance and Distrust: Women in the legal profession*, Melbourne & Auckland: Oxford University Press, 1996

Thornton, M. & Luker, T., 'The *Sex Discrimination Act* and Its rocky rite of passage', in M. Thornton (ed.), *Sex Discrimination in Uncertain Times*, Canberra: ANU Press, 2010, pp. 25–45

Wilson, A., *In Black and White: A young barrister's story of race and class in a broken justice system*, London: Endeavour, 2020

Chapter 2: How many women are silenced?

Contemporary newspaper resources and our own interviews form the backbone of this chapter. In the bibliography on the website, you will find the details of the cases, reports and academic work we cite in this chapter. But we imagine our readers will be most interested in knowing more about the women's stories we tell in this chapter, and in their own words. Shiori Ito, Mónica Roa López and Catalina Ruiz-

Navarro have all written their own books. We have also included reference to Louise Tickle's article for *Tortoise*, which tells the fascinating story of how the media agency overturned an injunction.

Griffiths v. Tickle [2021] EWHC 3365 (Fam)

Griffiths v. Tickle [2021] EWCA Civ 1882

Rosanna Flamer-Caldera v. Sri Lanka, Communication no. 134/2018, UN Doc CEDAW/C/81/D/134/2018, 21 February 2022, CEDAW

Ito, S. (translated by A.M. Powell), *Black Box: The memoir that sparked Japan's #MeToo movement*, New York: The Feminist Press, 2021

López, M.R., *Elefantes en la Sala: Una mirada íntima, crítica y amorosa a la familia*, Colombia: Ariel, 2022

Media Defence, 'Las Volcánicas: Sued for reporting on allegations of sexual abuse', Media Defence, 29 July 2021, <www.mediadefence.org/news/las-volcanicas-sued-for-reporting-on-allegations-of-sexual-abuse/>

Ruiz-Navarro, C., *Las mujeres que luchan se encuentran: Manual de feminismo pop latinamericano*, Barcelona: Grijalbo, 2019

Tickle, L., 'Griffiths v. Griffiths', *Tortoise*, 10 December 2021, <www.tortoisemedia.com/2021/12/10/griffiths-v-griffiths>

Chapter 3: What happens when women speak?

Between ourselves, we have been affectionately referring to this as 'the Australia chapter', since it tells a contemporary story about what happens when women in Australia speak—or try to speak—about their experiences or allegations of sexual assault and violence. In Australia, many of the women's stories have been reported in newspapers, magazines and social media. But outside of Australia, they might not be so well known. We relied upon these media resources to tell some of the stories, but we also drew on our interviews with Chanel Contos and Dhanya Mani. A number of the women whose stories we describe are writing their own books (███████████ Grace Tame and Chanel Contos), and we encourage you to read them when they become available. Some key resources relate to the Australian MeToo movement, and more recent movements. A range of material from various legal proceedings discussed can be found on the Federal Court website; it has been made available by the court due to the public interest in these matters.

Dyer v. Chrysanthou: <www.fedcourt.gov.au/services/access-to-files-and-transcripts/online-files/dyer-v-chrysanthou>

Porter v. ABC: <www.fedcourt.gov.au/services/access-to-files-and-transcripts/online-files/porter-v-abc>

R v. Lehrmann (No. 3) [2022] ACTSC 145

Rush v. Nationwide News: <www.fedcourt.gov.au/services/access-to-files-and-transcripts/online-files/rush-v-nationwide>

Crabb, A., 'Christian Porter is correct—this is an extremely unsatisfactory state of affairs', ABC News, 4 March 2021, <www.abc.net.au/news/2021-03-05/christan-porter-rule-of-law/13216806>

Dart Center for Journalism & Trauma, 'Reporting on Sexual Violence', 2011, <https://dartcenter.org/content/reporting-on-sexual-violence>

Ethics Advisory Committee of the Canadian Association of Journalists, 'Naming Sexual Assault Complainants in the Media: Ethical considerations for journalists', Canadian Association of Journalists, 16 February 2016, <https://caj.ca/images/downloads/Ethics/caj_ethics_report_sex_assault_revised_march_5.pdf>

Ferrier, T., 'The March4Justice women who are raring to rally: "A time of reckoning for Australia"', *The Guardian*, 10 March 2021, <www.theguardian.com/australia-news/2021/mar/10/the-march4justice-women-who-are-raring-to-rally-a-time-of-reckoning-for-australia>

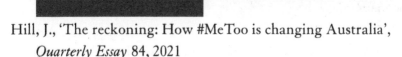

Hill, J., 'The reckoning: How #MeToo is changing Australia', *Quarterly Essay* 84, 2021

La Rosa, L., 'Trickle-down white feminism doesn't cut it', *Eureka Street*, 27 June 2018, <www.eurekastreet.com.au/article/trickle-down-white-feminism-doesn-t-cut-it>

Mani, D., 'Why victims of sexual harassment in politics are still forced to suffer in silence', *Women's Agenda*, 24 March 2019, <https://womensagenda.com.au/latest/why-victims-of-sexual-harassment-in-politics-are-still-forced-to-suffer-in-silence>

O'Connell, K., 'The MeToo movement in Australia: Silenced by defamation and disbelief', in Noel, A. & Oppenheimer, D. (eds), *The Global #MeToo Movement: How social media propelled a historic movement and the law responded*, Washington: Full Court Press, 2020, pp. 341–53

Chapter 4: Her guidebook to his playbook

This was the first chapter we sat down to write, based on our own experiences of legalling news stories at various national newspapers. The chapter was significantly enriched by our interviews with Pia Sarma and Gill Phillips, two legal media powerhouses. Due to the legal risks associated with this chapter, we decided to explain the different legal steps in reference to Jeffrey Epstein. The chapter is therefore indebted to the investigative work of journalists who contributed to the uncovering of Epstein's abuse and those who have written since about the media's failure—because of legal risks—to publish women's stories about his abuse earlier.

Chotiner, I., 'Why didn't *Vanity Fair* break the Jeffrey Epstein story?', *The New Yorker*, 8 February 2022, <www.newyorker. com/news/annals-of-communications/why-didnt-vanity-fair-break-the-jeffrey-epstein-story>

Folkenflik, D., 'A dead cat, a lawyer's call and a 5-figure donation: How media fell short on Epstein', *All Things Considered*, NPR, 22 August 2019, <www.npr.org/2019/08/22/753390385/a-dead-cat-a-lawyers-call-and-a-5-figure-donation-how-media-fell-short-on-epstei>

Kale, S., '"Everyone failed these young, Black girls": Journalist Jim DeRogatis on his decades-long battle to expose R Kelly', *The Guardian*, 4 May 2022, <www.theguardian.com/us-news/2022/may/04/everyone-failed-these-young-black-girls-journalist-jim-derogatis-on-his-decades-long-battle-to-expose-r-kelly>

Pogrund, G., 'Charlie Elphicke: The predator MP and his protection racket', *The Sunday Times*, 26 March 2022, <www. thetimes.co.uk/article/charlie-elphicke-the-predator-mp-and-his-protection-racket-3kb30pl6w>

Chapter 5: Contracted to silence

This chapter largely draws on Jen's perspective, and on our
conversations with Zelda Perkins, an incredible campaigner. It
has also benefited from conversations with legal experts in the
United Kingdom and Australia. We drew upon the investigative
reporting by the journalists in the United States and the United
Kingdom who broke the Harvey Weinstein story, as well as
an analysis of the leading legal judgment on this issue in the
United Kingdom, Jen's submissions to the Women and Equalities
Committee and the committee's subsequent reports.

ABC and ors v. Telegraph Media Group Ltd [2018] EWHC 2177 (QB)
ABC and ors v. Telegraph Media Group Ltd [2018] EWCA Civ 2329

Farrow, R., 'Harvey Weinstein's secret settlements', *The New Yorker*,
21 November 2017, <www.newyorker.com/news/news-desk/
harvey-weinsteins-secret-settlements>
Garrahan, M., 'Harvey Weinstein: How lawyers kept a lid on sexual
harassment claims', *Financial Times*, 24 October 2017, <www.
ft.com/content/1dc8a8ae-b7e0-11e7-8c12-5661783e5589>
Gordon, J.S., 'Silence for Sale', University of Sydney Law School
Legal Studies Research Paper Series, no. 20/34, vol. 17, June
2020, pp. 1109, 1111
Marriage, M., 'Men only: Inside the charity fundraiser where
hostesses are put on show', *Financial Times*, 24 January
2018, <www.ft.com/content/075d679e-0033-11e8-9650-
9c0ad2d7c5b5>
Newell, C., 'The British #MeToo scandal which cannot be revealed',
The Telegraph, 23 October 2018, <www.telegraph.co.uk/
news/2018/10/23/british-metoo-scandal-cannot-revealed>
Proops, A., McColgan, A., Connor, N. & Robinson, J., 'Submission
to the Women and Equalities Committee on Sexual Harassment

and the Abuse of Non-Disclosure Agreements (NDAs)', 2019, <http://data.parliament.uk/writtenevidence/committeeevidence. svc/evidencedocument/women-and-equalities-committee/ sexual-harassment-in-the-workplace/written/80878.html>

Chapter 6: Defamation on trial

This chapter provides a general overview of libel and defamation law in the United Kingdom and Australia. We were very pleased to have been able to cite the musical *Hamilton!* alongside academic work, case law and the work of journalists in this chapter. We also draw upon our own work in this area in the United Kingdom and the perspective we have gained as practitioners in the field. This is a book for a broad audience, so the chapter aims to give readers a general overview of libel. Those who wish to read further on this topic might want to delve into *Gatley on Libel and Slander* for UK defamation law and the two defamation texts on Australian law we cite below. The details of other sources that enriched our thinking for this chapter are also provided.

Craig v. MacGregor [2019] NZHC 2247 and [2021] NZCA 156
Economou v. De Freitas [2018] EWCA Civ 2591
Lachaux v. Independent Print Ltd [2015] EWHC 620; [2019] 3 WLR 18; [2021] EWHC 1797 (QB)
Lee v. Brown [2022] EWHC 1699 (QB)
Porter v. ABC: <www.fedcourt.gov.au/services/access-to-files-and-transcripts/online-files/porter-v-abc>
Rush v. Nationwide News Pty Ltd (No. 7) [2019] FCA 496 (see also <www.fedcourt.gov.au/services/access-to-files-and-transcripts/online-files/rush-v-nationwide>)
Stocker v. Stocker [2016] EWHC 474 (QB)
Stocker v. Stocker [2019] UKSC 17
Tölle v. Croatia, Application no. 41987/13, 10 December 2020, ECtHR

Edmondson, A., *In Sullivan's Shadow: The use and abuse of libel law during the long civil rights struggle*, Amherst: University of Massachusetts Press, 2019

George, P., *Defamation Law in Australia*, 3rd ed., Chatswood: LexisNexis Australia, 2017

Parkes, R. et al. (eds), *Gatley on Libel and Slander*, 13th ed., London: Sweet and Maxwell, 2022

Pring, G.W. & Canan, P., *SLAPPS: Getting sued for speaking out*, Philadelphia: Temple University Press, 1996

Rolph, D., *Defamation Law*, Sydney: Thompson Reuters, 2015

Chapter 7: Her truth on trial, twice

This chapter is about the two high-profile defamation trials in the United Kingdom and the United States involving Amber Heard's allegations of domestic and sexual abuse against her ex-husband, Johnny Depp. It is written from Jen's perspective based on her experience representing Amber in the UK proceedings and on the publicly available material and commentary on the US trial (Jen did not act for Amber in the United States). The key resources we used to write this chapter were: the reported UK judgment in the case Depp brought against *The Sun,* the subsequent appeal judgment, the trial transcripts and court documents (for the UK trial) and court files relating to the US case that Depp brought against Amber. All information contained in this chapter is already available on the public record or from Jen's personal perspective. In respect of the UK trial, journalist Nick Wallis has compiled most of the relevant court documents on his website, including submissions and witness statements. The US trial materials are available on the website of Fairfax County, Virginia.

John Christopher Depp II v. News Group Newspapers Ltd and Dan Wootton [2020] EWHC 2911 (QB)

John Christopher Depp II v. News Group Newspapers Ltd and Dan Wootton [2021] EWCA Civ 423

Fairfax County's website: <www.fairfaxcounty.gov/circuit/high-profile-cases>Nick Wallis's website: <www.nickwallis.com/depp-trial>
Nick Wallis's website: <www.nickwallis.com/depp-trial>

Heard, A., 'Opinion: Amber Heard: I spoke up against sexual violence—and faced our culture's wrath. That has to change', *The Washington Post*, 18 December 2018, <www.washingtonpost.com/opinions/ive-seen-how-institutions-protect-men-accused-of-abuse-heres-what-we-can-do/2018/12/18/71fd876a-02ed-11e9-b5df-5d3874f1ac36_story.html>

Chapter 8: What about her rights?

The vast majority of the sources we drew upon for this chapter are legal decisions from different jurisdictions around the world. A full list of the cases is available on the website. We are indebted to lawyers and colleagues who sent us cases, some of which are difficult to obtain online. These cases are likely to be the tip of the iceberg, especially since many legal proceedings which take place at the level of the magistrates' courts do not result in reported judgments. Some of the cases from the African continent are particularly difficult to find online. For those seeking further information about those cases, the organisation ISLA published a report after we finished writing our book. It is called 'Defending Women Who Speak: Proposing legal defences in cases against sexual violence victims by their attackers', and is available online in the ISLA Insights series. In addition, the Constitutional Court of Colombia handed down a judgment in a case in which we provided support to the Special Rapporteur on Freedom of Expression. We have included below our amicus brief in that case. The judgment is only available in Spanish.

Anees Petersen v. Daniell Segerman, Case no. H1028/19, 26 November 2020

Anees Petersen v. Daniell Segerman, Case no. A177-21, 24 March 2022

Economou v. De Freitas [2018] EWCA Civ 2591

Lachaux v. Independent Print Ltd and another [2019] UKSC 27

Malizole Daniel Mdlekeza v. Megan Gallie, in the High Court of South Africa, Case no. 15490-2020, 20 April 2021

Tölle v. Croatia, Application no. 41987/13, 10 December 2020, ECtHR

T-061/22, Acción de tutela promovida por Fabian Sanabria Sánchez contra Mónica Godoy Ferro, judgment of 23 February 2022, Constitutional Court of Colombia

T-275/21, judgment of 18 August 2021, Constitutional Court of Colombia

T-361/19, judgment of 12 August 2019, Constitutional Court of Colombia

Expert Opinion, In the Matter of the Constitutional Challenge to Article 22.4.2 of Law 559 of 2000 of the Colombian Criminal Code, <www.ohchr.org/sites/default/files/2022-02/Colombia-Constitutional-Court.pdf>

Gray, M., *Liar Lawsuits: Defamation and sexual violence in Canada*, Vancouver: UBC Press (forthcoming)

Srinivasan, A., *The Right to Sex*, London: Bloomsbury, 2021

Conclusion

Rather than list the sources we relied upon, which you can find online, here we point to a number of campaigns and websites that readers can access for more information on these issues and what is being done to free her speech.

https://cantbuymysilence.com
https://southallblacksisters.org.uk
www.teachusconsent.com
https://volcanicas.com

INDEX